WORK

and the

LIFE

of the

SPIRIT

WORK
and the
LIFE
of the
SPIRIT

edited by

DOUGLAS THORPE

with a foreword by
Thomas Moore

MERCURY HOUSE ◆ SAN FRANCISCO

Published in the United States of America by Mercury House, San Francisco, California, a nonprofit publishing company devoted to the free exchange of ideas and guided by a dedication to literary values.

United States Constitution, First Amendment: Congress shall make no law respecting an establishment of religion, or prohibiting the free exercise thereof; or abridging the freedom of speech, or of the press; or the right of the people peaceably to assemble, and to petition the Government for a redress of grievances.

Mercury House and colophon are registered trademarks of Mercury House, Incorporated.

Printed on recycled, acid-free paper and manufactured in the United States of America.

Cover art: *Shepherdesses Preparing Wool* (detail).
Les Secrets de l'histoire naturelle contenant les merveilles et choses mémorables du monde.
MS Fr. 22971, fol. 38; French, c. 1485. Bibliothèque Nationale, Paris.

Library of Congress Cataloguing-in-Publication Data:
Work and the life of the spirit / edited by Douglas Thorpe ;
with a foreword by Thomas Moore.
p.   cm.
Includes bibliographical references.
ISBN 1-56279-099-4 (pbk. : alk. paper)
1. Work—Religious aspects. 2. Vocation. I. Thorpe, Douglas, 1953–   .
BL65.W67W67   1998   97-20133
291.2'2—DC21   CIP

9 8 7 6 5 4 3 2 1
FIRST EDITION

This book is dedicated to Arthur and Katherine Thorpe,

who have helped to bring it to fruition

Today, like every other day, we wake up empty
and frightened. Don't open the door to the study
and begin reading. Take down a musical instrument.

Let the beauty we love be what we do.
There are hundreds of ways to kneel and kiss the ground.
— *Jalalludin Rumi,*
version by John Moyne & Coleman Barks

Eternity is in love with the productions of time.
— *William Blake*

TABLE OF CONTENTS

THE HUNT
73

CULTIVATION
113

HOME-WORK
141

ARTS, CRAFTS & HAND-WORK
175

FROM THE CITY TO SABBATH
245

EPILOGUE
255

SOURCES
273

PERMISSIONS
295

NOTES
301

ACKNOWLEDGMENTS
307

Thomas Moore

—————

FOREWORD

Work is one of the most far-reaching mysteries in a human life. Because it is so common and so much a part of everyday life, it's tempting to consider work only on a literal level—as a way of making a living. Yet, along with family, marriage, children, and friendship, work is what makes life worth living and accounts for meaning and deep satisfaction. C.G. Jung claimed that we have an instinct for creativity. If we understand creativity not merely as a personal virtue, but as the very work of our lives, then we might understand the importance of our jobs and even our so-called avocations.

To see the spiritual implications of work, it might help to expand our usual definition, recognizing the soul's work in service to our communities, our care for our children, making a home, traveling when the spirit moves us, and expressing our thoughts and reflections in publications, large and small, in letters and visits to friends and neighbors, and in painting, dance, gardening, and a variety of other forms of expression. It's a mistake to limit our idea of work to our job, and then consider the rest of life secondary.

In my years in a Catholic monastery, I learned the ancient traditional philosophy according to which work, especially ordinary manual labor, is as much a part of the spiritual life as meditation and ritual. I also recall the idea that ritual itself is a form of work, and that the word *work*—*ergon* in Greek—is contained in our word "liturgy." This monastic view is one we could recover today, appreciating the spiritual implications of our ordinary chores and activities.

But I wouldn't want to become too precious or abstract in redefining work. For most of us, to re-imagine work in practical terms might demand a challenging and radical shift in the way we live our lives. Indeed, in the past few years I have heard from dozens of people how they have made extraordinary sacrifices, quitting stable and well-paying jobs, in order to find work that is both more meaningful and closer to their nature.

Nor is this philosophy a mere abstraction for me. I have always made every effort to find work that would be in accord with my heart, and for most of my life I made very little money but almost always felt at home in my work. I didn't have children for many years, and so it was possible to live sparsely and find satisfaction at a highly spiritual level. Now I do have children, and I find myself working harder and worrying more about security. Still, the tension between doing work that addresses deep emotions and making a living is a creative dialectic. Without both sides of this tension I might become either unrealistically irresponsible about work or too pragmatic, and thus neglect my heart.

Living a creative life is a profound human need. When this craving goes unfulfilled, we may become depressed, aimless, and deeply dissatisfied. Ordinarily we don't connect our emotional conflicts and bitter moods with work, but rather focus our attention on relationships and our past; yet work reaches deep into the heart, making and sustaining an essential sense of personal worth, vitality, and meaningfulness.

If we were to appreciate more fully the connection between work and our general emotional state, we might withdraw our attention from narcissistic preoccupation with self and find the soul at work in the world. Then we might also realize that it isn't enough to consider work only in relation to personal and individual issues of meaning and emotion, but that work always implicates family, neighborhood, community, nation, and the globe itself. If the soul is to be served adequately, it isn't sufficient to find meaningful work for the individual; we also have to examine our social, corporate, and political views on work.

Around the globe at this very moment, children are being forced to work for next to no pay under extremely inhumane conditions, women are being harassed sexually and are being paid unfairly in relation to men, men and women are forced economically to work at jobs that are in every way dehumanizing, racial inequities still taint almost every profession and trade, and many of our highly educated and experienced male executives, depressed and disillusioned, are walking the streets in search of just bearable positions. The impact of these conditions on individuals, families, and the national soul is indescribable, and yet we seem not to appreciate the profoundly disturbing impact of heart-wounding work. Our public discussions of work address the minimal concerns of simply having a job and taking home a paycheck, however small.

In this dismal context I am heartened by this book that offers a wide spectrum of wisdom connecting work with the great philosophical and spiritual issues. The only way to breathe soul back into work is to deepen and broaden our imagination of work itself. In all areas of life and culture, we urgently need a desecularizing awakening of deep imagination, but perhaps work should be placed at or near the top of our list of priorities.

If we were to work with our hearts instead of at odds with them, with genuine attention to meaning and emotion, and with a spiritual vision instead of pragmatic resignation, we might stir the soul in all areas of public and private life. Then work would become a means and an avenue toward a renaissance of culture, a rebirth that is begging to happen in this end time of an ambitious century of productivity and a millennium of decreasing attention to values and necessities of the heart.

WORK
and the
LIFE
of the
SPIRIT

———⇒➤●◄⇐———

Silence remaind & every one resumd his Human Majesty
 And many conversed on these things as they labourd at the furrow
Saying: It is better to prevent misery, than to release from misery
It is better to prevent error, than to forgive the criminal:
Labour well the Minute Particulars, attend to the Little-ones:
And those who are in misery cannot remain so long
If we do but our duty: labour well the teeming Earth.

— *William Blake, from* Jerusalem

PROLOGUE

There was a time when the Will of the Lord, Whose hand has the power to create and destroy all things, unleashed an endless torrent of pain and sickness over the Earth. The air grew heavy with the moisture of tears, and a dim exhalation of sighs clouded it over. Even the legions that surround His throne were not immune to the hovering sadness. One angel, in fact, was so deeply moved by the sufferings he saw below, that his soul grew quite restless. When he lifted his voice in song with the others, a note of perplexity sounded among the strains of pure faith; his thoughts rebelled and contended with the Lord. He could no longer understand why death and deprivation need serve as connecting links in the great Chain of Events. Then one day, he felt to his horror that the eye of All-Being was piercing his own eye and uncovering the confusion in his heart. Pulling himself together, he came before the Lord, but when he tried to talk, his throat dried up. Nevertheless, the Lord called him by name and gently touched his lips. Then the angel began to speak. He begged God to place the administration of the Earth in his hands for a year's time, that he might lead it to an era of well-being. The angelic bands trembled at this audacity. But at that same moment, Heaven grew bright with the radiance of God's smile. He looked at the suppliant with great love, as He announced His agreement. When the angel stood up again, he too was shining.

And so a year of joy and sweetness visited the earth. The shining angel poured the great profusion of his merciful heart over the most anguished of her children, on those who were benumbed and terrified by want. The groans of the sick and dying no longer disturbed the world's deep, surging harmony. The angel's companion in the steely armor, who only a short time before had been rushing and roaring through the air, stepped aside now, waiting peevishly with lowered sword, relieved of his official duties. The Earth floated through a fecund sky that left her with the burden of new vegetation. When summer was at its height, people moved singing through the full, yellow fields; never had such abundance existed in the memory of living man. At harvest time, it seemed likely that the walls would burst or the roofs fly off, if they were going to find room to store their crops.

Proud and contented, the shining angel basked in his own glory. For by the time the first snow of winter covered the valleys, and dominion over the earth reverted into God's hands, he had parcelled out such an enormous bounty, that the people of earth would surely be enjoying his gifts for many years to come.

But one cold day, late in the year, a multitude of voices rose heavenwards in a great cry of anguish. Frightened by the sound, the angel journeyed down to earth and, dressed as a pilgrim, entered the first house along the way. The people there, having threshed the grain and ground it into flour, had then started baking bread – but, alas, when they took the bread out of the oven it fell to pieces and the pieces were unpalatable; they filled the mouth with a disgusting taste, like clay. And this was precisely what the angel found in the second house and in the third and everywhere he set foot. People were lying on the floor, tearing their hair and cursing the Lord of the World, who had deceived their miserable hearts with His false blessing.

The angel flew away and collapsed at God's feet. Lord, he cried, help me to understand where my power and judgment were lacking.

Then God raised his voice and spoke: Behold a truth which is known to me from the beginning of time, a truth too deep and dreadful for your delicate, generous hands, my sweet apprentice – it is this, that the earth must be nourished with decay and covered with shadows that its seeds may bring forth – and it is this, that souls must be made fertile with flood and sorrow, that through them the Great Work may be born.

—*Martin Buber*, The Angel and the World's Dominion

INTRODUCTION

The *American Heritage Dictionary* defines it as "physical or mental effort or activity directed toward the production or accomplishment of something; toil, labor." Synonyms include *drudgery, travail.* Like most of our famous four-letter words, this one flows directly from its Anglo-Saxon roots: in Old English *we(o)rc* means "act, deed, work." Its Indo-European root is little different: *werg:* "to do."

For millennia there has been little romance in the word, and no wonder. Work is just *work.* It's always for something else, always something better. It pays the rent, pays for the car and the mortgage; it pays the dentist and the doctor, for the clothes, books, CDs, vacation. It pays for prestige; for "the good life." Or, more simply, for security. As one janitor commented, "retirement is the occupational goal."[1]

Most of the work gathered in this book leads us off that familiar road. Yet I might easily have subtitled the book *Foundations* to suggest that the less common paths these essays tread could indeed be seen as primary — as salvational, in the root sense of the word: from *salve,* as in healing or making whole. They present a ground we might build upon.

This book does not intend to address directly the ways most of us now live and work (in air-conditioned offices, at desks and in front of computer screens), although this might come in a subsequent volume. It is not filled with "how-to" essays; it will not give you specifics about how to find a better (or better-paying) job. It is, rather, "why to": it looks to underlying truths.

The general thesis that runs through the volume can be put in many ways. Ananda K. Coomaraswamy (quoting Meister Eckhart) says that, "It is immaterial what the work may be, but it is essential that the artist should be wholly given to it ... it is working for the love of God in any case, because the perfection of the work is 'to prepare all creatures to return to God.'"[2]

The key, I think, is in these two sentences. First, to be given wholly to the work, however mundane it may appear. True labor involves commitment, discipline, love; it becomes a kind of marriage. And true work is not simply for oneself but "to prepare all creatures." However great the delight one takes, and however solitary the work may be, it is still work done for love. As with any true marriage, the relationship between the worker and her labor is not for herself alone; an entire community is implicated.

"O Earth," writes Rilke, "what, if not transformation, is your urgent command?"3 A good definition not only of the function of art, but, at its highest, of all human labor, which of necessity enters into the materials of the world, changing that world even as the one who works upon it is changed. This is the marriage — the curse and blessing — of labor.

Wendell Berry suggests that good work has to do with "harmony":

> Harmony is one phase, the good phase, of the inescapable dialogue between culture and nature. In this phase, humans consciously and conscientiously ask of their work: Is this good for us? Is this good for our place? And the questioning and answering in this phase is minutely particular: It can occur only with reference to particular artifacts, events, places, ecosystems, and neighborhoods.... Good workmanship — that is, careful, considerate, and loving work — requires us to think considerately of the whole process, natural and cultural, involved in the making of wooden artifacts, because the good worker does not share the industrial contempt for "raw material." The good worker loves the board before it becomes a table, loves the tree before it yields the board, loves the forest before it gives up the tree.4

Or try this, from Gary Snyder: Real work is "what is to be done."5 This may sound obvious, but while we may think that what we are doing must be done the truth can be quite different. Much of our work isn't necessary at all: It makes nothing of value, contributes to nothing essential, changes nothing, or does so only for the worse — meaning that the work only contributes to further alienation from ourselves, from the earth, and thus from the holy.

"The dignity of toil is undermined when its necessity is gone."6 Berry, quoting here from Kathleen Raine, suggests that we must find work that needs to be done, and do it in such a way that takes the worker deeper into her own life, connecting her with her own body, her mind and spirit, even as it connects her with all that lies outside: her tools, her neighbors, and the place that she inhabits. How can her work connect her with herself if it does not do so through her tools, her place, her medium?

At some point distinctions collapse. As we work we slowly realize that we are the material we work upon. We find the world as our own body.

Indeed, I wonder if it isn't this way for that son of a Nazarene carpenter. As he walks through the towns and deserts of Palestine, as he heals and listens and teaches, it must become clearer and clearer — to himself, as well as to others — just who he is. And isn't *this* his essential work, this slow revelation that shows itself *through* his work? Daily the Promise takes on form as he labors, leading him at last to Jerusalem, where he knows he is to complete himself by giving himself away. And where he comes not as conqueror but as lover, as outraged mother: "O Jerusalem, Jerusalem, killing the prophets and stoning those who are sent to you! How often would I have gathered your children together as a hen gathers her brood under her wings, and you would not!" (Matt. 23:37)

In Jerusalem he walks off all the known charts. It's no wonder that no one understands who he is. His life and death become a kind of koan, ungraspable, beyond definition. He finds himself as the Way that abandons all known ways. In the end, so thoroughly has he become it that he cannot separate himself from a single sparrow, a mustard seed. At last whatever he is stands revealed as synonymous with the force that drives the world. Call it Logos, Tao, Son of God, *Ruach HaKodesh:* In Him all work becomes charged with the grandeur of God. It all transforms.

He is a model of the wayless Way. He is the axe handle we both hold and work upon, always at hand should we need to know how it's shaped.7

There is deep satisfaction in a job well done. I know it, however dimly, as I sit here writing at my grandfather's battered oak desk. I know it as I watch Sid, my neighbor, digging in his garden, or as I watch Kathryn and Bob up the hill from me laying bricks or putting laundry on the line to dry. And, while they may never see it, I include them in my work — as (who knows?) in some fashion they may include me in theirs.

Watching them work brings pleasure; I know the delight they take in small tasks rightly done. Seeing it makes me want to sing, and so the singing becomes part of the work I give. And at moments, however pointless the song may seem, somewhere beyond the back fence it opens out into mystery.

So a song too may be necessary; it awakens us again to who we are. This, after all, is what it means to make a place inhabitable. It is more than a secure roof and a solid floor, although being well built, being *just,* is part of what it needs. Building well, whether a foundation, a poem, or a simple greeting at the store, brings something forth, something that exists not as mine but as the essential imaginative body I share with the world, and experience again in the work I do. This is the marriage we make in our working upon the world.

It's the way Chuang Tzu's woodcarver finds the right tree in the forest, fasting and praying "until I was collected in the single thought / Of the bell stand." Only then does he go to the forest, searching for the right tree until "the bell stand also appeared in it, clearly, beyond doubt."8

Is it merely human pride to suggest that the "potential" for this tree included a beautiful bell stand? Or to suggest that salmon or deer might "willingly" surrender their life to the right hunter, the one who recognizes a relative in the creature whose life he is taking? I am not one who is gifted in the language of trees and salmon, and so I cannot say for sure. And yet something in me wants to claim that the world is meant for transformation: This is what right work teaches. And the great human gift to the world is our awareness of this meaning, and our desire, at our best, to assist.

A note on the organization of the book: We have been taught that human culture develops – for better or worse – from its origins in the hunting/gathering societies of the Paleolithic to the agricultural societies of the Neolithic, which in turn make possible (or even necessary) the development of storage sites for excess food, walls to defend the storage sites, armies to defend the walls ... and thus cities, which may be (depending on your point of view) the ultimate home of *techne:* human craft and skill. From the beginning this has been a deeply ambiguous development, registered in our ambivalence about the city, which is both Pandemonium and Paradise, Babylon and Jerusalem. Witness the story of Cain and Abel, which, as the *Oxford Annotated Bible* says, "reflects the tension between farmers and semi-nomads." Cain, the disgruntled, rejected, and finally murderous farmer, is also the founder of the first city – which might explain a lot.

This book attempts to move as human culture moves, recognizing that boundaries are fluid, and narrow distinctions between craft and art, and even between hunting and cultivation, finally collapse. We reach, nonetheless, in this wandering way, to the modern city, with its associated industries and professions, which bear so little resemblance to the life that humans have lived for thousands of years – lives of hunting and gathering, spinning and weaving, milking and butchering, singing and storytelling; lives intimately engaged with stone and wood, with seeds and animals. We've rowed a long way up this stream to where I now sit in Seattle before a computer screen and keyboard, listening to music recorded half a world away and then encoded on a tiny plastic disk.

And this is where we stop, at least for now. We reach the pass, let us say; gazing in one direction – the direction that this book takes – we see who we have been (at our best) for thousands of years. Turning in another direction we suddenly find ourselves standing above a modern city. We gaze down from a distant hill upon that busy hive of lights and noise – a scene most of us know well.

To stop here, as I've said, is my intention. To go further, to get a sense of how work feels to many Americans in the latter half of the twentieth century, read Studs Terkel, talk to your friends and family, or simply take a look in the mirror. Most of us after all *live there.* This is, for the most part, about something else: a book of foundations, which intends to raise questions, to look back and down into a world and a way of being in it that most of us have left behind.

The world was all before them John Milton writes of Adam and Eve. Such has been the truth for each of us, as it is now the truth for my daughter, and perhaps for yours. My hope is that this collection will provide them – and us – with a reminder of the way work still might be.

– D.T.

ORIGINS & FIRST THOUGHTS

The way a culture understands its origins reflects upon its sense of work – and vice versa. Most famously to many readers of this book will be the creation story of the Hebrews, wherein the original man and woman are literally drawn from the soil of a paradise (or a wilderness, depending upon one's interpretation of "Eden"), which they are invited to "dress and keep" (Gen. 2:15). With the failure to heed the warnings about that central tree of knowledge, however, the creatures of the soil lose contact with their source. Exiled, they must struggle to make themselves at home in the new world before them. Creation now comes with struggle; life arises out of suffering.

Compare such an understanding of human labor to the excerpts from the other works presented here. To take just one example, consider the Navajo Creation Story, where there is an emergence of the human – and all of life – from a previous place (there are in fact four worlds "below" this one), leading to a wandering and a settling that is, in essence, coincident with the development of what we consider civilization: above all, cultivation and crafts.

Consider too what the Laguna Pueblo novelist and poet Leslie Marmon Silko says about the Emergence and Migration:

> The Emergence was an emergence into a precise cultural identity. Thus, the Pueblo stories about the Emergence and Migration are not to be taken as literally as the anthropologists might wish. Prominent geographical features and landmarks that are mentioned in the narratives exist for ritual purposes, not because the Laguna people actually journeyed south for hundreds of years from Chaco Canyon or Mesa Verde, as the archeologists say, or eight miles from the site of the natural springs at Paguate to the sandstone hilltop at Laguna.
>
> The eight miles ... are actually a ritual circuit, or path, that marks the interior journey the Laguna people made: a journey of awareness and imagination in which they emerged from being within the earth

and all-included in the earth to the culture and people they became, differentiating themselves for the first time from all that had sur-rounded them.[1]

Emergence is an imaginative process into a kind of self-knowledge, a process not unlike the journey of Adam (*adamah*, meaning "ground, soil") into an aware-ness of who he is, which means in part an awareness of whence he comes. For the human at least, "emergence" — the birth from the mother, as from the earth herself — seems synonymous with consciousness.

This process, however, takes many different forms. As Silko suggests, for the Pueblo "the journey was an interior process of the imagination, a growing aware-ness that being human is somehow different from all other life.... Yet, we are all from the same source: awareness never deteriorated into Cartesian duality, cutting off the human from the natural world."

One parallel example, from an early Wendell Berry essay. He is describing the work that went into tearing down an old building — one with many memories at-tached to it — and building another:

> The next afternoon I cleared the weeds and bushes off the building site, and with that my sadness at parting with the old house began to give way to the idea of the new. I was going to build the new house several feet higher up the slope than the old one, and to place it so that it would look out between the two big sycamores. Unlike a wild place, a human place gone wild can be strangely forbidding and even depressing. But that afternoon's work made me feel at home here again. My plans suddenly took hold of me, and I began to visualize the new house as I needed it to be and as I thought it ought to look. My work had made the place inhabitable, had set my imagination free in it. I began again to belong to it.[2]

"My sadness at parting ... began to give way to the idea of the new.... I began again to belong." This is a definition of work that could have been spoken by Adam and Eve.

> The World was all before them, where to choose
> Thir place of rest and Providence thir guide:
> They hand in hand with wand'ring steps and slow,
> Through Eden took thir solitary way.[3]

"Cursed is the ground because of you; in toil you shall eat of it all the days of your life; thorns and thistles it shall bring forth to you.... In the sweat of your face you shall eat bread...." All of this is true enough. We resist work; we want to re-main as children, irresponsible, dependent and blissfully, unconsciously, at home. Yet there the glory is: "My work had made the place inhabitable." This is the human predicament. If work results from alienation, at the same time it brings a reminder of home. And it is not just the comfort but the beauty that matters, that which speaks of order, justice, community, connection.

Call it a taste of the truly good life: the shelters we build, the clothes we stitch and weave, the food we eat, the wine we drink and the music we make during the long, dark nights – what is it all but our attempt once again to belong? And, at its best, our brief reminder that we do, naturally, through no effort of our own.

At its worst, of course, such labor deteriorates into Babel, building in arrogance, bringing only more disorder. The "good life" becomes sheer extravagance; we build larger, we drink more, trying to satisfy a thirst that will never be satisfied with substitutes. We seek to build our way out of the world (and out of work), confusing the New Jerusalem with indoor plumbing, central heating, or mai tai's with little umbrellas on a Caribbean beach. The freedom is illusory and brief, and usually built on someone else's back. All we have accomplished is to make ourselves more comfortable in our prisons – at a cost to someone else, and to the earth itself.

We learn our lessons slowly, painfully, and with much confusion and destruction. We lord it over life, forgetting who we are, that from which we are made. Forgetting, as Blake told Denise Levertov in a dream, that "'The will is given us that / we may know the / delights of surrender.'"4

All We

All we who make
Things transitory and good
Cannot but take
When walking in a wood
Pleasure in everything
And the maker's solicitude,
Knowing the delicacy
Of bringing shape to birth.
To fashion the transitory
We gave and took the ring
And pledged ourselves to earth.

– Edwin Muir

Little need be added to the clarity and directness of Edwin Muir's poem; it is, as Hayden Carruth has commented, "shaped of earth, not perdurable, in fact transitory, but nevertheless ingrained with the maker's love and the most lasting elements of human nature and experience."5

"Things transitory and good." These are the words of one who shapes well, and who takes care and delight in the shaping – and who, in doing so, sees himself as part of a larger shaping, a larger pattern circumscribed upon the earth.

The pieces in this section range from as early as Genesis to as recent as the past few years. They are, at times, theoretical; at other times poetic (and sometimes, as in Eckhart, a bit of both). They all, I hope, provide a useful way into a large subject. While there is certainly no attempt to be definitive, and without suggesting any simple uniformity of perspective, these "First Thoughts" do suggest a common thread, one spelled out in Muir's poem – an understanding of the value of work in human life and society.

While works such as the *Gita* and the *Diné bahane'* might feel remote in ways, Langland's prologue to *Piers Plowman* carries us into a very familiar world. Langland's vision remains piercing, funny, and prophetic. I suspect that Wendell Berry and Gary Snyder – along with Dorothee Soelle, E.F. Schumacher, and Walt Whitman (among other guiding spirits for this book) – would proudly acknowledge themselves as his spiritual descendents.

Eckhart is another story, of course. Difficult at times, still in his vernacular (German versus Latin) sermons there remains a common, colloquial touch. Almost Langland's contemporary (and Rumi's!), he shared with Long Will a sharp eye for the particular. Ananda K. Coomaraswamy provides a wonderfully erudite commentary on Eckhart, viewed from both a Western and richly Eastern perspective.

We end with Whitman and the Norwegian poet Olav Hauge. Whitman is inevitable here, as a singer and celebrator of work in all of its forms. "I was there," he chants; the self he weaves out of this "kosmos" is the body enlarged to include everything and everyone.

Hauge is something else again. A Norwegian who makes his living through the keeping of an orchard, in his allusion to *The Odyssey* (Laertes, Odysseus's father, leaves his palace for his garden when Odysseus fails to return from Troy) he returns us to the everyday, and to the nonheroic. Hauge's poetry reminds me (like Frost's, curiously) of the comment that Native American poet Joy Harjo has made about the relationship between writing poetry and "digging piles of earth with a stick: smell it, form it."[6] It's a reminder that *compose* and *compost* are close neighbors.

Navajo

—➤●◄—

THE EMERGENCE
from *Diné bahane': The Navajo Creation Story*

It is also said that late in the autumn of that year the newcomers heard a distant voice calling to them from far in the east.

They listened and waited, listened and waited. Until soon they heard the voice again, nearer and louder than before. They continued to listen and wait, listen and wait, until they heard the voice a third time, all the nearer and all the louder.

Continuing to listen, they heard the voice again, even louder than the last time, and so close now that it seemed directly upon them.

A moment later they found themselves standing among four mysterious beings. They had never seen such creatures anywhere before. For they were looking at those who would eventually become known as *Haashch'ééh dine'é*.

In the language of *Bilagáana* the White Man, that name means Holy People. For they are people unlike the earth-surface, people who come into the world today, live on the ground for a while, die at a ripe old age, and then move on. These are intelligent people who can perform magic. They do not know the pain of being mortal. They are people who can travel far by following the path of the rainbow. And they can travel swiftly by following the path of the sunray. They can make the winds and the thunderbolts work for them so that the earth is theirs to control when they so wish....

Without speaking the Holy People made signs to those who were gathered there, as if to give them instructions. But the exiles could not understand their gestures. So they stood by helplessly and watched.

And after the gods had left, the people talked about that mysterious visit for the rest of that day and all night long, trying to determine what it meant.

—➤●◄—

As for the gods, they repeated their visit four days in a row. But on the fourth day, *Bits'íís łizhin* the Black Body remained after the other three departed. And when he was alone with the onlookers, he spoke to them in their own language. This is what he said:

"You do not seem to understand the Holy People," he said.

"So I will explain what they want you to know.

"They want more people to be created in this world. But they want intelligent people, created in their likeness, not in yours.

"You have bodies like theirs, true enough.

"But you have the teeth of beasts! You have the mouths of beasts! You have the feet of beasts! You have the claws of beasts!

"The new creatures are to have hands like ours. They are to have feet like ours. They are to have mouths like ours and teeth like ours. They must learn to think ahead, as we do.

"What is more, you are unclean!

"You smell bad.

"So you are instructed to cleanse yourselves before we return twelve days from now."

That is what *Bits'íís łizhin* the Black Body said to the insect people who had emerged from the first world to the second, from the second world to the third, and from the third world to the fourth world where they now lived.

⟫●⟪

Accordingly, on the morning of the twelfth day the people bathed carefully. The women dried themselves with yellow corn meal. The men dried themselves with white corn meal.

Soon after they had bathed, they again heard the distant voice coming from far in the east.

They listened and waited as before, listened and waited. Until soon they heard the voice as before, nearer and louder this time.

They continued to listen and wait, listen and wait, until they heard the voice a third time as before, all the nearer and all the louder.

Continuing to listen as before, they heard the voice again, even louder than the last time, and so close now that it seemed directly upon them, exactly as it had seemed before. And as before they found themselves standing among the same four *Haashch'ééh dine'é*, or Holy People, as *Bilagáana* the White Man might wish to call them.

Bits'íís doott'izh the Blue Body and *Bits'íís łizhin* the Black Body each carried a sacred buckskin. *Bits'íís łigaii* the White Body carried two ears of corn.

One ear of corn was yellow. The other ear was white. Each ear was completely covered at the end with grains, just as sacred ears of corn are covered in our own world now.

Proceeding silently, the gods laid one buckskin on the ground, careful that its head faced the west. Upon this skin they placed the two ears of corn, being just as careful that the tips of each pointed east. Over the corn they spread the other buckskin, making sure that its head faced east.

Under the white ear they put the feather of a white eagle.

And under the yellow ear they put the feather of a yellow eagle.

Then they told the onlooking people to stand at a distance.

So that the wind could enter.

Then from the east *Nílch'i łigai* the White Wind blew between the buckskins. And while the wind thus blew, each of the Holy People came and walked four times around the objects they had placed so carefully on the ground.

As they walked, the eagle feathers, whose tips protruded slightly from between the two buckskins, moved slightly.

Just slightly.

So that only those who watched carefully were able to notice.

And when the Holy People had finished walking, they lifted the topmost buckskin.

And lo! The ears of corn had disappeared.

In their place there lay a man and there lay a woman.

———— ❊ ————

The white ear of corn had been transformed into our most ancient male ancestor. And the yellow ear of corn had been transformed into our most ancient female ancestor.

It was the wind that had given them life: the very wind that gives us our breath as we go about our daily affairs here in the world we ourselves live in!

When this wind ceases to blow inside of us, we become speechless. Then we die.

In the skin at the tips of our fingers we can see the trail of that life-giving wind.

Look carefully at your own fingertips.

There you will see where the wind blew when it created your most ancient ancestors out of two ears of corn, it is said.

Hebrew

from

THE BOOK OF GENESIS

These are the generations of the heavens and the earth when they were created.

In the day that the Lord God made the earth and the heavens, when no plant of the field was yet in the earth and no herb of the field had yet sprung up – for the Lord God had not caused it to rain upon the earth, and there was no man to till the ground; but a mist went up from the earth and watered the whole face of the ground – then the Lord God formed man of dust from the ground, and breathed into his nostrils the breath of life; and man became a living being. And the Lord God planted a garden in Eden, in the east; and there he put the man whom he had formed. And out of the ground the Lord God made to grow every tree that is pleasant to the sight and good for food, the tree of life also in the midst of the garden, and the tree of the knowledge of good and evil.

A river flowed out of Eden to water the garden, and there it divided and became four rivers....

The Lord God took the man and put him in the garden of Eden to till and keep it. And the Lord God commanded the man, saying, you may freely eat of every tree of the garden; but of the tree of the knowledge of good and evil you shall not eat, for in the day that you eat of it you shall die....

Now the serpent was more subtle than any other wild creature that the Lord God had made. He said to the woman, "Did God say, 'You shall not eat of any tree of the garden'?" And the woman said to the serpent, "We may eat of the fruit of the trees of the garden, but God said, 'You shall not eat of the fruit of the tree which is in the midst of the garden, neither shall you touch it, lest you die.'" But the serpent said to the woman, "You shall not die. For God knows that when you eat of it your eyes will be opened, and you will be like God, knowing good and evil."...

The Lord God said to the serpent, "because you have done this, cursed are you above all cattle, above all wild animals; on your belly you shall go, and dust you shall eat all the days of your life."...

To the woman he said, "I will greatly multiply your pain in childbearing; in pain you shall bring forth children, yet your desire shall be for your husband, and he shall rule over you."

And to Adam he said, "Because you have listened to the voice of your wife, and have eaten of the tree of which I commanded you, 'You shall not eat of it,' cursed is the ground because of you; in toil you shall eat of it all the days of your life; thorns and thistles it shall bring forth to you; and you shall eat the plants of the field. In the sweat of your face you shall eat bread till you return to the ground, for out of it you were taken; you are dust, and to dust you shall return."

Saint Paul

---

from
SECOND LETTER TO THE THESSALONIANS

Now we command you, brethren, in the name of our Lord Jesus Christ, that you keep away from any brother who is living in idleness and not in accord with the tradition that you received from us. For you yourselves know how you ought to imitate us; we were not idle when we were with you, we did not eat any one's bread without paying, but with toil and labor we worked night and day, that we might not burden any of you. It was not because we have not that right, but to give you in our conduct an example to imitate. For even when we were with you, we gave you this command: If any one will not work, let him not eat.

Hesiod

—>●<—

from
WORKS AND DAYS

I mean you well, Perses, you great idiot, and I will tell you.
Look, badness is easy to have, you can take it by handfuls
 without effort. The road that way is smooth and starts here beside you.
But between us and virtue the immortals have put what will make us
sweat. The road to virtue is long and goes steep up hill,
hard climbing at first, but the last of it, when you get to the summit
(if you get there) is easy going after the hard part.

That man is all-best who himself works out every problem
and solves it, seeing what will be best late and in the end.
That man, too, is admirable who follows one who speaks well.
He who cannot see the truth for himself, nor, hearing it from others,
store it away in his mind, that man is utterly useless.
As for you, remember what I keep telling you over and over:
work, O Perses, illustrious-born, work on, so that Famine
will avoid you, and august and garlanded Demeter
will be your friend, and fill your barn with substance of living;
Famine is the unworking man's most constant companion.
Gods and men alike resent that man who, without work
himself, lives the life of the stingless drones,
who without working eat away the substance of the honeybees'
hard work; your desire, then, should be to put your works in order
so that your barns may be stocked with all livelihood in its season.
It is from work that men grow rich and own flocks and herds;
by work, too, they become much better friends of the immortals.
[and to men too, for they hate the people who do not labor].
Work is no disgrace; the disgrace is in not working;
and if you do work, the lazy man will soon begin to be envious
as you grow rich, for with riches go nobility and honor.
It is best to work, at whatever you have a talent for doing,

without turning your greedy thought toward what some other man
possesses, but take care of your own livelihood, as I advise you.
Shame, the wrong kind of shame, has the needy man in convoy,
shame, who does much damage to men, but prospers them also,
shame goes with poverty, but confidence goes with prosperity.

Hindi

---

from
BHAGAVAD GITA

[Note: The entire *Gita* consists of a long dialogue between Krishna, the main speaker, who "is in truth a manifestation of the Supreme Deity in human form.... The other speaker ... is Arjuna.... The conversation between Arjuna and Krishna is supposed to take place just before the battle which is the main theme of the great epic" (Edgerton).]

Arjuna said:
1. Of renunciation, great-armed one,
I desire to know the truth,
And of abandonment, Hrsikesa,
Severally, Slayer of Kesin.

The Blessed One said:
2. The renouncing of acts of desire
Sages call renunciation.
The abandonment of all action-fruits
The wise call abandonment.

3. That it must be abandoned as sinful, some
Wise men say of action;
That actions of worship, gift, and austerity
Must not be abandoned, say others.

4. Hear my decision in this matter
Of abandonment, best of Bharatas;
For abandonment, O man-tiger,
Is reputed to be threefold.

5. Actions of worship, gift, and austerity
Must not be abandoned, but rather performed;
Worship, gift, and austerity
Are purifiers of the wise.

6. However, these actions
With abandonment of attachment and fruits
Must be performed: this, son of Prtha, is My
Definite and highest judgment.

7. But abandonment of a (religiously) required
Action is not seemly;
Abandonment thereof owing to delusion
Is reputed to be of the nature of darkness.

8. Because it is troublesome, what action
One abandons thru fear of bodily affliction,
Such a man performs an abandonment that is of the nature of passion;
By no means shall he get any fruit of (this) abandonment.

9. Simply because it ought to be done, when action
That is (religiously) required is performed, Arjuna,
Abandoning attachment and fruit,
That abandonment is held to be of goodness.

10. He loathes not disagreeable action,
Nor does he cling to agreeable (action),
The man of abandonment who is filled with goodness,
Wise, whose doubts are destroyed.

11. For a body-bearing (soul) can not
Abandon actions without remainder;
But he who abandons the fruit of action
Is called the man of (true) abandonment.

12. Undesired, desired, and mixed –
Threefold is the fruit of action
That ensues after death for those who are not men of abandonment,
But never for men of renunciation.

. . . .

23. Obligatory, free from attachment,
Done without desire or loathing,
By one who seeks no fruit from it, action
Such as this is called of goodness.

24. But action which by one seeking desires,
Or again by one who is selfish,
Is done, with much weary labor,
That is declared to be of passion.

25. Consequences, loss, injury (to others),
And (one's own) human power disregarding,
Owing to delusion, when action is undertaken,
It is declared to be of darkness.

26. Free from attachment, not talking of himself,
Full of steadfastness and energy,
Unchanged in success or failure,
Such an agent is called one of goodness.

27. Passionate, seeking the fruits of action,
Greedy, injurious, impure,
Full or joy and grief, such an agent
Is celebrated as one of passion.

28. Undisciplined, vulgar, arrogant,
Tricky, dishonest, lazy,
Despondent, and procrastinating,
Such an agent is said to be of darkness.

29. The distinction of intelligence and of firmness, also,
Threefold according to the Strands, hear
Fully expounded
In their several forms, Dhanamjaya.

30. Activity and cessation from it,
Things to be done and not to be done, danger and security,
Bondage and release, that which knows these
Is the intelligence that is of goodness, son of Prtha.

31. Whereby right and upright,
And things to be done and not to be done,
Are understood incorrectly,
That intelligence, son of Prtha, is of passion.

32. Right as unright what
Conceives, obscured by darkness,
And all things contrary (to the truth),
That intelligence, son of Prtha, is of darkness.

33. The firmness with which one holds fast
The activities of the mind, life-breaths, and senses,
And which is unswerving in discipline,
That firmness is of goodness, son of Prtha.

34. But when to religion, love, and wealth
With firmness he holds fast, Arjuna,
With attachment, desirous of the fruits,
That firmness is of passion, son of Prtha.

35. Whereby sleep, fear, sorrow,
Despondency, and pride,
The foolish man does not let go,
That firmness is of darkness, son of Prtha.

36. But now the threefold happiness
Hear from Me, bull of Bharatas.
That in which he comes to delight thru long practice (only),
And comes to the end of suffering,

37. Which in the beginning is like poison,
But in maturity like nectar,
That is called the happiness of goodness,
Sprung from serenity of soul and of intellect.

38. (Springing) from union of the senses and their objects,
That which in the beginning is like nectar,
In maturity like poison,
That happiness is recorded as of passion.

39. Which both in the beginning and in its consequence
Is a happiness that deludes the self,
Arising from sleep, sloth, and heedlessness,
That is declared to be of darkness.

40. There is no thing, whether on earth,
Or yet in heaven, among the gods,
No being which free from the material-nature-born
Strands, these three, might be.

41. Of brahmans, warriors, and artisans,
And of serfs, scorcher of the foe,
The actions are distinguished
According to the Strands that spring from their innate nature.

42. Calm, (self-)control, austerities, purity,
Patience, and uprightness,
Theoretical and practical knowledge, and religious faith,
Are the natural-born actions of brahmans.

43. Heroism, majesty, firmness, skill,
And not fleeing in battle also,
Generosity, and lordly nature,
Are the natural-born actions of warriors.

44. Agriculture, cattle-tending, and commerce
Are the natural-born actions of artisans;
Action that consists of service
Is likewise natural-born to a serf.

45. Taking delight in his own special kind of action,
A man attains perfection;
Delighting in one's own special action, success
How one reaches, that hear!

46. Whence comes the activity of beings,
By whom this all is pervaded,
Him worshiping by (doing) one's own appropriate action,
A man attains perfection.

47. Better one's own duty, (even) imperfect,
Than another's duty well performed.
Action pertaining to his own estate
Performing, he incurs no guilt.

48. Natural-born action, son of Kunti,
Even tho it be faulty, one should not abandon.
For all undertakings by faults
Are dimmed, as fire by smoke.

49. His mentality unattached to any object,
Self-conquered, free from longings,
To the supreme perfection of actionlessness
He comes thru renunciation.

50. Having attained perfection, how to Brahman
He also attains, hear from Me,
In only brief compass, son of Kunti;
Which is the highest culmination of knowledge.

51. With purified mentality disciplined,
And restraining himself with firmness,
Abandoning the objects of sense, sounds and the rest,
And putting away desire and loathing,

52. Cultivating solitude, eating lightly,
Restraining speech, body, and mind,
Devoted to the discipline of meditation constantly,
Taking refuge in dispassion,

53. From egotism, force, pride,
Desire, wrath, and possession
Freed, unselfish, calmed,
He is fit for becoming Brahman.

54. Having become Brahman, serene-souled,
He neither grieves nor longs;
Alike to all beings,
He attains supreme devotion to Me.

55. Thru devotion he comes to know Me,
What My measure is, and who I am, in very truth;
Then, knowing Me in very truth,
He enters into (Me) straightway.

56. Even tho all actions ever
He performs, relying on Me,
By My grace he reaches
The eternal, undying station.

57. With thy thoughts all actions
Casting upon Me, devoted to Me,
Turning to discipline of mentality,
Keep thy mind ever fixed on Me.

58. If thy mind is on Me, all difficulties
Shalt thou cross over by My grace;
But if thru egotism thou
Wilt not heed, thou shalt perish.

59. If clinging to egotism
Thou thinkest 'I will not fight!',
Vain is this thy resolve;
(Thine own) material nature will coerce thee.

60. Son of Kunti, by thine own natural
Action held fast,
What thru delusion thou seekest not to do,
That thou shalt do even against thy will.

61. Of all beings, the Lord
In the heart abides, Arjuna,
Causing all beings to turn around
(As if) fixed in a machine, by his magic power.

62. To Him alone go for refuge
With thy whole being, son of Bharata;
By His grace, supreme peace
And the eternal station shalt thou attain.

63. Thus to thee has been expounded the knowledge
That is more secret than the secret, by Me;
After pondering on it fully,
Act as thou thinkest best.

64. Further, the highest secret of all,
My supreme message, hear.
Because thou art greatly loved of Me,
Therefore I shall tell thee what is good for thee.

65. Be Me-minded, devoted to Me;
Worshiping Me, revere Me;
And to Me alone shalt thou go; truly to thee
I promise it – (because) thou art dear to Me.

66. Abandoning all (other) duties,
Go to Me as thy sole refuge;
From all evils I thee
Shall rescue: be not grieved!

67. This on thy part to no one not endowed with austerity,
Nor ever to one not devoted,
Nor to one not obedient, must be told,
Nor to one who murmurs against Me.

68. Whoso this supreme secret
Shall make known to My devotees,
Showing utmost devotion to Me,
Shall go just to Me, without a doubt.

69. And not than he among men
Is there any who does things more pleasing to Me;
Nor shall there be than he to Me
Any other dearer on earth.

70. And whoso shall study this
Colloquy on duty between us two,
By him with knowledge-worship I
Would be worshiped: so I hold.

71. With faith, and not murmuring against it,
What man even hears it,
He too shall be released, and the fair worlds
Of men of virtuous deeds shall he attain.

72. Has this been heard, son of Prtha,
By thee with concentrated thought?
Has the confusion of ignorance
In thee been destroyed, Dhanamjaya?

Arjuna said:
73. Destroyed the confusion; attention (to the truth) is won,
By Thy grace, on my part, O Changeless One;
I stand firm, with doubts dispersed;
I shall do Thy word.

ISHA UPANISHAD

1. The Great One dwells
in all this, and in all
that moves in this mobile universe.
Enjoy things by
giving them up, not by craving
some other man's substance.

2. Engaged in works
hope to live
here for a hundred years —
it's what you receive,
nothing else.
There is no one for karma
to cling to.

3. There are worlds
they call sunless,
turbulent,
covered with gloom —
those who
violate spirit
depart after death
into them —

4. The Immobile One's
swifter than thought,
not even a god
can approach it.
Stands, yet outflanks what runs;
holds the waters
the Hidden Female let forth.

5. Moves,
and does not move.
Is distant,
is near.
It inhabits all this,
stays outside of it all.

6. Who sees
all breathing creatures
as self, self
in everything breathing,
no longer shrinks
from encounter.

7. When the spectator
of this unity
regards all creatures as Self,
who can suffer,
who be misled?

8. It is out traveling —
bright, bodiless, pure,
unflawed,
unpierced by evil.
   All objects
have in their self-nature
been arranged precisely about us
by that presence —
poet, and thinker.

9. They enter a turbulent
darkness, who
cultivate ignorance —
a yet thicker darkness
who are addicted to
knowledge.

10. It is different
from knowledge — different also
from what you do not know —
this we heard
from the steadfast ones
who opened our eyes.

11. Who is cunning
towards knowledge and ignorance,
with ignorance
moves across death,
with knowledge reaches
the deathless —

12. They enter a turbulent
darkness, who
cultivate unmanifest worlds —
a yet thicker darkness
who are addicted
to empirical worlds.

13. Different
from what you can see —
different also
from what goes unseen —
this we heard
from the steadfast ones
who opened our eyes.

14. Who is cunning
towards loss and creation,
with loss
crosses death,
with creation reaches
the deathless —

15. A golden solar disc
hides the gateway
into the Real —
remove it O Nourisher,
so I can see
the Unwavering.

16. O Nourisher, sole Seer,
judge of the dead,
 O sun, offspring of the Father of Creatures,
fan out your rays,
draw up lustre —
    that most
splendrous form, yours —
I would see — that is —
the I am

17. Animate breath
   is undying
but the body ends in ashes —
Om —
   oh volition, remember,
remember that which was done,
remember
that which was
done —

18. O Fire,
knower of every
   creature's breath,
take us along the good road,
far from deviant evil —
we offer you
   precious verse.

Andrew Schelling

WORK IN *ISHA UPANISHAD* & *BHAGAVAD GITA*

Humans get utterly confounded by the notion of work. That's why a poem like *Isha Upanishad* comes sharp as a breeze through the pines to us. For reasons not easy to articulate it seems to resolve a few thorny issues. No one knows who wrote or compiled its verses. The best scholarship says it was put together in the eighth or seventh century BC, making it one of the earliest strictly philosophical statements known. Lao-tzu's *Taoteching* and the fragments of Herakleitos – two texts that share *Isha's* tone and tough dialectic – come centuries later. What the three books hold in common are some elegant ideas about life, work, and what you do with the rewards of working.

Enjoy things by giving them up, says the poet. How interesting! Notice that this is not crabby moralizing or some puritanic hatred of pleasure. The counsel is to enjoy things, not cling to them. Blake said it like this:

> He who binds to himself a joy
> does the winged life destroy
> He who kisses the joy as it flies
> lives in Eternity's sunrise.

A few bedrock facts crop up in *Isha.* First among them, that each of us has a single precious human lifetime. *Hope for a hundred years,* the poem counsels. In India that was a symbolic way of saying a full human life, which is basically a shape cut into time. You devise that shape, that human shape, largely by what you do in this world as you move among its people and things.

It helps to read a few other *Upanishads* along with *Isha.* I recommend the good translations by Juan Mascaro and S. Radakrishnan. More prosaic, less cryptic, they flesh out ideas that come kernel-like, nutty, and hard-to-get-at in *Isha. Brihad-Aranyaka Upanishad* gives a few deceptively simple guidelines for action, addressed respectively to gods, humans, and demons. Interestingly, the anonymous poet of that old book (ca. 800 BC) claims to have heard the lessons directly from nature – in the crashing of thunder. "Da, Da, Da." All the poet does is interpret the mystic thunder syllables. *Damyata, dana, dayadhvam.*

These are: *self-restraint*, which pertains to gods and god-like folk, those beings who live where pleasures and possessions are in abundance. For ordinary humans, the thunder says *be generous.* The task is to counter archaic proclivities toward greed, which I'd guess is a deep genetic trait of *homo sapiens*. It probably comes from several hundred thousand years living as foragers and hunters – which made us edgy due to scarce and uncertain food supplies, and competition from other predators. Therefore generosity. Finally, for bitter, angry demon types, the teaching is – *compassion.*

So a deliberately cultivated attitude. Detachment, liberality. In every situation the most practical act a human can undertake is to give things up or away. Remember that to the *Upanishad* thinkers *things* may be material. But there are also intellectual things (such as good ideas, shapely ideas, art) and spiritual things such as benedictions and teachings. Among human failings it would seem stinginess is the greatest.

Years after the composition of *Isha Upanishad*, probably about the first century of the common era, an anonymous poet inserted *Bhagavad Gita* into the midst of *The Mahabharata* (ca. 500 BC–AD 500), India's enormous epic poem. Cast in devotional and religious terms, *Bhagavad Gita* builds on the thought of the *Upanishads* and gives them a subtle elegant inflection. Your deeds are your own, it counsels, but not the rewards of your work. The poem is worth reading repeatedly through the years, and no brief commentary could hope to interpret or paraphrase it. For modern ears a tentative translation might run: get as free as possible from the profit motive.

I bring up the profit motive because with the rise of industrial capitalism the human population of our planet seems to have passed through some barrier. It is very, very difficult to look back now and see how things must once have been. The ground and purpose of everyone's work have completely shifted since the day when *Isha* was familiar thought. Even the folk who first heard *Bhagavad Gita* lived in a vastly different world. At present, nearly everyone undertakes work specifically to acquire things. What sort of things? Exactly those things that one's neighbor possesses – "some other man's substance" as the *Upanishad* has it. What does an American get when he buys a child's toy produced in a Chinese work camp, or a shirt stitched together in a Philippine sweatshop? What about cars? Gas? Electricity? Fruit shipped up from Mexico?

The right to make money is the principal & most fiercely defended value for a twentieth-century American. It is central and respectable in the way, say, erotics was for Sappho, or religion for San Juan de la Cruz. The entire system is loaded to produce people with few other requirements from work than that it turn them a profit. By profit I mean money and things above and beyond what's needed to live. Real necessities – food, clothes, shelter, companionship, membership in the community – were once rather few.

How many people now work with the express purpose of giving things up or away? Artists? Teachers? Doctors? I don't ask this to condemn individuals, but to point out the way the market economy has altered what it means to be human. For one thing it insists on an inordinate attachment to, and belief in, things of the pragmatic world.

Isha is quite clear, without needing to locate them, that a variety of worlds exist. According to the old mythology you inhabit them depending on how you have led your previous life. Some worlds it calls demonic or sunless. Torpid, dark, full of delusion. As a figure of speech the poem suggests you go after death to these worlds. With a little psychological prowess we moderns would say the gates to these worlds are here, now, at the exact moment we act. Worlds are states of mind.

It seems likely that for centuries poems like *Isha Upanishad* helped an entire civilization keep track of its finest thought. It must have clarified what it meant to be human — all the conflicted ideas about knowledge and work; how to regard belongings; what to expect when your human life runs out. But for our world? Each passing year seems to make people less human. A predatory economy chews up everything in its path — the workers, the materials, the machines — turning them all into icons to be bought and sold or discarded as waste. Unions get busted, wilderness dwindles each minute, dignity gets farther away. Against all this, what could *Isha* mean? Or *Bhagavad Gita* with its haunting tenderness?

These poems no longer serve as documents of a culture's coherence. They come to contemporary ears as voices from far outside. Voices — along with *Taoteching* and a few very necessary other texts — for the subculture of resistance. A dissident community that still lives by old dictates of poetry and generosity. The bravest members of this scattered subculture even try to modify the course of civilization by quietly applying tenets of the old poems to social activism.

A note of caution though. We need to cast a sceptical eye at even the inspired elder texts. One of *Bhagavad Gita's* best known passages reads "Better to perform your own duty however poorly, than another person's, however well." It took the Sanskrit and Tibetan scholar Jan Willis, who adores the poem, to point out to me that you can hear behind that passage priests and politicians telling common workers, servants, ditch diggers, marginal farmers, "stay in your place, do your job." Jan, a black woman, grew up in Mississippi. This is not incidental. She came into adulthood with a similar voice in her ear. But there was another voice, the dissident one known as the Civil Rights Movement. So — what I got from her careful conversation: *never read uncritically.* Test every thought. Test each line of every poem against personal insight. Don't hang on to opinion or learning or life or work or anything. Enjoy yourself. Work hard. And try to be generous.

How funny we humans must look to our fellow creatures. Fretting every day over work, hanging onto things with an inane attachment, flipping the pages of books. How eccentric. As though we could clarify our lives simply by consulting a few ink-marks on paper. Yet what luck! To have *Isha Upanishad* and *Bhagavad Gita*, to have so many good books to guide us. Crickets or draft-horses or snowshoe hares doubtless go somewhere else. But they do recognize generosity when they meet it.

Lao-tzu

—⇒◗◆◖⇐—

TAOTECHING #2

All the world knows beauty
but if that becomes beautiful
this becomes ugly
all the world knows good
but if that becomes good
this becomes bad
the coexistence of have and have not
the coproduction of hard and easy
the correlation of long and short
the codependence of high and low
the correspondence of note and noise
the coordination of first and last
is endless
thus the sage performs effortless deeds
and teaches wordless lessons
he doesn't start all the things he begins
he doesn't presume on what he does
he doesn't claim what he achieves
and because he makes no claim
he suffers no loss

translated by Red Pine

Saint Benedict

from
THE RULE OF SAINT BENEDICT

4 First of all, every time you begin a good work, you must pray to him most earnestly to bring it to perfection. 5 In his goodness, he has already counted us as his sons, and therefore we should never grieve him by our evil actions. 6 With his good gifts which are in us, we must obey him at all times that he may never become the angry father who disinherits his sons, 7 nor the dread lord, enraged by our sins, who punishes us forever as worthless servants for refusing to follow him to glory.

8 Let us get up then, at long last, for the Scriptures rouse us when they say: *It is high time for us to arise from sleep* (Rom. 13:11). 9 Let us open our eyes to the light that comes from God, and our ears to the voice from heaven that every day calls out this charge: 10 *If you hear his voice today, do not harden your hearts* (Ps. 94 [95]:8). 11 And again: *You that have ears to hear, listen to what the Spirit says to the churches* (Rev. 2:7). 12 And what does he say? *Come and listen to me, sons; I will teach you the fear of the Lord* (Ps. 33[34]:12). 13 *Run while you have the light* of life, *that the darkness* of death *may not overtake you* (John 12:35).

William Langland

---

from
PIERS PLOWMAN

One sweet summer, when the sun was soft,
I got me into wool as if I were a blessed sheep –
Dressed like some shepherd or unholy hermit –
And went wide in the world wonders to hear.
But on a May morning on the Malvern Hills
A marvel befell me, from Fairyland methought.
I was weary with wandering and went to rest
Under a broad bank by the stream's side;
And as I lay and leaned over those waters
I slipped into slumber, it swayed so merrily.

Then I dreamed a marvelous dream –
That I was in a wilderness, I never knew where.
But as I gazed East, high up towards the sun
I saw a tower on a hill, truly made,
a deep dale beneath, a dungeon therein,
With deep ditches, dark and dreadful of sight.
A fair field full of folk I found there between –
Of all manners of men, both the mean and rich,
working and wandering as the world requires.

Some put themselves to the plough, playing full seldom,
Seeding and sowing they toiled true and hard,
Working to produce what wasters in gluttony consume.
And some dressed in pride, tricked out in fine array.
In prayers and penance many put themselves out;
All for the love of Our Lord they lived true lives
In hope to have heavenly bliss –
As anchorites and hermits they keep to their cells
With no longing to go loafing about the land
Or indulge their bodies with luxurious living.

And some chose trade; they succeeded the more
Since it seems in our sight that such men thrive –

And some made mirth as minstrels best can,
getting gold with their glee – guiltless I believe –
But jesters and chatterers, Judas's children,
Fake such fantasies and make themselves fools
Who have the wit to work if they would;
What Paul preaches I won't prove here:
Those who speak such shit are the devil's own.…

There too hundreds in coifs of silk hovered about –
Lawyers, it seemed, that served at the Bar,
Pleading for pennies and pounding out the law,
And not one for love of Our Lord loosed their lips once.
You might better measure mist on the Malvern Hills
 Than get a murmer from their mouths till money be shown!

Barons and burgers and peasants too
I saw in this assembly, as you shall hear later;
Bakers and brewers and butchers in plenty,
Wool-weavers and workers of linen,
Tailors and tinkers and toll-collectors,
Masons and miners and many other crafts-folk:
All kinds of laborers running for a living –
Ditchers and diggers who do their deeds ill –
Shoddy workmen who sing bawdy songs
All the day long –
Cooks and their knaves crying "hot pies, real hot!
Fat pigs and geese! Get 'em while they're hot!"
Tavern men tell the same:
"White wine of Alsace, wine of Gascony,
Rhine and La Rochelle to wash down the roast!"
– All this I saw sleeping, and seven times more.

modernized by Douglas Thorpe

Meister Eckhart

SERMON 39
Iustus in perpetuum vivet et apud dominum est merces eius

One reads a short saying in today's epistle spoken by the wise man: "The just lives in eternity."

I have already spoken at times about what a just man is, but now shall explain it differently or in a different sense: A just person is one who has been informed by and transformed into justice. The just man lives in God and God in him because God is born in the just man and the just man in God. In every virtue of the just man God is born, and he is filled with joy by every virtue of the just man. But not just by every virtue, rather, by every work of the just man, however small it may be, if it is performed by the just man in justice, it fills God with joy. He is delighted through and through because nothing remains in his ground that is not animated by joy. This fact is for the less discerning to believe and for the enlightened to know.

The just man seeks nothing in his works. Those that seek something in their works or those who work because of a "why" are servants and hired hands. And so, if you want to be informed by and transformed into justice, have no [specific] intention in your works and form no "why" in yourself, either in time or in eternity, either reward or happiness, either this or that. Such works are, in fact, dead. Even if you form God within yourself, whatever works you perform for a [specific] purpose are all dead, and you ruin good works. You do not just ruin good works; you also commit sin because you act just like a gardener who is supposed to plant a garden but only pulls out the trees and expects to get paid for it. This is how you ruin good works. And so, if you want to live and want your works to live, you must be dead to all things and have become nothing. It is a characteristic of creatures that they make something out of something, while it is a characteristic of God that he makes something out of nothing. Therefore, if God is to make anything in you or with you, you must first have become nothing. Hence go into your own ground and work there, and the works that you work there will all be living. This is why he says, "The just lives." Because he is just he works, and his works live.

Now he says, "His reward is with God" (Wis. 5:16). On this point only a few words. He says "with" because the just man's reward is where God himself is. The happiness of the just man and God's happiness are one happiness because the just man is only happy where God is happy. St. John says, "The Word was with God"

(John 1:1). He says "with," and this is why the just man is like God: God is justice. Therefore, whoever is in justice is in God and *is* God.

Now let us say more about the word "just." He does not say "the just *human being*" or "the just *angel*"; he simply says "the just." The Father gives birth to his Son the just and the just his Son. All the virtues of the just and every work that has been performed by the virtue of the just is nothing else but the Son being born of the Father. This is why the Father never rests but spends his time urging and prodding, so that the Son be born in me, as the scripture says: "Neither for Zion's sake am I silent nor for Jerusalem's sake do I rest until the just appears and shines forth like lightning" (Isa. 62:1). *Zion* means the summit of life, and *Jerusalem* means the summit of peace. However, neither for the summit of life nor for the summit of peace does God ever rest, but [he] urges and prods always that the just appear. In the just nothing should work but God alone. If it happens that anything from without moves you to work, the works are really all dead. And if it happens that God moves you from without to work, these works are all dead. If your works are to live, God must move you from within, in the innermost of the soul, if they really are to live. There is where your life is; there alone is where you live.

I say further: If one virtue seems greater to you than another and if you esteem it more than another, then you do not cherish it as it exists in justice and God does not yet work in you. As long as a person esteems or cherishes one virtue more [than another], he does not cherish or take them as they exist in justice, nor is he just. The just man takes and performs all virtues in justice, since they are justice itself.

The scripture says: "Before the created world I am" (Sir. 24:14). He says "before" and "I am." This means: Where man is above time in eternity, there he works one work with God. Some people ask: How can a person perform works that God worked a thousand years ago or a thousand years hence, and they do not understand it. In eternity there is neither before nor after. Hence what happened a thousand years ago or will happen a thousand years from now or is happening now is all simply one in eternity. Therefore, whatever God did or created a thousand years ago or a thousand years hence he is doing now; it is simply all one work. Thus a man who is above time in eternity works together with God whatever God worked a thousand years ago or a thousand years hence. And this is for wise people to know and for the less wise to believe.

St. Paul says, "We are eternally chosen in the Son" (Cf. Ep. 1:4). Hence we should never rest until we become that which we eternally have been in him; for the Father urges and prods that we be born in the Son and become the same thing that the Son is. The Father gives birth to his Son, and in giving birth the Father has so much peace and delight that he consumes his whole nature in it. All that is in God moves him to give birth. His ground, his essence, and his being all move the Father to give birth.

Sometimes a light becomes perceptible in the soul, and a person thinks it is the Son; but is only a light. Whenever the Son appears in the soul, the love of the Holy

Spirit also appears. Therefore, I say: The Father's being consists in giving birth to the Son; the Son's being consists in my being born in him and like him; the Holy Spirit's being lies in my catching fire in him and becoming totally melted and becoming simply love. Whoever is thus inside of love and is totally love thinks that God loves no one but him alone, nor can he love anyone nor be loved by anyone than by him [God] alone.

Some teachers claim that the spirit takes its happiness from love; others claim that it takes it in seeing God. I say, however, it takes it neither from love nor from knowing nor from seeing. Now one could ask: In eternal life does not the spirit see God? Yes and no. Insofar as the spirit is born, it does not look up to or see God. But insofar as it is being born, it sees God. Therefore the happiness of the spirit consists in its having been born and not in its being born; for it lives where the Father lives: in oneness and in the nakedness of being. Therefore, turn away from all things and take yourself purely in being, for whatever is outside of being is accident and accidents result in "why."

That we live in eternity, may God help us. Amen.

Ananda K. Coomaraswamy

from
MEISTER ECKHART'S VIEW OF ART

With respect to his "staying with creatures to keep them in being" (427, cf. 261), Eckhart thinks of God as a mother (the creations both of God and man are in the nature of children begotten and conceived), and it will not be overlooked that in so far as man takes care of things that have been made and preserves them from decay, he is working temporarily in the analogy of God's maternal maintenance. All man's working in creation, preservation, and destruction is temporal analogy of God's simultaneous expression, maintenance, and resolution, *srsti, sthiti, laya*. But "yonder no work is done at all" (238); "if the carpenter were perfect at his work he would not need materials; he would no sooner think a house than, lo, it would be made," as is the case "with the works in God; he thinks them and behold they are" (238); or again, "a carpenter building a house will first erect it in his mind and, were the house enough subject to his will, then, materials apart, the only difference between them would be that of begetter and suddenly begotten ... (as) it is in God ... one God, there being no distinction of outpouring (*abhisrsti*) and outpoured (*abhisarga*)" (72).

Alike in man and God, the "art" (intuition-expression) is and remains wholly in the artist; but "think not it is with God as with a human carpenter, who works or works not as he chooses, who can do or leave undone at his good pleasure. It is not thus with God; but finding thee ready, he is obliged to act, to overflow into thee; just as the sun must needs burst forth when the air is bright, and is unable to contain itself" (23). The "being ready" is otherwise expressed as matter's being "insatiable for form" (18); so God "must do, willy-nilly" (162), according to his nature, without a why. In man this becomes what has been called the gratuitousness of art: "man ought not to work for any why, not for God nor for his glory nor for anything at all that is outside him, but only for that which is his being, his very life within him" (163, cf. *Brhadaranyaka Upanisad*, IV, 5, 6); "have no ulterior purpose in thy work" (149), "work as though no one existed, no one lived, no one had ever come upon the earth" (308); "All happiness to those who have listened to this sermon. Had there been no one here I must have preached it to the poor-box" (143).

"God and God's will are one, for if I am a man and if I mean to do real work entirely without or free from will ... I should do my works in such a way that they entered not into my will.... I should do them simply at the will of God" (308), "Above all lay no claim to anything. Let go thyself, and let God act for thee" (308). The artist has some "inkling" (47) of God's manner of working "willingly but not by will, naturally and not by nature" (225) when he has acquired mastery and the habit (*habitus, slistatva*) of his work and does not hesitate but "can go ahead without a qualm, not wondering, am I right or am I doing wrong? If the painter had to plan out every brush mark before he made his first he would not paint at all" (141). Still, "Heaven does more than the carpenter who builds a house" (II, 209).

"Inspired by his art" (II, 211), "as much like his ideal as he can" (252), and "working for work's sake," sound to modern ears like art for art's sake. But "art" and "his ideal" have not here their modern sentimental connotations, they represent nothing but the artist's understanding of his theme, the work to be done (*krtârtha*); working for "the real intention of the work's first cause" (252) is not working for the sake of the workmanship, as the modern doctrine implies; "working for work's sake" means in freedom, without ulterior motive, easily (cf. *Bhagavad Gita, passim*). To work according to the "dearest conception of his art" (97), that is with all the skill and care he can command, is merely honest, and "By honest I mean doing one's best at the moment" (II, 95), having "good grounds for thinking no one else could do the work as well" (II, 90), and standing for "perfection in temporal works" (II, 92), the "careful" being "those who let nothing hinder them in their work" (II, 90).

The first cause of the work and the good of the work to be done are one and the same, "the ultimate end (*prayojana*) of the work is ever the real intention (*artha*) of the work's first cause" (252), "when the carpenter builds a house his first intention is a roof (that is, the idea of shelter), and that is (actually) the finish of the house" (196). No man being a rational being works for no end: "The builder hewing wood and stone because he wants to build a house 'gainst summer's heat and winter's chill is thinking first and last about the house, excepting for the house he would never hew a single stone or do a hand's turn of the work" (II, 72).

The good of the work is its immediate physical good, not its edifying purpose. Actual work requires a worldly wisdom, industry, and cunning, not to be confused with vision, but matter of fact, and with due regard to the material (II, 93): for instance, "A celebrant (of the mass) over-much intent on recollection is liable to make mistakes. The best way is to try and concentrate the mind before and afterwards, but when actually saying it to do so quite straightforwardly" (II, 175). A work may be undertaken *ad majorem gloriam Dei* or to any more immediate end, but the end can only be enjoyed in the prospect or in completion of the work. In action the workman is nothing but a tool, and should use himself accordingly, concerned with the work and not with its results; he can and should be totally absorbed in the work, like the "heathen philosopher who studied mathematics ... in pursuance of his art ... too much absorbed to see or hear his enemy" (12). Working thus is not for the sake of or to display skill, but to serve, and praise the first cause of the work, that is, the subject imaged in the artist's mind "without idea of ownership" (35). It is immaterial what the work may be, but it is essential that the artist should be wholly given to it, "it is all the same to him what he is loving" (II, 66), it is working for the love of God in any case, because the perfection of the work is "to prepare all creatures to return to God" (143) as "in their natural mode (they) are exemplified in divine essence" (253), and this will hold good even if the painter paints his own portrait, God's image in himself. He is no true workman but a vainglorious showman who would astonish by his skill; "any proper man ought to be ashamed for good people to know of this in him" (II, 51); having his art which he is expected to practice, he should take his artfulness and cunning for granted. If by reason of his skill he gets a good report in the world, that is to be taken as the "gift of God" (143), not as his due who should work "as though no one existed" (308). Similarly as to wages, the workman is indeed worthy of his hire, but if he is "careful" for anything but the good of the work to be done, he is no workman but a "thrall and hireling" (149).

Working in the world "at some useful occupation" (22) is by no means any hindrance to the perfecting of the man, and though "praying is a better act than spinning" (II, 8) a man should relinquish "rapture" to engage in any activity that may be required of him by way of service (II, 14, etc.), and even that "without which I cannot get into God, is work, vocation, or calling in time, which interferes not one whit with eternal salvation" (II, 93). "To be in the right state one of two things has to happen: either he must find God and learn to have him in his works, or else things and works must be abandoned altogether. But no one in this life can be without activities, human ones, and not a few at that, so man has to learn to find his God in everything" (II; cf. *Bhagavad Gita* III, 33); even for the religious "active life bridges the gaps in the life of contemplation," and, "Those who lead the contemplative life and do no outward works, are most mistaken and all on the wrong tack"; "No person can in this life reach the point at which he is excused from outward works" (425 cf. *Bhagavad Gita* III, 16 and 25); therefore "'work in all things' and 'fulfil thy destiny'" (165). Still more in the case of one "who knows nothing of the truth from within, if he woo it without (he) shall find it too within" (440). In any case "God's purpose in the union (*yoga*) of contemplation is fruitfulness in works" (16).

Jalaluddin Rumi

from
THE MATHNAWI

From you this ebb and flow comes, O Lord,
or else this sea of mine is still.
Unperplex me. I'm a desert camel
starved and burdened by my own free will.
Let the load drop —
let me live and graze
on the meadow of your infinite body.
I shall roll as you turn me, right or left,
true as a ball down the green felt.
Hundreds of thousands of years I've spent flying
like dust through the air —
only at night do I remember
and escape from this cross of myself
into the infinite pastures of spirit;
only in sleep do I nurse again
from the milk of your magnificence.
All the world flees this desert of the self —
all know its snare, memory
and consciousness ripening
into hell. Like me they flee
from self to selflessness —
winged by night in wine and dreams,
by day in the wonders of
all engrossing work.

version by Douglas Thorpe

Hadewijch

LIVING IN THE RHYTHM OF THE TRINITY

> Be generous and zealous for every virtue,
> But do not apply yourself to any one virtue.
> Fail not with regard to a multitude of things,
> But perform no particular work.
> Have good will and compassion for every need,
> But take nothing under your protection.
> This I wished long since to tell you,
> For it lies heavy on my heart;
> May God give you to understand what I mean,
> Solely in the one nature of Love.

The things I order you in these verses were ordered me by God. Therefore I desire in my turn to order you the same things, because they belong perfectly to the perfection of Love, and because they belong perfectly and wholly in the Divinity. The attributes I mentioned here are perfectly the divine Nature. For to be generous and zealous is the Nature of the Holy Spirit; this is what is his proper Person. And not to apply oneself to a particular work is the Nature of the Father; through this he is the one Father. This pouring out and keeping back are the pure Divinity and the entire Nature of Love.

> Fail not with regard to a multitude of things,
> But perform no particular work.

The first of these verses expresses the power of the Father, whereby he is God almighty. The second verse expresses his just will, with which his justice works its unknown mighty works. These works are deep and dark, unknown and hidden for all who, as I said, are below this Unity of the Godhead but nevertheless render service (and, indeed, chivalrously) to each of the Three Persons, according to the verses I placed first in each couplet:

> To be favorable and zealous for every virtue,
> And not to fail with regard to a multitude of things,
> And to have compassionate good will for every need.

This seems indeed to be the most perfect life one can attain on earth. And you have heard this continually, for I always recommended it above all; and I also experienced it above all, and rendered service accordingly and worked chivalrously until the day it was forbidden me.

The verses that come second in each of the three couplets I have composed express the perfection of the Unity and of Love, and according to justice treat of Love as one being, one sole Love, and nothing else. O *Deus!* This is a frightening being who, at one and same time engulfs in unison such hatred and such charity!

Have good will and compassion for every need.

That was the Son in what is proper to his Person. He was purely this and did purely this.

But take nothing under your protection.

Thus his Father engulfed him in himself; this cruel great work ever belongs to the Father. Yet it is the Unity of purest love in the Divinity: so that this Unity is also just with the justice of love and includes this Devotion, this Manhood, and this Power; nor would it have anyone left in need. And it includes one's charity and compassion for those in hell and purgatory; for those unknown to God (Matt. 25:12; Luke 13:25), or who are known to him but still stray outside his dearest will; and for loving souls, who have more sorrow than all the rest, since they lack what they love. Justice takes up all this into itself. And yet each Person separately has given out what is proper to him, as I have said.

But the just nature of the Unity, in which Love belongs to Love and is perfect fruition of herself, does not seek after virtues, virtuous tendencies, or particular works, however pure or of however pure authority they are; and it does not give its protection, out of mercy, to any need, mighty though it is to enrich.

For in that fruition of Love there never was and never can be any other work than that one fruition in which the one almighty Deity is Love.

What was forbidden me (as I told you it was forbidden) was to have on earth any undueness of love; that is, to stand in awe of nothing outside of Love, and to live in love so exclusively that everything outside of Love should be utterly hated and shunned; therefore for those outside of Love, to have no inclination and no virtuous acts, to perform no particular works that might assist them, and to have no mercy that might protect them, but to remain constantly in the fruition of Love. But when this fruition grows less or passes away, all three of the forbidden works should indeed be performed, as justly owed. When anyone seeks Love and undertakes her service, he must do all things for her glory, for during all this time he is human and needy; and then he must work chivalrously in all things, be generous, serve, and show mercy, for everything fails him and leaves him in want. But when by fruition man is untied to Love, he becomes God, mighty and just. And will, work, and might have an equal part in his justice, as the Three Persons are in one God.

These prohibitions were laid upon me on Ascension Day, four years ago, by God the father himself, at the moment when his Son came upon the altar. At this coming, I received a kiss from him, and by this token I was shown what follows. Having been made one with him, I came before his Father. There the Father took the Son to himself with me and took me to himself with the Son. And in this Unity into which I was taken and where I was enlightened, I understood this Essence and knew it more clearly than, by speech, reason, or sight, one can know anything that is knowable on earth.

Although I forbid you some works and command the others, you will in either case have to serve much. But lack of discrimination regarding the things I have said, this I forbid you as those works were forbidden me by God's will. But you must still labor at the works of Love, as I long did, and as his friends did and still do. For my part I am devoted to these works at any hour and still perform them at all times: to seek after nothing but Love, and advance nothing but Love. How you are to do or omit each of these things, may God, our Beloved, teach you.

E. F. Schumacher

BUDDHIST ECONOMICS

"Right livelihood" is one of the requirements of the Buddha's Noble Eightfold Path. It is clear, therefore, that there must be such a thing as Buddhist economics.

Buddhist countries have often stated that they wish to remain faithful to their heritage. So Burma: "The New Burma sees no conflict between religious values and economic progress. Spiritual health and material well-being are not enemies: they are natural allies." Or: "We can blend successfully the religious and spiritual values of our heritage with the benefits of modern technology." Or: "We Burmans have a sacred duty to conform both our dreams and our acts to our faith. This we shall ever do."

All the same, such countries invariably assume that they can model their economic development plans in accordance with modern economics, and they call upon modern economists from so-called advanced countries to advise them, to formulate the policies to be pursued, and to construct the grand design for development, the Five-Year Plan or whatever it may be called. No one seems to think that a Buddhist way of life would call for Buddhist economics, just as the modern materialist way of life has brought forth modern economics.

Economists themselves, like most specialists, normally suffer from a kind of metaphysical blindness, assuming that theirs is a science of absolute and invariable truths, without any presuppositions. Some go as far as to claim that economic laws are as free from "metaphysics," of "values" as the law of gravitation. We need not, however, get involved in arguments of methodology. Instead, let us take some fundamentals and see what they look like when viewed by a modern economist and a Buddhist economist.

There is universal agreement that a fundamental source of wealth is human labour. Now, the modern economist has been brought up to consider "labour" or work as little more than a necessary evil. From the point of view of the employer, it is in any case simply an item of cost, to be reduced to a minimum if it cannot be eliminated altogether, say, by automation. From the point of view of the workman, it is a "disutility"; to work is to make a sacrifice of one's leisure and comfort, and wages are a kind of compensation for the sacrifice. Hence the ideal from the point of view of the employer is to have output without employees, and the ideal from the point of view of the employee is to have income without employment.

The consequences of these attitudes both in theory and in practice are, of course, extremely far-reaching. If the ideal with regard to work is to get rid of it, every method that "reduces the work load" is a good thing. The most potent method, short of automation, is the so-called "division of labour" and the classical example is the pin factory eulogised in Adam Smith's *Wealth of Nations*. Here it is not a matter of ordinary specialisation, which mankind has practiced from time immemorial, but of dividing up every complete process of production into minute parts, so that the final product can be produced at great speed without anyone having had to contribute more than a totally insignificant and, in most cases, unskilled movement of his limbs.

The Buddhist point of view takes the function of work to be at least threefold: to give a man a chance to utilise and develop his faculties; to enable him to overcome his ego-centredness by joining with other people in a common task; and to bring forth the goods and services needed for a becoming existence. Again, the consequences that flow from this view are endless. To organize work in such a manner that it becomes meaningless, boring, stultifying, or nerve-wracking for the worker would be little short of criminal; it would indicate a greater concern with goods than with people, an evil lack of compassion and a soul-destroying degree of attachment to the most primitive side of this worldly existence. Equally, to strive for leisure as an alternative to work would be considered a complete misunderstanding of one of the basic truths of human existence, namely that work and leisure are complementary parts of the same living process and cannot be separated without destroying the joy of work and the bliss of leisure.

From the Buddhist point of view, there are therefore two types of mechanization which must be clearly distinguished: one that enhances a man's skill and power and one that turns the work of man over to a mechanical slave, leaving man in a position of having to serve the slave. How to tell the one from the other? "The craftsman himself," says Ananda K. Coomaraswamy, a man equally competent to talk about the modern West as the ancient East, "can always, if allowed to, draw the delicate distinction between the machine and the tool. The carpet loom is a tool, a contrivance for holding warp threads at a stretch for the pile to be woven round them by the craftsmen's fingers; but the power loom is a machine, and its significance as a destroyer of culture lies in the fact that it does the essentially human part of the work." It is clear, therefore, that Buddhist economics must be very different from the economics of modern materialism, since the Buddhist sees the essence of civilization not in a multiplication of wants but in the purification of human character. Character, at the same time, is formed primarily by a man's work. And work, properly conducted in conditions of human dignity and freedom, blesses those who do it and equally their products. The Indian philosopher and economist J.C. Kumarappa sums the matter up as follows:

> If the nature of the work is properly appreciated and applied, it will
> stand in the same relation to the higher faculties as food is to the
> physical body. It nourishes and enlivens the higher man and urges him

to produce the best he is capable of. It directs his free will along the proper course and disciplines the animal in him into progressive channels. It furnishes an excellent background for man to display his scale of values and develop his personality.

If a man has no chance of obtaining work he is in a desperate position, not simply because he lacks an income but because he lacks this nourishing and enlivening factor of disciplined work which nothing can replace. A modern economist may engage in highly sophisticated calculations on whether full employment "pays" or whether it might be more "economic" to run an economy at less than full employment so as to ensure a greater mobility of labour, a better stability of wages, and so forth. His fundamental criterion of success is simply the total quantity of goods produced during a given period of time. "If the marginal urgency of goods is low," says Professor Galbraith in *The Affluent Society*, "then so is the urgency of employing the last man of the last million men in the labour force." And again: "If ... we can afford some unemployment in the interest of stability – a proposition, incidentally, of impeccably conservative antecedents – then we can afford to give those who are unemployed the goods that enable them to sustain their accustomed standard of living."

From a Buddhist point a view, this is standing the truth on its head by considering goods as more important than creative activity. It means shifting the emphasis from the worker to the product of work, that is, from the human to the subhuman, a surrender to the forces of evil. The very start of Buddhist economic planning would be a planning for full employment, and the primary purpose of this would in fact be employment for everyone who needs an "outside" job: it would not be the maximization of employment nor the maximization of production. Women, on the whole, do not need an "outside" job, and the large-scale employment of women in offices or factories would be considered a sign of serious economic failure. In particular, to let mothers of young children run wild would be as uneconomic in the eyes of a Buddhist as the employment of a skilled worker as a soldier in the eyes of a modern economist.

While the materialist is mainly interested in goods, the Buddhist is mainly interested in liberation. But Buddhism is "The Middle Way" and therefore in no way antagonistic to physical well-being. It is not wealth that stands in the way of liberation but the attachment to wealth; not the enjoyment of pleasurable things but the craving for them. The keynote to Buddhist economics, therefore, is simplicity and nonviolence. From an economist's point of view, the marvel of the Buddhist way of life is the utter rationality of its pattern – amazingly small means leading to extraordinarily satisfactory results.

For the modern economist this is very difficult to understand. He is used to measuring the "standard of living" by the amount of annual consumption, assuming all the time that a man who consumes more is "better off" than a man who consumes less. A Buddhist economist would consider this approach excessively irrational: since consumption is merely a means to human well-being, the aim should be to obtain the maximum of well-being with the minimum of consumption. Thus, if the purpose of clothing is a certain amount of temperature comfort and an attractive appearance, the task is to attain this purpose with the smallest possible effort, that is, with the smallest annual destruction of cloth and with the help of designs that involve the smallest possible input of toil. The less toil there is, the more time and strength is left for artistic creativity. It would be highly uneconomic, for instance, to go in for complicated tailoring, like the modern West, when a much more beautiful effect can be achieved by the skillful draping of uncut material. It would be the height of folly to make material so that it should wear out quickly and the height of barbarity to make anything ugly, shabby, or mean. What has just been said about clothing applies equally to all other human requirements. The ownership and the consumption of goods is a means to an end, and Buddhist economics is the systematic study of how to attain given ends with the minimum of means.

Modern economics, on the other hand, considers consumption to be the sole end and purpose of all economic activity, taking the factors of production – land, labour, and capital – as the means. The former, in short, tries to maximize human satisfactions by the optimal pattern of consumption, while the latter tries to maximize consumption by the optimal pattern of productive effort. It is easy to see that the effort needed to sustain a way of life which seeks to attain the optimal pattern of consumption is likely to be much smaller than the effort needed to sustain a drive for maximum consumption. We need not be surprised, therefore, that the pressure and strain of living is very much less in, say, Burma than it is in the United States, in spite of the fact that the amount of labour-saving machinery used in the former country is only a minute fraction of the amount used in the latter.

Simplicity and nonviolence are obviously closely related. The optimal pattern of consumption, producing a high degree of human satisfaction by means of a relatively low rate of consumption, allows people to live without great pressure and strain and to fulfill the primary injunction of Buddhist teaching: "Cease to do evil; try to do good." As physical resources are everywhere limited, people satisfying their needs by means of a modest use of resources are obviously less likely to be at each other's throats than people depending upon a high rate of use. Equally, people who live in highly self-sufficient local communities are less likely to get involved in large-scale violence than people whose existence depends on worldwide systems of trade.

From the point of view of Buddhist economics, therefore, production from local resources for local needs is the most rational way of economic life, while dependence on imports from afar and the consequent need to produce for export to unknown and distant peoples is highly uneconomic and justifiable only in exceptional cases and on a small scale. Just as the modern economist would admit that a high rate of consumption of transport services between a man's home and his place of work signifies a misfortune and not a high standard of life, so the Buddhist economist would hold that to satisfy human wants from faraway sources rather than from sources nearby signifies failure rather than success. The former tends to take statistics showing an increase in the number of ton/miles per head of the population carried by a country's transport system as proof of economic progress, while to the latter – the Buddhist economist – the same statistics would indicate a highly undesirable deterioration in the pattern of consumption.

Another striking difference between modern economics and Buddhist economics arises over the use of natural resources. Bertrand de Jouvenel, the eminent French political philosopher, has characterized "Western man" in words which may be taken as a fair description of the modern economist:

> He tends to count nothing as an expenditure, other than human effort; he does not seem to mind how much mineral matter he wastes and, far worse, how much living matter he destroys. He does not seem to realize at all that human life is a dependent part of an ecosystem of many different forms of life. As the world is ruled from towns where men are cut off from any form of life other than humans, the feeling of belonging to an ecosystem is not revived. This results in a harsh and improvident treatment of things upon which we ultimately depend, such as water and trees.

The teaching of the Buddha, on the other hand, enjoins a reverent and nonviolent attitude not only to all sentient beings but also, with great emphasis, to trees. Every follower of Buddha ought to plant a tree every few years and look after it until it is safely established, and the Buddhist economist can demonstrate without difficulty that the universal observation of this rule would result in a high rate of genuine economic development independent of any foreign aid. Much of the economic decay of southeast Asia (as of many other parts of the world) is undoubtedly due to a heedless and shameful neglect of trees.

Modern economics does not distinguish between renewable and nonrenewable materials, as its very method is to equalize and quantify everything by means of a money price. Thus, taking various alternative fuels, like coal, oil, wood, or water-power: the only difference between them recognized by modern economics is relative cost per equivalent unit. The cheapest is automatically the one to be preferred, as to do otherwise would be irrational and "uneconomic." From a Buddhist point of view, of course, this will not do; the essential difference between nonrenewable fuels like coal and oil on the one hand and renewable fuels like wood and water-power cannot be simply overlooked. Nonrenewable goods must be used only if they are indispensable, and then only with the greatest care and the most meticulous concern for conservation. To use them heedlessly or extravagantly is an act of violence, and while complete nonviolence may not be attainable on this earth, there is nonetheless an ineluctable duty on man to aim at the ideal of nonviolence in all he does.

Just as a modern European economist would not consider it a great economic achievement if all European art treasures were sold to America at attractive prices, so the Buddhist economist would insist that a population basing its economic life on nonrenewable fuels is living parasitically, on capital instead of income. Such a way of life could have no permanence and could therefore be justified only as a purely temporary expedient. As the world's resources of nonrenewable fuels – coal, oil, and natural gas – are exceedingly unevenly distributed over the globe and undoubtedly limited in quantity, it is clear that their exploitation at an ever-increasing rate is an act of violence against nature which must almost inevitably lead to violence between men.

This fact alone might give food for thought even to those people in Buddhist countries who care nothing for the religious and spiritual values of their heritage and ardently desire to embrace the materialism of modern economics at the fastest possible speed. Before they dismiss Buddhist economics as nothing better than a nostalgic dream, they might wish to consider whether the path of economic de-velopment outlined by modern economics is likely to lead them to places where they really want to be. Towards the end of his courageous book *The Challenge of Man's Future*, Professor Harrison Brown of the California Institute of Technology gives the following appraisal:

> Thus we see that, just as industrial society is fundamentally unstable and subject to reversion to agrarian existence, so within it the condi-tions which offer individual freedom are unstable in their ability to avoid the conditions which impose rigid organization and totalitar-ian control. Indeed, when we examine all of the foreseeable diffi-culties which threaten the survival of industrial civilization, it is difficult to see how the achievement of stability and the maintenance of individual liberty can be made compatible.

Even if this were dismissed as a long-term view there is the immediate question of whether "modernization" as currently practiced without regard to religious and spiritual values, is actually producing agreeable results. As far as the masses are con-cerned, the results appear to be disastrous – a collapse of the rural economy, a ris-ing tide of unemployment in town and country, and the growth of a city prole-tariat without nourishment for either body or soul.

It is in the light of both immediate experience and long-term prospects that the study of Buddhist economics could be recommended even to those who believe that economic growth is more important than any spiritual or religious values. For it is not a question of choosing between "modern growth" and "traditional stag-nation." It is a question of finding the right path of development, the Middle Way between materialist heedlessness and traditionalist immobility, in short, of finding "Right Livelihood."

Dorothee Soelle

WORK AS
SELF-EXPRESSION

Several years ago I discovered the meaning of work when I contacted the teacher of my youngest child, then a first-grader at an excellent school in Manhattan. One day I became impatient with my daughter's progress at school. They had not yet taught her, at age six, to read or write. So I visited her teacher to ask when the children would start to work. "Work!" he scoffed. "What do you mean? You're talking about work! Can't you see what's going on here? Don't you see that these strong workers, these children, are building a town with their blocks?" He sent me home with this response, a response I was to mull over and benefit from in the ensuing years. His response changed my mind, moving me from a myopic, production-oriented perspective on work to a more humane understanding of work. I discovered the meaning of work in its three essential dimensions: self-expression, social-relatedness, and reconciliation with nature by way of this experience.

These three dimensions of human labor are spiritual as well as material. The spiritual dimension of work is all too easily overlooked. When I questioned the teacher about my child's progress, for example, I displayed a spiritually impoverished perspective on work. Here I attempt to take the flesh-and-blood human being seriously as a worker who realizes God's image through work. E.F. Schumacher, to whom I am greatly indebted, observes in his *Good Work* that "the question of what work does to the worker is hardly ever asked."[7] This is true. It was certainly true of me as a mother six years ago. I was not thinking about what work did to the worker, even to the elementary-school worker, and yet how the work affects the worker is a most important question. If we neglect this question, we will restrict human work to one purpose only, namely, to provide necessary, useful goods and services – as if that could be accomplished without reflecting on the author of work, the worker. The biblical creation narrative teaches us, as other religious and wisdom traditions do, that the purposeful activity of producing is linked to the human striving for perfection. Work enables "every one of us to use and thereby perfect our gifts like good stewards."[8] Schumacher recovers for us the dignity of the worker, or the steward, and the yearning for self-perfection and creativity that underlies human activity. If we understand life as a school, a training ground in which we strive to become something more than we are at present, then work becomes creative praxis.

Good work gives the person a chance to utilize and to develop her faculties. We have to learn "to reject meaningless, boring, stultifying, or nerve-wracking work," as Schumacher maintains, "in which a man (or a woman) is made the servant of a machine or a system."[9] I concur with Schumacher that it is extremely important to teach people to reject unsatisfying, pointless, or nerve-wracking work. Work should be a joy in our lives, and it is crucial for our attainment of full personhood. Thomas Aquinas said that there can be no joy in life without joy in work. The opposite of this joy in medieval philosophy is laziness, or *acedia*, the meaning of which is closer to depression, listlessness, lack of energy, malaise, and laziness in a more existential sense than the word in English conveys. *Acedia* was a severe problem among the cloistered monks and nuns of medieval society, where it was considered to be a sign of the "sadness of the soul" bereft of joy and energy. If we never experience the joy of life in our work, we never mature as full persons. We must not settle for less than work that is good for the worker. We need work for our development, for the perfection of our souls.

Unfortunately, most forms of work are utterly unsatisfying, boring, and meaningless:

> Mechanical, artificial, divorced from nature, utilizing only the smallest part of man's potential capabilities, [work] sentences the great majority of workers to spending their lives in a way which contains no worthy challenge, no stimulus to self-perfection, no chance of development, no element of Beauty, Truth, or Goodness.[10]

Look for these elements in our work. Where are they? A contemporary of Marx stated that "the subdivision of labor is the assassination of a people."[11] The subdivision of labor is a direct attack on the element of beauty, truth, or goodness in work. The extreme forms of labor division are all destructive to our potentials in that they make only partial use of them. In understanding what good work means and what it does to the worker, the paradigm of the artist is most relevant. There is an element of art in good work. Art, like all good work, enables us to release the power of our imaginations and to become persons as we use this power to come up with an invention, a new solution to a problem, a new way of working. In this sense, the worker-artist collaborates with God in creating, and she or he experiences this labor, praxis, self-activity as pleasure and enjoyment. Art pleases the intellect and the senses, and so does good work.

The vision of self-expression and self-fulfillment in work is more than a utopian dream of people who suffer under the curse tradition of meaningless work. A theology of work must have a visionary, prophetic, or utopian element. As the Book of Proverbs says, "Where there is no vision, the people perish" (29:18, KJV). If there are both repressive and liberating traditions in Christianity, the task of theology is to uncover, to unmask, to critique the repressive tradition and to reveal the true meaning of human work and the identity of its agent, the worker. Good work is a basic human need. We destroy the human being if work means functioning without joy, without fulfillment, without imagination. If we labor under this curse tradition, then we have to recall for ourselves that fulfilling work is a human need. We need to understand ourselves as co-creators who require constructive and joyful work in which we are challenged to develop our creative potential.

The sense of wholeness implied in the concept of good work as a basic human need is marred especially by the division of labor we experience from early childhood onward. As every adequate critique of culture maintains, modern education has produced a variety of specialists who, in common parlance, know more and more about less and less. One result of this intellectual and emotional underdevelopment is "the inability of the person to develop self-government and to interact critically with the surrounding social order."[12] The depoliticization of society is a grave consequence of unfulfilling work in which no self-expression is permitted. People are trained to use such a minuscule part of their brains, such a limited range of their capacities, that their potentials never reach fruition. If at a certain point they are given the opportunity to move beyond these confines, people often fail, as was the case in Yugoslavia for a time. The capitalist countries watched what turned out to be a long experiment in Yugoslavian worker self-governance and just gloated. "We always told you that workers were unable to manage a factory" was the gist of their rebuff as the new Yugoslavian system of worker self-governance indeed catapulted into mismanagement, the bankruptcy of factories, and corruption. This was hardly surprising inasmuch as mismanagement, bankruptcy, and corruption had plagued the Yugoslavian capitalist system for centuries. It took considerable time and effort before the new class of self-ruled workers learned how to use freedom responsibly and to combine the economic goal of high productivity with the social goal of enhancing the dignity of workers through self-government. Although beset with problems, the Yugoslavian experiment is now functioning. It represents one of the most important workers' experiments based on a democratic understanding of self-rule and management in our time.

Schumacher aptly summarizes what young, rebellious people would say about work and their hopes for meaningful work:

> I don't want to join the rat race. Not be enslaved by machines, bureaucracies, boredom, ugliness. I don't want to become a moron, robot, commuter.... I want to deal with people, not masks. People matter. Nature matters. Beauty matters. Wholeness matters. I want to be able to *care*.[13]

This is a beautiful summary of how most people actually feel. It is the intent of the Green party in West Germany, for example, to forge a program that will overcome meaningless work in favor of a wholistic understanding of work which in turn will retard and impede the death of human creativity we experience in industrial society. The same aspiration has been articulated in the works of utopian socialists, the prescientific socialists before Marx such as Fourier, Proudhon, Weitling, and others, who envisioned a society in which the inequitable division of labor would not exist and people would find fulfillment in their work.

Another dream for the emergence of meaningful work was embodied in the Catholic Worker movement, which strongly emphasized labor as a free gift rather than as a commodity to be bought and sold. In his *Easy Essays,* the self-taught philosopher Peter Maurin (1877–1949), whom Dorothy Day called "a genius, a saint, an agitator, a writer, a lecturer, a poor man, and a shabby tramp, all in one,"[14] envisioned a society "based on creed instead of greed" and voluntary poverty. He proposed a "green revolution," in which unemployed people would become self-employed working the land, and rooted as he was in the personalist philosophy of traditional Catholicism, he inveighed against the dehumanizing effects of industrialized labor:

> Carlyle says:
> "He who has found his work
> let him look for no other blessedness."
> Bur workmen
> cannot find happiness
> in mechanized work.
> As Charles Devas says:
> "The great majority having to perform
> some mechanized operation
> which requires little thought
> and allows no originality
> and which concerns an object
> in the transformation of which,
> whether previous or subsequent,
> they have no part,
> cannot take pleasure in their work."
> Eric Gill says:
> "The notion of work has been separated
>   from the notion of art.
> The notion of useful has been separated
>   from the notion of beautiful.
> The artist, that is to say,
>   the responsible workman,
>   has been separated from all other workmen.
> The factory hand
>   has no responsibility for what he produces.
> He has been reduced to a sub-human condition
>   of intellectual irresponsibility.
> Industrialism has released the artist
>   from the necessity of making anything useful.
> Industrialism has also released the workman
>   from making anything amusing."[15]

As co-founders of the Catholic Worker movement, Peter Maurin and Dorothy Day shared a unique vision of how the Christian tradition could contribute to a thoroughly new understanding of work. They claimed that "labor was related to thought and that thought was not a commodity but a spiritual faculty."[16] Every worker in his or her work must be related to thought and should be taught to think. The Friday night meetings of the Catholic Worker brought together "educational workers" or "cultural workers" (as I would call myself) and production workers for the purpose of "clarifying" their thinking and their roles in order to achieve shared goals. These people had learned to channel their freedom away from the acquisitive society by keeping in mind "that means had to harmonize with the ultimate ends pursued."[17]

If one is part of an acquisitive society, one tends to think of work as neutral, because only the end matters, not the means. The end is money, so people think about money and work for more of it. The end eventually defines everything, and the importance of the means recedes. This philosophical system is a travesty, because when consideration of means is discarded our relationships to one another and to the earth degenerate. One of the strong claims in the philosophy of nonviolence is that the means change the ends. This is true for the workplace. Good work must therefore be understood as an end in itself and not just as a means to get something else.

What does work do to the worker? If we overlook this question, we are doomed to understand work only in terms of its exchange value and thereby to destroy the self-expression of the worker. There is strong support for a personalistic approach to work in an encyclical letter of Pope John Paul II, *Laborem exercens*, which provides insights into a new theology of work.[18] Emerging from the philosophical tradition of Christian personalism represented by such thinkers as Jacques Maritain, Emmanuel Mounier, and the Russian exile Nikolai Berdyaev, John Paul here extends the principles of a Christian understanding of the person to the realm of labor. The pope's emphasis on the subjectivity of the worker, grounded in her having been made in the image of God, is the point of departure for critiquing both capitalism and state socialism as systems that deny the dignity of the worker in her work. "Human subjectivity is the locus of divine presence."[19] This is the deepest reason for the priority of labor over capital. And the subjectivity of the worker, the need for self-expression, responsibility, and creativity, cannot be taken away from her even under alienating conditions.

Despite alienating work, the human being remains a subject and never totally becomes an object. One strength of the encyclical is its emphasis on human dignity even under debasing conditions. Created in the image of God, the worker cannot wholly lose his subjectivity. We should reflect on this aspect of *Laborem exercens* in light of the Polish workers' movement in the 1980s and the struggle of "Solidarity" against state socialism. The principle of the "priority of labor over capital" applies to state socialism as well as to advanced capitalism and provides a tool for radical criticism of both systems. New forms of cooperative ownership and cooperative management in a decentralized democratic form of socialism are envisioned and partially realized in the Yugoslavian model of socialism. The papal encyclical is critical of those trends in Marx and Marxism that define the human being as an assemblage of social relations and forces, without understanding the power of the subjects which transcends a merely positivistic view of the human historical project. It is wrong to define human beings solely by the forces of production and the social relations determined by these modes. To define humanity in this way is to overlook that God is redemptively at work in present history and calls people to struggle against those powers that constrict and violate humanity.

The encyclical starts with the human person, who "is made in the visible universe an image and likeness of God . . . and . . . is placed in it in order to subdue the earth. From the beginning therefore he is called to work."[20] The theological foundation of the encyclical is the understanding of the human being as a worker. God has created people to be creators and to realize their humanity through work. The human being actualizes herself, becomes the subject she is meant to be, becomes truly herself, through work. In good work, we discover who we are, we assume responsibility for ourselves and others, and we lay the foundations for our own future and society's future.

The encyclical draws a helpful distinction between the subjective and the objective sides of labor. The objective side refers to the product of labor; it signifies not only the goods produced by the worker, but also the machines and technology used for their production. Technology, according to the pope, should be our ally:

> It facilitates . . . work, perfects, accelerates, and augments it. It leads to an increase in the quantity of things produced by work and in many cases improves their quality. However it is also a fact that in some instances technology can cease to be man's ally and become almost his enemy, as when the mechanization of work "supplants" him, taking away all personal satisfaction and the incentive to creativity and responsibility, when it deprives many workers of their previous employment or when, through exalting the machine, it reduces man to the status of its slave.[21]

In this sense, the objective side of labor has its own dialectic: it can be either an ally of the worker or an enemy.

Because work is never to be understood simply in its objective sense, the encyclical clarifies what work does to the worker. The pope speaks about the "gospel of work," which is given implicitly in "the fact that the one who, while being God, became like us in all things devoted most of the years of his life on earth to manual work at the carpenter's bench."[22] Whereas the ancient world considered manual work unworthy of free men and therefore the lot of slaves, Christianity "brought about a fundamental change of ideas in this field."[23] When God, incarnate in Jesus, became a worker, our understanding of work was finally freed from the tradition of the curse. The new dignity of the worker appears in this gospel of work. The encyclical states:

> The basis for determining the value of human work is not primarily the kind of work being done, but the fact that the one who is doing it is a person. The sources of the dignity of work are to be sought primarily in the subjective dimension, not in the objective one.[24]

The distinction between the subjective and the objective sides of labor is neither value-free nor merely descriptive. It gives priority to what work does to the worker not to what her work produces. Responsibility and self-realization are of greater value and importance than the commodities produced.

Out of this revaluation of the subjective meaning of work over its objective goals follows another principle, namely, the priority of labor over capital. These principles, the priority of the subjective side of labor over its objective side and the priority of labor over capital, are interdependent. In a capitalist economy, labor is seen from its objective side alone (as I saw the "labor" of my first-grade daughter). The worker is treated as an object and thus easily experiences herself as the object of the machinery, the product, and the industrial process. Workers lose the sense of being subjects and agents of their own lives. Capital achieves priority over human life. But "justice means that capital is made to serve labor."[25]

We humans have an undeniable need for self-expression. Labor, in its subjective dimension, is a way to fulfill this need. Because the Christian faith is not neutral to essential human needs, Christians must claim work as the self-expression of the worker. Saying that God is already redemptively at work in present history is a statement of faith in the human project as willed by the source of life, even if the objective conditions seem hopeless. To claim God as the source of our co-creative power as workers moves us beyond determinism. God and the claim of an absolute human dignity are interdependent.

Wendell Berry

HEALTH AND WORK

The modern urban-industrial society is based on a series of radical disconnections between body and soul, husband and wife, marriage and community, community and the earth. At each of these points of disconnection the collaboration of corporation, government, and expert sets up a profit-making enterprise that results in the further dismemberment and impoverishment of the Creation.

Together, these disconnections add up to a condition of critical ill health, which we suffer in common – not just with each other, but with all other creatures. Our economy is based upon this disease. Its aim is to separate us as far as possible from the sources of life (material, social, and spiritual), to put these sources under the control of corporations and specialized professionals, and to sell them to us at the highest profit. It fragments the Creation and sets the fragments into conflict with one another. For the relief of the suffering that comes of this fragmentation and conflict, our economy proposes, not health, but vast "cures" that further centralize power and increase profits: wars, wars on crime, wars on poverty, national schemes of medical aid, insurance, immunization, further industrial and economic "growth," etc.; and these, of course, are followed by more regulatory laws and agencies to see that our health is protected, our freedom preserved, and our money well spent. Although there may be some "good intention" in this, there is little honesty and no hope.

Only by restoring the broken connections can we be healed. Connection *is* health. And what our society does its best to disguise from us is how ordinary, how commonly attainable, health is. We lose our health – and create profitable diseases and dependences – by failing to see the direct connections between living and eating, eating and working, working and loving. In gardening, for instance, one works with the body to feed the body. The work, if it is knowledgeable, makes eating both nourishing and joyful, not consumptive, and keeps the eater from getting fat and weak. This is health, wholeness, a source of delight. And such a solution, unlike the typical industrial solution, does not cause new problems.

The "drudgery" of growing one's own food, then, is not drudgery at all. (If we make the growing of food a drudgery, which is what "agribusiness" does make of it, then we also make a drudgery of eating and of living.) It is – in addition to being the appropriate fulfillment of a practical need – a sacrament, as eating is also, by which we enact and understand our oneness with the Creation, the conviviality of one body with all bodies. This is what we learn from the hunting and farming rituals of tribal cultures.

As the connections have been broken by the fragmentation and isolation of work, they can be restored by restoring the wholeness of work. There is work that is isolating, harsh, destructive, specialized or trivialized into meaninglessness. And there is work that is restorative, convivial, dignified and dignifying, and pleasing. Good work is not just the maintenance of connections – as one is now said to work "for a living" or "to support a family" – but the *enactment* of connections. It *is* living, and a way of living; it is not support for a family in the sense of an exterior brace or prop, but is one of the forms and acts of love.

To boast that now "ninety-five percent of the people can be freed from the drudgery of preparing their own food" is possible only to one who cannot distinguish between these kinds of work. The former deputy assistant secretary [James E. Bostic, Jr.] cannot see work as a vital connection; he can see it only as a trade of time for money, and so of course he believes in doing as little of it as possible, especially if it involves the use of the body. His ideal is apparently the same as that of a real-estate agency which promotes a rural subdivision by advertising "A home-life of endless vacation." But the society that is so glad to be free of the drudgery of growing and preparing food also boasts a thriving medical industry to which it is paying $500 per person per year. And that is only the down payment.

We embrace this curious freedom and pay its exorbitant cost because of our hatred of bodily labor. We do not want to work "like a dog" or "like an ox" or "like a horse" – that is, we do not want to use ourselves as beasts. This as much as anything is the cause of our disrespect for farming and our abandonment of it to businessmen and experts. We remember, as we should, that there have been agricultural economies that used people as beasts. But that cannot be remedied, as we have attempted to do, by using people as machines, or by not using them at all.

Perhaps the trouble began when we started using animals disrespectfully: as "beasts" – that is, as if they had no more feeling than a machine. Perhaps the destructiveness of our use of machines was prepared in our willingness to abuse animals. That it was never necessary to abuse animals in order to use them is suggested by a passage in *The Horse in the Furrow*, by George Ewart Evans. He is speaking of how the medieval ox teams were worked at the plow: "... the ploughman at the handles, the team of oxen – yoked in pairs or four abreast – and the driver who walked alongside with his goad." And then he says: "It is also worth noting that in the Welsh organization ... the counterpart of the driver was termed *y geilwad* or the "caller." He walked *backwards* in front of the oxen singing to them as they worked. Songs were specially composed to suit the rhythm of the oxen's work ..."

That seems to me to differ radically from our customary use of any living thing.

The oxen were not used as beasts or machines, but as fellow creatures. It may be presumed that this work used people the same way. It is possible, then, to believe that there is a kind of work that does not require abuse or misuse, that does not use anything as a substitute for anything else. We are working well when we use ourselves as the fellow creatures of the plants, animals, materials, and other people we are working with. Such work is unifying, healing. It brings us home from pride and from despair, and places us responsibly within the human estate. It defines us as we are: not too good to work with our bodies, but too good to work poorly or joylessly or selfishly or alone.

Walt Whitman

from

SONG OF MYSELF

9

The big doors of the country barn stand open and ready,
The dried grass of the harvest-time loads the slow-drawn wagon,
The clear light plays on the brown gray and green intertinged,
The armfuls are pack'd to the sagging mow.

I am there, I help, I came stretch'd atop of the load,
I felt its soft jolts, one leg reclined on the other,
I jump from the cross-beams and seize the clover and timothy,
And roll head over heels and tangle my hair full of wisps.

10

Alone far in the wilds and mountains I hunt,
Wandering amazed at my own lightness and glee,
In the late afternoon choosing a safe spot to pass the night,
Kindling a fire and broiling the fresh-kill'd game,
Falling asleep on the gather'd leaves with my dog and gun by my side.

The Yankee clipper is under her sky-sails, she cuts the sparkle and scud,
My eyes settle the land, I bend at her prow or shout joyously from the deck.

The boatmen and clam-diggers arose early and stopt for me,
I tuck'd my trowser-ends in my boots and went and had a good time;
You should have been with us that day round the chowder-kettle.

I saw the marriage of the trapper in the open air in the far west, the bride was a red girl,
Her father and his friends sat near cross-legged and dumbly smoking, they had moccasins
　　to their feet and large thick blankets hanging from their shoulders,
On a bank lounged the trapper, he was drest mostly in skins, his luxuriant beard and curls
　　protected his neck, he held his bride by the hand,
She had long eyelashes, her head was bare, her coarse straight locks descended upon her
voluptuous limbs and reach'd to her feet.

The runaway slave came to my house and stopt outside,
I heard his motions crackling the twigs of the woodpile,
Through the swung half-door of the kitchen I saw him, limpsy and weak,
And went where he sat on a log and led him in and assured him,
And brought water and fill'd a tub for his sweated body and bruis'd feet,
And gave him a room that enter'd from my own, and gave him some coarse clean clothes,
And remember perfectly well his revolving eyes and his awkwardness,
And remember putting plasters on the galls of his neck and ankles;
He staid with me a week before he was recuperated and pass'd north,
I had him sit next me at table, my fire-lock lean'd in the corner.

. . . .

12

The butcher-boy puts off his killing-clothes, or sharpens his knife at the stall in the market,
I loiter enjoying his repartee and his shuffle and break-down.

Blacksmiths with grimed and hairy chests environ the anvil,
Each has his main-sledge, they are all out, there is a great heat in the fire.

From the cinder-strew'd threshold I follow their movements,
The lithe sheer of their waists plays even with their massive arms,
Overhand the hammers swing, overhand so slow, overhand so sure,
They do not hasten, each man hits in his place.

13

The negro holds firmly the reins of his four horses, the block swags underneath on its tied-over chain,
The negro that drives the long dray of the stone-yard, steady and tall he stands pois'd on one leg on the string-piece,
His blue shirt exposes his ample neck and breast and loosens over his hip-band,
His glance is calm and commanding, he tosses the slouch of his hat away from his fore head,
The sun falls on his crispy hair and mustache, falls on the black of his polish'd and perfect limbs.

I behold the picturesque giant and love him, and I do not stop there,
I go with the team also.

In me the caresser of life wherever moving, backward as well as forward sluing,
To niches aside and junior bending, not a person or object missing,
Absorbing all to myself and for this song.

Oxen that rattle the yoke and chain or halt in the leafy shade, what is that you express in your eyes?
It seems to me more than all the print I have read in my life.

My tread scares the wood-drake and wood-duck on my distant and day-long ramble,
They rise together, they slowly circle around.

I believe in those wing'd purposes,
And acknowledge red, yellow, white, playing with me,
And consider green and violet and the tufted crown intentional,
And do not call the tortoise unworthy because she is not something else,
And the jay in the woods never studied the gamut, yet trills pretty well to me,
And the look of the bay mare shames silliness out of me.

. . . .

15

The pure contralto sings in the organ loft,
The carpenter dresses his plank, the tongue of his foreplane whistles its wild ascending lisp,
The married and unmarried children ride home to their Thanksgiving dinner,
The pilot seizes the king-pin, he heaves down with a strong arm,
The mate stands braced in the whale-boat, lance and harpoon are ready,
The duck-shooter walks by silent and cautious stretches,
The deacons are ordain'd with cross'd hands at the altar,
The spinning-girl retreats and advances to the hum of the big wheel,
The farmer stops by the bars as he walks on a First-day loafe and looks at the oats
      and rye,
The lunatic is carried at last to the asylum a confirm'd case,
(He will never sleep any more as he did in the cot in his mother's bed-room;)
The jour printer with gray head and gaunt jaws works at his case,
He turns his quid of tobacco while his eyes blur with the manuscript;
The malform'd limbs are tied to the surgeon's table,
What is removed drops horribly in a pail;
The quadroon girl is sold at the auction-stand, the drunkard nods by the bar-room stove,
The machinist rolls up his sleeves, the policeman travels his beat, the gate-keeper marks
who pass,
The young fellow drives the express-wagon, (I love him, though I do not know him;)
The half-breed straps on his light boots to compete in the race,
The western turkey-shooting draws old and young, some lean on their rifles, some sit
      on logs,
Out from the crowd steps the marksman, takes his position, levels his piece;
The groups of newly-come immigrants cover the wharf or levee,

As the woolly-pates hoe in the sugar-field, the overseer views them from his saddle,
The bugle calls in the ball-room, the gentlemen run for their partners, the dancers bow
  to each other,
The youth lies awake in the cedar-roof'd garret and harks to the musical rain,
The Wolverine sets traps on the creek that helps fill the Huron,
The squaw wrapt in her yellow-hemm'd cloth is offering moccasins and bead-bags for
  sale,
The connoisseur peers along the exhibition-gallery with half-shut eyes bent sideways,
As the deck-hands make fast the steamboat the plank is thrown for the shore-going
  passengers,
The young sister holds out the skein while the elder sister winds it off in a ball, and stops
  now and then for the knots,
The one-year wife is recovering and happy having a week ago borne her first child,
The clean-hair'd Yankee girl works with her sewing-machine or in the factory or mill,
The paving-man leans on his two-handed rammer, the reporter's lead flies swiftly over
  the note-book, the sign-painter is lettering with blue and gold.
The canal boy trots on the tow-path, the book-keeper counts at his desk, the shoemaker
  waxes his thread,
The conductor beats time for the band and all the performers follow him,
The child is baptized, the convert is making his first professions,
The regatta is spread on the bay, the race is begun, (how the white sails sparkle!)
The drover watching his drove sings out to them that would stray,
The pedler sweats with his pack on his back, (the purchaser higgling about the odd cent;)
The bride unrumples her white dress, the minute-hand of the clock moves slowly,
The opium-eater reclines with rigid head and just-open'd lips,
The prostitute draggles her shawl, her bonnet bobs on her tipsy and pimpled neck,
The crowd laugh at her blackguard oaths, the men jeer and wink to each other,
(Miserable! I do not laugh at your oaths nor jeer you;)
The President holding a cabinet council is surrounded by the great Secretaries,
On the piazza walk three matrons stately and friendly with twined arms,
The crew of the fish-smack pack repeated layers of halibut in the hold,
The Missourian crosses the plains toting his wares and his cattle,
As the fare-collector goes through the train he gives notice by the jingling of loose change,
The floor-men are laying the floor, the tinners are tinning the roof, the masons are
  calling for mortar,
In single file each shouldering his hod pass onward the laborers;
Seasons pursuing each other the indescribable crowd is gather'd, it is the fourth of
  Seventh-month, (what salutes of cannon and small arms!)
Seasons pursuing each other the plougher ploughs, the mower mows, and the winter-
  grain falls in the ground;
Off on the lakes the pike-fisher watches and waits by the hole in the frozen surface,

The stumps stand thick round the clearing, the squatter strikes deep with his axe,
Flatboatmen make fast towards dusk near the cotton-wood or pecan-trees,
Coon-seekers go through the regions of the Red river or through those drain'd by the
    Tennessee, or through those of the Arkansas,
Torches shine in the dark that hangs on the Chattahooche or Altamahaw,
Patriarchs sit at supper with sons and grandsons and great-grandsons around them,
In walls of adobie, in canvas tents, rest hunters and trappers after their day's sport,
The city sleeps and the country sleeps,
The living sleep for their time, the dead sleep for their time,
The old husband sleeps by his wife and the young husband sleeps by his wife;
And these tend inward to me, and I tend outward to them,
And such as it is to be of these more or less I am,
And of these one and all I weave the song of myself.

Olav Hauge

EVERYDAY

You've left the big storms
behind you now.
You didn't ask then
why you were born,
where you came from, where you were going to,
you were just there in the storm,
in the fire.
But it's possible to live
in the everyday as well,
in the grey quiet day,
set potatoes, rake leaves,
carry brushwood.
 There's so much to think about here in the world,
one life is not enough for it all.
After work you can fry pork
and read Chinese poems.
Old Laertes cut briars,
dug round his fig trees,
and let the heroes fight on at Troy.

translated by Robin Fulton

THE HUNT

Paleolithic Cave Painting

I stop in the shadows along the muskeg's upper edge, and think back over the years with the Koyukon people. What stands out for me at this moment is a special wisdom of their tradition – to expect nothing of nature, but to humbly receive its mystery, beauty, food, and life. In return, Koyukon people show the same respect toward nature that is shown towards humans, acknowledging that spirit and sacredness pervade all things. If I understand correctly, their behavior toward nature is ordered around a few simple principles: Move slowly, stay quiet, watch carefully, be ever humble, show no hint of arrogance or disrespect. And if they follow one overarching commandment, it is to approach all life, of which humans are a part, with humility and restraint. All things are among the chosen.[1]

To talk about hunting as "work" may be misleading, given that the very idea of "work" is a product of a perspective entirely foreign to other traditions and cultures. "What today stands for work," Ivan Illich writes, "namely, wage labor, was a badge of misery all through the Middle Ages." Indeed, one category of destitution – along with orphan, widow, and victim of a recent act of God – was "heads of family totally dependent on wage work."[2]

Under such a system leisure and work become opposites. Leisure is "vacation," a brief flash of time when we attempt to empty our minds of everything significant, anything taxing. But – as Paul Shepard suggests – "Thought to the primitive man is not autonomous and detached 'work,' and it always involves a confrontation revealing a 'thou,' not an 'it,' for the 'whole creation' is a being."

Leisure, he concludes, "is not idleness nor spare time. It is 'listening to the essence of things.'"[3]

There is hardly a better way to describe the relationship that traditional hunters invite between themselves, the land, and the animal. The work *requires* such leisure. It requires profound attention, a patience and discipline that most of us would find impossible. Which is why a hunter/trapper such as John Haines – who is also a profound writer – can so readily see that the activity of hunting requires, at its purest form, the same kind of concentration, the same *leisure* – that art requires (or vice versa). This is a *seeing into* that life itself requires if it is to have any depth and meaning.

Always such attention brings us up against the fact of death; and surely one way of understanding our culture is to see it as one driven above all by a desire *not* to see death, not to face the connection between life and death that hunting (and eating) should require. In that way we prefer to remain on the surface – and indeed to pave over the surface, eliminating accident and chance. And of course one result of this is the removal as well of leisure in the sense that Paul Shepard (and Joseph Pieper behind him) is using the word. True leisure invites depth. Vacation, on the other hand, invites a kind of pure surface, a nonengagement with the land, with other people (especially those native to the area), and with one's self.

I suspect that the current problem with overwork, however much we may wish to blame someone else, rests with our fear of slowing down, of taking some real leisure and actually *looking*.

In her short story "Storyteller," Leslie Marmon Silko describes the revenge a young native Alaskan woman takes against the white shopkeeper who was responsible for the deaths of her parents: Using her own body as the sexual bait, she lures him onto the ice and to his death. She is the hunted, but so too is he – only he is unaware of it. And she, knowing herself as both hunted and hunter, is the one who survives. As Silko says in a subsequent essay,

> Although the white trader possessed every possible garment, insulation, heating fuel, and gadget ever devised to protect him from the frozen tundra environment, he still dies ... because the white man had not reckoned with the true power of that landscape, especially not the power that the Yupik woman understood instinctively and

that she used so swiftly and efficiently. The white man had reckoned with the young woman and had determined he could overpower her. But the white man failed to account for the conjunction of the landscape with the woman. The Yupik woman had never seen herself as anything but a part of that sky, that frozen river, that tundra. The river's ice and the blinding white are her accomplices, and yet the Yupik woman never for a moment misunderstands her own relationship with that landscape.

There is nothing sentimental about this relationship: the woman too is in danger of dying on that ice, and indeed knows that someday, in some way, she will succumb to its force – as will we all.[4]

MAGIC WORDS FOR HUNTING CARIBOU

You, you caribou
yes you
    long legs
yes you
    long ears
you with the long neck hair —
From far off you're little as a louse:
Be my great swan, fly to me;
big bull
    cari-bou-bou-bou.

Put your footprints on this land —
this land I'm standing on
is rich with the plant food you love.
See, I'm holding in my hand
 the reindeer moss you're dreaming of —
so delicious, yum, yum, yum —
Come, caribou, come.

Come on, move them bones,
move your leg bones back and forth
and give yourself to me.

I'm here,
I'm waiting
    just
        for
            YOU
you, you, caribou
APPEAR!
COME HERE!

translated by Edward Field

Barry Lopez

from
SAINT LAWRENCE
ISLAND, BERING SEA

The mountain in the distance is called Sevoukuk. It marks the northwest cape of Saint Lawrence Island in the Bering Sea. From where we are on the ice, this eminence defines the water and the sky to the east as far as we can look. Its western face, a steep wall of snow-streaked basalt, rises above a beach of dark cobbles, riven, ice-polished, ocean-rolled chips of Sevoukuk itself. The village of Gambell is there, the place I have come from with the Yup'ik men, to hunt walrus in the spring ice.

We are, I believe, in Russian waters; and also, by a definition to them even more arbitrary, in "tomorrow," on the other side of the international date line. Whatever political impropriety might be involved is of little importance to the Yup'ik, especially while they are hunting. From where blood soaks the snow, then, and piles of meat and slabs of fat and walrus skin are accumulating, from where ivory tusks have been collected together like exotic kindling, I stare toward the high Russian coast. The mental categories, specific desires, and understanding of history among the people living there are, I reflect, nearly as different from my own as mine are from my Yup'ik companions'.

I am not entirely comfortable on the sea ice butchering walrus like this. The harshness of the landscape, the vulnerability of the boat, and the great size and power of the hunted animal combine to increase my sense of danger. The killing jars me, in spite of my regard for the simple elements of human survival here.

We finish loading the boats. One of the crews has rescued two dogs that have either run off from one of the Russian villages or been abandoned out here on the ice. Several boats gather gunnel to gunnel to look over the dogs. They have surprisingly short hair and seem undersize to draw a sled, smaller than Siberian huskies. But the men assure me these are typical Russian sled dogs.

We take our bearing from the far prominence of Sevoukuk and turn home, laden with walrus meat, with walrus hides and a few seals, with crested auklets and thick-billed murres, with ivory and Russian dogs. When we reached shore, the four of us put our shoulders to the boat to bring it high up on the beach. A young man in the family I am staying with packs a sled with what we have brought back. He pulls it away across the snow behind his Honda three-wheeler, toward the house. Our meals. The guns and gear, the harpoons and floats and lines, the extra clothing and portable radios are all secured and taken away. I am one of the last to leave the beach, still turning over images of the hunt.

No matter what sophistication of mind you bring to such events, no matter what breadth of anthropological understanding, no matter your fondness for the food, your desire to participate, you have still seen an animal killed. You have met the intertwined issues – What is an animal? What is death? – in those large moments of blood, violent exhalation, and thrashing water, with the acrid odor of burned powder in the fetid corral smells of a walrus haul-out. The moments are astounding, cacophonous, also serene. The sight of men letting bits of meat slip away into the dark green water with mumbled benedictions is as stark in my memory as the suddenly widening eyes of the huge, startled animals.

I walk up over the crest of the beach and toward the village, following a set of sled tracks. There is a narrow trail of fresh blood in the snow between the runners. The trail runs out at a latticework of drying racks for meat and skins. The blood in the snow is a sign of life going on, of other life going on. Its presence is too often confused with cruelty.

I rest my gloved fingers on the driftwood meat rack. It is easy to develop an affection for the Yup'ik people, especially when you are invited to participate in events still defined largely by their own traditions. The entire event – leaving to hunt, hunting, coming home, the food shared in a family setting – creates a sense of well-being easy to share. Viewed in this way, the people seem fully capable beings, correct in what they do. When you travel with them, their voluminous and accurate knowledge, their spiritual and technical confidence, expose what is insipid and groundless in your own culture.

I brood often about hunting. It is the most spectacular and succinct expression of the Eskimo's relationship with the land, yet one of the most perplexing and disturbing for the outsider to consider. With the compelling pressures of a cash-based economy to contend with, and the ready availability of modern weapons, hunting practices have changed. Many families still take much of their food from the land, but they do it differently now. "Inauthentic" is the criticism most often made of their methods, as though years ago time had stopped for the Yup'ik.

But I worry over hunting for another reason – the endless reconciliation that must be made of Jacob with his brother Esau. The anguish of Gilgamesh at the death of his companion Enkidu. We do not know how exactly to bridge this gap between civilized man and the society of the hunter. The Afrikaner writer Laurens van der Post, long familiar with Kalahari hunting peoples as archetypal victims of our prejudice, calls the gap between us "an abyss of deceit and murder" we have created. The existence of such a society alarms us. In part this is a trouble we have with writing out our history. We adjust our histories in order to elevate ourselves in the creation that surrounds us; we cut ourselves off from our hunting ancestors, who make us uncomfortable. They seem too closely aligned with insolent, violent, predatory animals. The hunting cultures are too barbaric for us. In condemning them, we see it as "inevitable" that their ways are being eclipsed. Yet, from the testimony of sensitive visitors among them, such as van der Post and others I have mentioned in the Arctic, we know that something of value resides with these people.

I think of the Eskimos compassionately as *hibakusha* — the Japanese word for "explosion-affected people," those who continue to suffer the effects of Hiroshima and Nagasaki. Eskimos are trapped in a long, slow detonation. What they know about a good way to live is disintegrating. The sophisticated, ironic voice of civilization insists that their insights are only trivial, but they are not.

I remember looking into a herd of walrus that day and thinking: do human beings make the walrus more human to make it comprehensible or to assuage loneliness? What is it to be estranged in this land?

It is in the land, I once thought, that one searches out and eventually finds what is beautiful. And an edge of this deep and rarefied beauty is the acceptance of complex paradox and the forgiveness of others. It means you will not die alone.

I looked at the blood in the snow for a long time, and then turned away from the village. I walked north, toward the spot where the gravel spit on which the houses stand slips under the sea ice. It is possible to travel in the Arctic and concentrate only on the physical landscape — on the animals, on the realms of light and dark, on movements that excite some consideration of the ways we conceive of time and space, history, maps, and art. One can become completely isolated, for example, in the intricate life of the polar bear. But the ethereal and timeless power of the land, that union of what is beautiful with what is terrifying, is insistent. It penetrates all cultures, archaic and modern. The land gets inside us; and we must decide one way or another what this means, what we will do about it.

Richard Nelson

THE GIFTS OF DEER

Cold, clear, and calm in the pale blue morning. Snow on the high peaks brightening to amber. The bay a sheet of gray glass beneath a faint haze of steam. A November sun rises with the same fierce, chill stare of an owl's eye.

I stand at the window watching the slow dawn, and my mind fixes on the island. Nita comes softly down the stairs as I pack gear and complain that I've slept too late for these short winter days. A few minutes later, Ethan trudges out onto the cold kitchen floor, barefoot and half asleep. We make no direct mention of hunting, to avoid acting proud or giving offense to the animals. I say only that I'll go to the island and look around; Ethan says only that he would rather stay at home with Nita. I wish he would come along so I could teach him things, but know it will be quieter in the woods with just Shungnak.

They both wave from the window as I ease the skiff away from shore, crunching through cakes of fresh-water ice the tide has carried in from Salmon River. It's a quick run through Windy Channel and out onto the freedom of Haida Strait, where the slopes of Kluksa Mountain bite into a frozen sky. The air stings against my face, but the rest of me is warm inside thick layers of clothes. Shungnak whines, paces, and looks over the gunwale toward the still distant island.

Broad swells lying in from the Pacific alternately lift the boat and drop it between smooth-walled canyons of water. Midway across the strait a dark line of chop descends swiftly from the north, and within minutes we're surrounded by whitecaps. There are two choices: either beat straight up into them or cut an easier angle across the waves and take the spray. I vacillate for a while, then choose the icy spray over the intense pounding. Koyukon elders often told me it's wrong to curse the wind or complain about the cold, but this morning I do it anyway.

A kittiwake sweeps over the water in great, vaulting arcs, its wings flexed against the surge and billow of the air. As it tilts its head passing over the boat, I think how clumsy we must look. The island's shore lifts slowly in dark walls of rock and timber that loom above the apron of snow-covered beach. Approaching the shelter of Sea Lion Point, the chop fades and the swell diminishes. I turn up along the lee, running between the kelp beds and the surf, straining to see if any deer are grazing on seaweed at the tide's edge.

Near the end of the point is a gut that opens into a tight, shallow anchorage. I ease the boat between the rocks, with lines of surf breaking close on either side.

The waves rise and darken, their edges sparkle in the sun, then long manes of spray whirl back as they turn inside out and pitch onto the reef. The anchor slips through ten feet of crystal water to settle among the kelp fronds and urchin-covered rocks. On a strong ebb the boat would go dry here, but today's tide range is only six feet. Before launching the punt, I pull the binoculars from my pack and warm them inside my coat so the lenses won't fog. Then I spend a few minutes scrutinizing the broad, rocky shore and the sprawls of brown grass along the timber's edge. A bunch of rock sandpipers flashes up from the shingle and an otter loops along the windrows of drift logs, but there are no signs of deer.

I can't help feeling a little anxious, because the season is drawing short and our year's supply of meat is not yet in. During the past few weeks, deer have been unusually wary, haunting the underbrush and slipping away at the least disturbance. I've come near a few, but these were young ones I stalked only for the luxury of seeing them from close range. Now that the rutting season has begun, there's a good chance of finding larger deer, and they'll be distracted by the search for mates.

A bald eagle watches from a tall hemlock as we bob ashore in the punt. Finally the bird lurches out, scoops its wings full of dense, cold air, and soars away beyond the line of trees. While I trudge up with the punt, Shungnak prances back and forth hunting for smells. The upper reaches are layered and slabbed with ice; slick cobbles shine like steel; frozen grass crackles underfoot. I lean the punt on a snow-covered log, pick up my rifle and small pack, and slip through the leafless alders into the forest.

My eyes adjust to the darkness, the deep green of boughs, and the somber, shadowy trunks. I feel safe and hidden here. The forest floor is covered with deep moss that should sponge gently underfoot. But today the softness is gone: frozen moss crunches with each step and brittle twigs snap, ringing out in the crisp air like strangers' voices. It takes a while to get used to this harshness in a forest that's usually wet and velvety and silent. I listen to the clicking of gusts in the high branches and think that winter has come upon us like a fist.

At the base of a spruce tree is a familiar white patch — a scatter of deer bones: ribs, legs, vertebrae, two pelvis bones, and two skulls with half-bleached antlers. I put them here last winter, saying they were for the other animals, to make clear they were not being thoughtlessly wasted. The scavengers soon picked them clean, the deer mice have gnawed them, and eventually they'll be absorbed into the forest again. Koyukon elders say it shows respect, returning animal bones to a clean, wild place instead of throwing them away with trash or discarding them in a garbage dump.

The long, quiet, methodical process of the hunt begins. I move deeper into the forest, ever mindful of treading the edge between protracted, eventless watching and the startling intensity of coming upon an animal, the always unexpected meeting of eyes. A deer could show itself at this moment, in an hour, in several hours, or not at all. Most of hunting is like this — an exercise in patient, isometric endurance and keen, hypnotic concentration. I lift my foot, step ahead, ease it down, wait, step again. Shungnak follows closely, as we work our way through a maze of windfallen trees, across the clear disks of frozen ponds, and around patches of snow beneath openings in the forest canopy. I remind myself there is probably a doe or a buck somewhere in this stretch of woods, perhaps close enough to hear a branch snap or a bough scratch against my clothes. Deep snow has forced the deer off Kluksa Mountain and Crescent Peak, so they're sure to be haunting these lowlands.

We climb a high, steep scarp that levels to a wooded terrace. After pausing to catch my breath, I stand atop a log and peer into the semi-open understory of twiggy bushes, probing each space with my eyes. A downy woodpecker's call sparks from a nearby tree. Several minutes pass. Then a huckleberry branch moves, barely shivers, without the slightest noise, not far ahead.

Amid the scramble of brush where I saw nothing a few minutes ago, a dim shape materializes, as if its own motion had created it. A doe steps into an open space, deep brown in her winter coat, soft and striking and lovely, dwarfed among the great trees, lifting her nose, looking right toward me. For perhaps a minute we're motionless in each other's gaze; then her head jerks to the left, her ears shift back and forth, her tail flicks up, and she turns away in the stylized gait deer always use when alarmed.

Quick as a breath, quiet as a whisper, the doe glides off into the forest. Sometimes when I see a deer this way I know it's real at the moment, but afterward it seems like a daydream.

As we move farther into the woods, I hope for another look at her and think a buck might have been following nearby. Any deer is legal game and I could almost certainly have taken her, but I'd rather wait for a larger buck and let the doe bring on next year's young. Shungnak savors the ghost of her scent that hangs in the still air, but she has vanished.

Farther on, the snow deepens to a continuous cover beneath smaller trees, and we cross several sets of deer tracks, including some big prints with long toe drags. I poke my fingers into one track and feel its edges: still soft and fluffy, with no hint of the crustiness that develops in a few hours when snow is disturbed in cold weather. The powder helps to muffle our steps, but it's hard to see very far because the bushes are heavily loaded. The thicket becomes a lattice of white on black, every branch spangled in a thick fur of jeweled flakes. We move through it like eagles cleaving between tumbled columns of cloud. New siftings occasionally drift down when the treetops are touched by the breeze.

I stop for a while, not to watch for deer so much as to catch my balance in this feathery mosaic of snow, with its distracting beauty and dizzying absence of relief. A Koyukon word keeps running through my mind: *duhnooyh,* "clumps of powdery snow clinging on branches." In the old days, pregnant women drank water melted from this snow, so their children would grow up to be nimble and light-footed. For the same reason, I heard people advise the young boys to drink water melted from surface powder, not from the dense, granular snow, called *tliyh,* which forms underneath during the course of winter. Koyukon elders sometimes told riddles to help teach their children these words, to test their cleverness, and to sharpen their attention to details of the natural world:

> *Wait, I see something: We are sitting all puffed up across from each other, in coats of mountain sheep skin.*
> *Answer: duhnooyh.*

Slots between the trunks ahead shiver with blue where a muskeg opens. I angle toward it, feeling no need to hurry, picking every footstep carefully, stopping often to stare into the jumbled crannies, listening for any splinter of sound, keeping my senses tight and concentrated. A raven calls from high above the forest, and as I catch a glimpse of it the same old questions run through my mind. It lofts and plays on the wind, then folds up and rolls halfway over, a strong sign of hunting luck. Never mind the issue of knowing; I'll assume the power is here and let myself be moved by it.

I turn to look at Shungnak, taking advantage of her sharper hearing and magical sense of smell. She lifts her nose to the fresh but nebulous scent of deer who must have come through here this morning. I watch her little radar ears, waiting for her to focus in one direction and hold it, hoping to see her body tense as it does when something moves nearby. But she only hears the twitching of red squirrels on dry bark. Shungnak and I have a very different opinion of the squirrels. They excite her more than any other animal because she believes she'll catch one someday. But for a hunter, they make distracting spurts of movement and sound, and their sputtering alarm calls alert the deer.

We approach a low, abrupt rise, covered with obscuring brush and curtained with snow. A lift of wind hisses in the high trees, then drops away and leaves us in near-complete silence. I pause to choose a path through a scramble of blueberry bushes and little windfalls ahead, then glance back at Shungnak. She has her eyes and ears fixed toward our left, directly across the current of breeze. She stands very stiff, quivering slightly, leaning forward as if she has already started to run but cannot release her muscles. I shake my finger and look sternly into her eyes as a warning to stay.

I listen as closely as possible, but hear nothing. I work my eyes into every dark crevice and slot among the snowy branches, but see nothing. I stand perfectly still and wait, then look again at Shungnak. Her head turns so slowly I can barely detect the movement, until finally she's looking straight ahead. Perhaps it's just another squirrel. I consider taking a few steps for a better view.

Then I see it.

A long, dark body appears among the bushes, moving up into the wind, so close I can scarcely believe I didn't see it earlier. Without looking away, I gently slide the breech closed and raise the rifle to my shoulder, almost certain that a deer this size will be a buck. Shungnak, now forgotten behind me, must be contorted with the suppressed urge to give chase.

The deer walks silently, determinedly along the little rise, never looking our way.

Then he turns straight toward us. Thick tines of his antlers curve over the place where I have the rifle aimed. I remember the Koyukon elders saying that animals come to those who have shown them respect, allowing themselves to be taken, in what is both a physical and spiritual passage. At a moment like this, it's easy to sense that despite my abiding doubt there is an invisible world beyond this one, a world filled with power and awareness, a world that demands recognition and exacts a price from those who ignore it.

It is a very large buck. He comes so quickly that I have no chance to shoot, and then he is so close I haven't the heart to do it. Fifty feet away, the deer lowers his head almost to the ground and lifts a slender branch that blocks his path. Snow shakes onto his neck and clings to the fur of his shoulders as he slips underneath. Then he half lifts his head and keeps coming. I ease the rifle down to watch, wondering how much closer he'll get. Just now he makes a long, soft rutting call, like the bleating of a sheep, except lower pitched and more hollow. His hooves tick against dry twigs hidden by the snow. I can almost feel the breeze blowing against his fur, the chill winnowing down through close-set hairs and touching his skin.

In the middle of a step he raises his head all the way up, and he sees me standing there — a stain against the pure white of the forest, a deadly interloper, the one utterly incongruous thing he has met here in all his life. He reaches his muzzle forward and draws in the affliction of our smell. A sudden spasm stuns him, so sharp and intense it's as if his fright spills out into the forest and tingles inside me like electricity. His front legs jerk apart and he freezes all askew, head high, nostrils flared, coiled and hard. I stare at him and wait, my mind snarled with irreconcilable emotions. Here is a perfect buck deer. In the Koyukon way, he has come to me; but in my own he has come too close. I am as congealed and transfixed as he is, as devoid of conscious thought. It's as if my mind has ceased to function and only my senses remain.

But the buck has no choice. He instantly unwinds in a burst of ignited energy, springs straight up from the snow, turns in midflight, stabs the frozen earth again, and makes four great bounds off to the left. His thick body seems to float, relieved of its own weight, as if a deer has the power to unbind itself from gravity.

The same deeper impulse that governs the flight of a deer governs the predator's impulse to pursue it. I watch the first leaps without moving a muscle. Then, not pausing for an instant of deliberation, I raise the rifle back to my shoulder, follow the movement of the deer's fleeing form, and wait until he stops to stare back. Almost at that moment, still moving without conscious thought, freed of the ambiguities that held me before, now no less animal than the animal I watch, my hands warm and steady and certain, acting from a more elemental sense than the ones that brought me to this meeting, I carefully align the sights and let go the sudden power.

The gift of the deer falls like a feather in the snow. And the rifle's sound has rolled off through the timber before I hear it.

I walk to the deer, now shaking a bit as accumulated emotions pour through me. Shungnak is already next to it, whining and smelling, racing from one side to the other, stuffing her nose down in snow full of scent. She looks off into the brush, searching back and forth, as if the deer that ran is somewhere else, still running. She tries to lick at the blood that trickles down, but I stop her out of respect for the animal. Then, I suppose to consummate her own frustrated predatory energy, she takes a hard nip at its shoulder, shuns quickly away, and looks back as if she expects it to leap to its feet again.

I whisper thanks to the animal, hoping I might be worthy of it, worthy of carrying on the life it has given, worthy of sharing in the larger life of which the deer and I are a part. Incompatible emotions clash inside me – elation and remorse, excitement and sorrow, gratitude and shame. It's always this way: the sudden encounter with death, the shock that overrides the cushioning of the intellect. I force away the sadness and remember that death is the spark that keeps life itself aflame: these deer we eat from, and the fish, and the plants that die to feed us.

It takes a few minutes before I settle down enough to begin the other work. Then, I tie a length of rope onto the forelegs, run it over a low branch, back down through a loop in the rope, and up over the branch again like a double pulley, so I can raise the animal above the ground. This done, I cut the dark, pungent scent glands from its hind legs, to prevent their secretions from tainting the meat. Next, I make a small incision through the belly skin, insert my hand to shield the knife blade from the distended stomach, and slice upward to make an opening about a foot long. Reaching inside, I loosen the stomach and intestines, then work them out through the incision, pulling carefully to avoid tearing the thin membranes and spilling stomach contents into the body cavity. The deer's inward parts feel very hot, slippery, and wet, as I suppose my own would if I could ever touch them. Finally the viscera slide out onto the ground: soft, bladderlike stomach and flaccid ribbons of intestine; a gray, shining mound, webbed with networks of veins and lacy fat, steaming into the cold, saturating the air with a rich odor of plant mulch and body fluids.

Next, I roll up my jacket sleeve and thrust my arm deep inside the deer, until I feel the diaphragm, a sheet of muscle that separates the abdomen from the chest. When I slice through it, a thick, hot rush of blood flows down my arm and sloshes into the vacant belly. There is a hollow, tearing sound as I pull the lungs free; and reaching up inside the chest, I can feel the firm, softball-sized muscle of the heart. The lungs are marbled creamy-pink and feel like soft, airy sponge. As I lay them beside the other organs, I whisper that these parts are left here as food for the animals. Shungnak wants to take some for herself but I make her stay away. Koyukon elders say the sensitivity and awareness leave an animal's remains slowly, and there are rules about what should be eaten by a dog. Shungnak will have her share of the scraps later on, when more of the life is gone.

The inside of the deer is now empty, except for the heart and the dark-purple liver, which I've left attached. I tie a short piece of cord around the end of the lower intestine to keep the remaining blood from flowing out when I carry the animal on my back. Then I poke a series of holes in the hide along either side of the belly incision and lace it shut with another cord. After lowering the deer onto the ground, I cut through the "knee" joints of the forelegs, leaving them attached by a stout tendon, then slice a hole in the hock – a space between the bone and tendon of the hind leg – and I toggle the forelegs through these openings. This way I can put my arms through the joined legs and carry the deer like a pack – not a trick to be used if there is the slightest chance another hunter might be around and mistake my burden for a live animal.

I barely have enough strength to lift the buck and trudge along, but there is plenty of time to work back toward the beach, stopping occasionally to rest and cool down. During one of these breaks, I hear two ravens in an agitated exchange of croaks and gurgles, and I wonder if those black eyes have already spotted the remnants. No pure philanthropist, if Raven gave this luck to me, it was only to create luck for himself. I remember how difficult it was, at first, to accept the idea of a sanctified creature having such a contradictory personality. The Raven described by elders like Grandpa William was both good and evil, sage and fool, benefactor and thief – embodiment of the human paradox. When Joe Stevens described an American president of dubious character, he said, "Just like Raven."

Half an hour later, sweating and exhausted, I push through the low boughs of the beachside trees, lay the animal down, and find a comfortable seat on the driftwood. Afternoon sun throbs off the water, but the north wind takes every hint of warmth out of it. Little gusts splay dark patterns across the anchorage; the boat paces on its mooring line; the strait races with whitecaps. I take a good rest, watching a fox sparrow flit among the alders and a bunch of crows hassle over some bit of food near the water's edge. At this low tide, Sea Lion Point has expanded to a flat sill of rock reaching out several hundred yards from the island's shore. The point has such scant relief that higher tides reduce it to a fraction of this size. The anchorage is nothing more than a gouge in the rocks, closely rimmed with breakers and jagged boulders, so it's only accessible to small skiffs whose pilots are either reckless or foolish. Despite its barren appearance, Sea Lion Point has extensive tide flats, ponds, and beds of estuarine grass that attract congregations of birds, especially during the spring and fall migrations.

Today, hundreds of gulls have gathered on the outer reaches of the point, all sitting with their beaks into the wind. They appear sluggish and languid, as if their sole purpose is to huddle together against the chill. But they're also keeping watch. When the breeze slacks to a momentary calm, a black foil sweeps out from the forest's edge. The eagle leans sharply down, half folds its wings, banks toward the gulls, and builds speed, falling and blurred and sinister. Gulls and crows swirl up like a handful of salt and pepper thrown into the wind. Clusters of ducks spray off the water in opposite directions. Shorebirds dazzle over the tangled skeins of kelp. A close formation of oystercatchers babbles across the anchorage in front of us.

The eagle shears through the scattering swarm, looking ponderous and clumsy, oddly outclassed by its darting prey. Carried into a steep climb by its momentum, the eagle swings around and drops again, legs dangling, unsheathed talons gaping in the frosted air. But the birds have whirled away, leaving an empty void like the eye of a storm. Its voice mingles with the cries and wails of the gulls, a shrill complaint amid easy laughter. Finally the eagle flaps off to a high perch. Swaying back and forth, jerking and flexing its wings for balance, it watches the crows dwindle away over the rocks, the gulls float down onto the flats again. All of the birds seem calm and unhurried, as if nothing of significance has happened, as if the whole thing has been only a game. The hoary quiet of winter returns, and the wait begins once more.

Though I feel satisfied, grateful, and contented sitting here, much remains to be done, and at this time of year the daylight ebbs quickly. Hunters are allowed more than one deer, so I'll stay on the island and take another look around tomorrow. As we idle from the anchorage, we pass within a few yards of lovely surf peeling across a smooth, triangular reef. If I had a surfboard and wetsuit it would be impossible to resist, no matter how frigid the air and water might be. I stop to watch a few waves pour over the shoals like liquid silver; then I follow the shore toward Bear Creek. By the time I've anchored and unloaded the boat, the wind has diminished and a growing winter chill sinks down in the pitched, hard shadow of Kluksa Mountain.

Bear Creek cabin is situated in a thicket well back from shore, hidden in summer but easily seen once the leaves have fallen. I split some half-dry wood, which hisses and sputters in the rusty stove, then reluctantly gives way to flames. After the fire starts crackling, I walk down to the creek. Dipping a bucket into a clear pool, I notice a few salmon bones scattered among the rocks and pebbles. I'm surprised to see them, but also surprised that so little would remain from the hordes of fish I watched here this fall. I had a similar feeling recently, when I went looking for the sperm whale carcass that beached last summer near Tsandaku Point. At first it seemed the storm swells had washed it away, but then I found a bare vertebra and a rib among the rocks. Eventually, I came across the skull — about ten feet long and weighing hundreds of pounds — half buried in the driftwood. Six months after the whale came ashore, scavengers and decay had taken every bit of flesh, gnawed or carried off the smaller bones, and left only a few fragments to wash in the surge.

After fetching water, I carry the deer inside the cabin and hang it from a low beam. Better to work on it now than wait, in case tomorrow brings more luck. The animal is dimly lit by a kerosene lantern and a blush of daylight through the windows. I feel strange in its presence, as if it still watches, still glows with something of its life, still demands that nothing be done carelessly and no offensive words be spoken in its presence. Grandpa William told me that a hunter should never let himself be deluded by pride or a false sense of dominance. It's not through his own power that a person takes life in nature, but through the power of nature that life is given to him.

After sharpening the knife, I slit the deer's skin along the whole length of its underside and down each leg to the hoof. Then I peel the soft hide away, using the blade to separate it from the muscles underneath, gradually revealing the inner perfection of the deer's body. When the skinning is finished, I follow an orderly sequence, cutting through crisp cartilage, severing the leg joints, brisket, ribs, vertebrae, and pelvis, following the body's own design to disarticulate bone from bone. Everything comes apart smoothly and easily, as deer becomes meat, animal becomes food, the most vital and fundamental transformation in all of living existence. There is no ugliness in it, only hands moving in concert with the beauty of an animal's shape. While I work with the deer, it's as if something has already begun to flow into me. I couldn't have understood this when I was younger and had yet to experience the process of one life being passed on to another.

Before I lived with the Eskimo people, I had never hunted and had never seen how game is prepared. But I was immediately fascinated by their skill at taking an animal into its component parts. The Eskimos always watched me closely and found my mistakes entertaining. If I did something uncharacteristically well, someone was likely to look bemused and declare: "Accident." They were passionate hunters and incredibly hard workers. When they hunted walrus, it took only a short while to stalk the animals but many hours to butcher them. As we pulled the skin-covered boat onto the ice, someone was sure to say, "Well, the excitement's over. Now it's time for the real work." But somehow, it never seemed like work to me, this deeply engaged process of learning about animals from the inside and out, of binding my own existence more closely to the lives that sustained me.

By the time I went to live with Koyukon people, I could skin and butcher animals; but I knew little about the delicate matter of keeping a right mind while working with them. Sarah and Joe Stevens were especially scrupulous about treating each animal as a sentient being and butchering it according to the traditional pattern, which was not only a technique but also a ritual of respect. They made certain that no usable part was wasted or tossed carelessly aside, that the meat was covered to keep dogs and scavengers away, and that it was well cached so nothing would spoil. Once, I met Sarah carrying a platter of meat to her neighbor's house, with a piece of cloth over it. She explained, "It wouldn't be right to leave this open to the air, like it doesn't mean anything." In this and other ways, she treated meat as a sacred substance, a medium of interchange between herself and the empowered world in which she lived. It seemed that everything she did in relationship to nature was both an activity and a prayer.

When I've finished with the deer, I put two slices from the hindquarter in a pan atop the stove. Scraps of meat and fat boil in a separate pot for Shungnak. She whines impatiently, perhaps remembering her sled dog days, when she lived mostly on meat and fish and bones. As soon as she's been fed, I sit on a sawed log and eat venison straight from the pan. No meal could be simpler, more satisfying, or more directly a part of the living process. I also savor a deep feeling of security in having this meat, bringing it home to freeze or can for the year ahead — pure food, taken from a clean, wild place, and prepared by our own efforts. There is a special intimacy in living directly from nature, nourishing my body from the same wildness that so elevates my spirit.

I wish Ethan were here to share this meal, so I could explain to him again that when we eat the deer, its flesh becomes our flesh. Each time we eat we should remember the deer and feel gratitude for what it has given us. And each time, we should carry a thought like a prayer inside: "Thanks to the animal and to all that made it – the island and the forest, the air, and the rain ..." I would tell Ethan that in the course of things, he and Nita and I are all generations of deer and of the life that feeds us. Like the deer, we also come from the island, and from the earth that sustains us and gives us breath.

Later, perched atop rocks near the mouth of Bear Creek, Shungnak and I look out over Haida Strait to the sea beyond. A distant winter sun sprawls against the horizon, thins to a mound of shivering flame, and drowns itself in the cold Pacific. The sky fades to violet, darkens, and relaxes, like a face losing expression at the edge of sleep. Silence hovers in the brittle woods.

A great blue heron glides down into the anchorage cove and stands motionless in the shallows, like the shadow of a pterodactyl against the Mesozoic sky. Every few minutes I notice the bird's stance and position have changed, but invisibly, like a clock's hands, so that I never actually see its legs move. Then I notice its head slowly lowering, its body tilting, its neck stretching forward. Suddenly it flashes out and draws back, and a fish wriggles on the dripping spear of its beak. The recoiling heron stands erect, flips the fish lengthwise, gulps it, and resumes hunting. Over the next few minutes, the bulge of the fish gradually moves down its serpentine neck.

I've watched herons many times before, admiring them as elegantly plumed, primeval works of art. But I never thought about their impeccable skill and patience as hunters. This event gives me a better sense of the way they live – the measured and timeless stalks, the penetrating eyes fixed at the water's edge, the shadows of prey moving below, the saber beak striking down, the sudden consummation of predatory impulse. Given a choice of birds, I would be a heron, or an owl, a falcon, an eagle. I love these quick, canny animals, perhaps because they seem closest to my own kind. To feel otherwise about predators would be like shrinking from the face in the mirror.

Dusk settles on the waters of Haida Strait, swallows the far peaks and inlets, drifts down through the surrounding forest, takes the island inside itself, and joins it with the sky. Sitting in the darkness, I feel overcome with gratitude and wish for a way to express it. Words seem frail and empty; offerings seem foreign and artificial. Perhaps just being here is enough, becoming wholly engaged with this place, touching it, eating from it, winding my life as tightly as possible into it. The island and I, turning ourselves ever more inside out.

Warm in my sleeping bag, I let the fire ebb to coals. The lamp is out. The cabin roof creaks in the growing chill. I drift toward sleep, pleased that there is no moon, so the deer will wait until dawn to feed. On the floor beside me, Shungnak jerks and whimpers in her dog's dreams.

Dawn. The cold fire of winter sun climbs a pallid wall of sky. Mountains stand out as sharp and clear as the sound of shattering glass. Clouds of steam rise above the open riffles of Bear Creek. The silver calm of Haida Strait is splotched with dark blue where an uncertain breeze touches down against it. Three goldeneye ducks drift in the anchorage, like smudges on a sheet of polished iron.

The temperature is twenty degrees, perhaps much colder back away from shore. Although it rarely drops to zero along this coast, sea humidity and gusty winds often intensify the chill. But even so, our winter is a far cry from that of Koyukon country, where temperatures average below zero for five months of the year and may hover at forty to sixty below for weeks. Not surprisingly, Koyukon elders treat cold weather as a conscious thing, with a potent and irritable spirit. They warn the younger ones to speak carefully about cold, lest they incite its frigid wrath. In the old days, children were even told not to throw snowballs, because the frivolity or annoyance could bring on bitter weather.

When Shungnak was born it was so cold that one of her littermates froze stiff. Thawed out behind the wood stove, he survived, although his tail eventually fell off. Perhaps because she grew up in that climate, and because the frozen landscape meant freedom and adventure for a sled dog, Shungnak still loves winter weather. As we walk back to the cabin, she prances around me, full of excited energy, anxious to get started with the day.

An hour later, I anchor the boat at Sea Lion Point. After paddling the punt ashore, I follow Shungnak to where our tracks from yesterday enter the woods. Just beyond the place of the buck, a pair of does drifts at the edge of sight and disappears. For an hour we angle north, then come slowly back deeper into the woods, moving crosswise to a growing easterly breeze. In two places, deer snort and pound away, invisible beyond a shroud of brush. Otherwise there is nothing.

We keep on in the same direction, probing first through snowy thickets, then through heavy forest with bare, frozen moss underneath. In a dense maze of young spruce, I come face to face with a red squirrel, clinging to the trunk of a dead tree. Luckily, Shungnak has lagged a few yards behind. And instead of scurrying to a high branch, the squirrel stays put, bold, curious and confident, apparently unconcerned about my intentions. I inch ahead, wait, then move again, until he's so close I could ruffle his fur if I blew hard enough.

The squirrel twitches this way and that on his skinny white tree, first head up, then head down, leaning out as if to get a closer look at me. He sticks effortlessly to the smooth wood, or actually hangs from it by the tips of his curved claws. Never satisfied to simply observe, I wonder how his claws can possibly be so sharp, and what keeps them from getting dull? The squirrel spends a long minute checking me out, constantly in motion, scratching up the tree and back down again, jerking from one angle to another, stitching his little feet, shaking his frizzy tail, shivering his long black whiskers. Then he jumps to a spruce just as close but with a slightly different angle. I can see the crenulations of his nose, the fine hairs on his snout, the quick pumping of his ribs, and my face reflecting on his bright indigo eye. When he's seen enough, he turns and jitters to a place above my head. I can tell he's ready to burst into a chatter, as squirrels often do after some deliberation, so I edge past and leave him alone.

A short while later we follow a familiar stretch of trail through a copse of shore pines and cedars. I kneel down to examine a bunch of deer bones in the snowless patch under a tree. Darkened by age and half covered with moss, they're hardly visible any more. I first came across them several years ago, when they still had a blanched white color, with bits of clinging skin, cartilage, and tufts of fur. It looked as if the deer had died only a few months before, and because the nearby tree trunk was heavily clawed, I guessed a bear had either killed the animal or scavenged its carcass. I always looked at the bones when I passed by, but never touched them because I wanted to see how long it took an animal's remains to vanish from the forest floor. Each year, a few more bones were missing or were cloaked over by the moss.

Last summer, I walked through here with a friend and showed him the bones. He touched several of them and pulled one out from the moss. Both of us were stunned by what he found: a hind-leg bone that had been fractured in several places while the deer was alive. It was so badly shattered that a piece the thickness of my index finger had stuck out almost two inches from the wound as indicated by a line where healing flesh had closed around it. The deer must have lived a long time after its terrible injury. Long enough so the fragments knitted themselves together, as if liquid bone had seeped into the wound and solidified as a porous, bulging, convoluted mass. Though gnarled and misshapen, the fused bone seemed almost as strong as a healthy one. But the deer's leg was considerably shortened and had a hollow ivory splinter piercing out from it. As we turned the bone in our hands, I marveled at the determination of living things, and of life itself, to carry on, to mend, and to become whole again after being torn apart.

What could have caused such a wound? It might have been a bad fall, an unskilled hunter's bullet, or a bear. Hardest of all to imagine was the agony this deer went through, the days and weeks of unrelievable pain, endured in solitude, through nights of rain and storm, burdened by the omnipresent danger of being discovered by a bear. Of course, it might have been another bear that eventually killed the animal. After my friend and I left the bones, the forest seemed less beautiful for a while, less a place of shelter than of violence and tragedy. At that same moment, some other animal was probably suffering toward death not far away — perhaps severed by an eagle's beak or broken by a bear, perhaps old and weakened, perhaps riven with disease — biting the moss in torment and fear. I thought, there is little mercy in nature, little to relieve the pain or loneliness of death. Many of the tragedies found in the human world are also found here. Then I realized that loving nature meant loving it all, accepting nature exactly as it is, not idealizing it or ignoring the hard truths, not reducing it to an imaginary world of peace and perfection. How could I crave the beauty of the flame without accepting the heat that made it?

Shortly after noon we come into a narrow muskeg with scattered shore pines and a ragged edge of brushy, low-growing cedar. I squint against the sharp glare of snow. It has that peculiar look of old powder, a bit settled and touched by wind, very lovely but without the airy magic of a fresh fall. I gaze up the muskeg's easy slope. Above the encroaching wall of timber, seamed against the deep blue sky, is the peak of Kluksa Mountain, with a great plume of snow streaming off in what must be a shuddering gale. It has a contradictory look of absoluteness and unreality about it, like a Himalayan summit suspended in midair over the saddle of a low ridge.

I move slowly up the muskeg's east side, away from the breeze and in the sun's full warmth. Deer tracks crisscross the opening, but none of the animals stopped here to feed. Next to the bordering trees, the tracks join as a single, hard-packed trail, showing the deer's preference for cover. Shungnak keeps her nose to the thickly scented snow. We come across a pine sapling that a buck has assaulted with his antlers, scattering twigs and flakes of bark all around. But his tracks are hardened, frosted, and lack sharpness, indicating they're at least a day old.

We slip through a point of trees, then follow the edge again, pausing long moments between footsteps. A mixed tinkle of crossbills and siskins moves through the high timber, and a squirrel rattles from deep in the woods, too far off to be scolding us. Shungnak picks up a strong ribbon of scent, but she hears nothing. I stop for a few minutes to study the muskeg's raveled fringe, the tangle of shade and thicket, the glaze of mantled boughs.

Then my eye barely catches a fleck of movement up ahead, near the ground and almost hidden behind the trunk of a leaning pine – perhaps a squirrel's tail or a bird. I slowly lift my hand to shade the sun, stand dead still, and wait to see if something is there. Finally it moves again.

At the very edge of the trees, almost out of sight in a little swale, small and furry and bright-tinged, turning one direction and then another, is the funnel of a single ear. Having seen this, I soon make out the other ear and the slope of a doe's forehead. Her neck is behind the leaning pine, but on the other side I can barely see the soft, dark curve of her back above the snow. She is comfortably bedded, gazing placidly into the distance, chewing her cud.

Shungnak has stopped twenty yards behind me in the point of trees and has no idea about the deer. I shake my finger at her until she lays her ears back and sits. Then I watch the doe again. She is fifty yards ahead, ten yards beyond the leaning tree, and still looking off at an angle. Her left eye is visible and she refuses to turn her head away, so it might be impossible to get closer. Perhaps I should just wait here, in case a buck is attending her nearby. But however improbable it might be under these circumstances, a thought is lodged in my mind: I can get near her.

My first step sinks down softly, but the second makes a loud budging sound, like stepping on a piece of toast. She snaps my way, stops chewing, and stares for several minutes. It seems hopeless, especially out here in an open field of crispy snow with only the narrow tree trunk for a screen. But she turns away and starts to chew again. I move just enough so the tree blocks her eye and the rest of her head, but I can still see her ears. Every time she chews they shake just a bit, so I watch them and step when her hearing is obscured by the sound of her own jaws.

Either this works or the deer has decided to ignore me, because after a while I've come close enough so the noise of my feet has to reach her easily. She should have jumped up and run long ago, but instead she lies there in serene repose. I deliberate on every step, try for the softest snow, wait long minutes before the next move, stalking like a cat toward ambush. I watch beyond her, into the surrounding shadows and across to the muskeg's farther edge, for the shape of a buck deer; but there is nothing. I feel ponderous, clumsy-footed, out of place, inimical. I should turn and run away, take fear on the deer's behalf, flee the mirrored image in my mind. But I clutch the cold rifle at my side and creep closer.

The wind refuses to blow and my footsteps seem like thunder in the still sunshine. But the doe only turns once to look my way, without even pointing her ears toward me, then stares off and begins to chew again.

I am ten feet from the leaning tree. My heart pounds so hard I think those enchanted ears should hear the blood rushing in my temples. Yet a strange assurance has come into me, a quite unmystical confidence. Perhaps she has decided I am another deer, a buck attracted by her musk or a doe feeding gradually toward her. My slow pace and lapses of stillness would not seem human. For myself, I have lost awareness of time; I have no feeling of patience or impatience. It's as if the deer has moved slowly toward me on a cloud of snow, and I am adrift in the pure motion of experience.

I take the last step to the trunk of the leaning pine. It's bare of branches, scarcely wider than my outstretched hand, but perfectly placed to break my odd profile. There is no hope of getting any closer, so I slowly poke my head out to watch. She has an ideal spot: screened from the wind, warmed by the sun, and with a clear view of the muskeg. I can see muscles working beneath the close fur of her jaw, the rise and fall of her side each time she breathes, the shining edge of her ebony eye.

I hold absolutely still, but her body begins to stiffen, she lifts her head higher, and her ears twitch anxiously. Then instead of looking at me she turns her face to the woods, shifting her ears toward a sound I cannot hear. A few seconds later, the unmistakable voice of a buck drifts up, strangely disembodied, as if it comes from somewhere underneath the snow. I huddle as close to the tree as I can, press against the hard dry bark, and peek around its edge.

There is a gentle rise behind the doe, scattered with sapling pines and bushy juniper. A rhythmic crunching of snow comes invisibly from the slope, then a bough shakes ... and a buck walks easily into the open sunshine.

Focusing completely on the doe, he comes straight to her and never sees my intrusive shape just beyond. He slips through a patch of small trees, stops a few feet from where she lies, lowers his head and stretches it toward her, then holds this odd pose for a long moment. She reaches her muzzle to one side, trying to find his scent. When he moves up behind her she stands quickly, bends her body into a strange sideways arc, and stares back at him. A moment later she walks off a bit, lifts her tail, and puts droppings in her tracks. The buck moves to the warm ground of her bed and lowers his nose to the place where her female scent is strongest.

Inching like a reptile on a cold rock, I have stepped out from the tree and let my whole menacing profile become visible. The deer are thirty feet away and stand well apart, so they can both see me easily. I am a hunter hovering near his prey and a watcher craving inhuman love, torn between the deepest impulses, hot and shallow-breathed and seething with unreconciled intent, hidden from opened eyes that look into the nimbus of sun and see nothing but the shadow they have chosen for themselves. In this shadow now, the hunter has vanished and only the watcher remains.

Drawn by the honey of the doe's scent, the buck steps quickly toward her. And now the most extraordinary thing happens. The doe turns away from him and walks straight for me. There is no hesitation, only a wild deer coming along the trail of hardened snow where the other deer have passed, the trail in which I stand at this moment. She raises her head, looks at me, and steps without pausing.

My existence is reduced to a pair of eyes; a rush of unbearable heat flushes through my cheeks; and a sense of absolute certainty fuses in my mind.

The snow blazes so brightly that my head aches. The deer is a dark form growing larger. I look up at the buck, half embarrassed, as if to apologize that she's chosen me over him. He stares at her for a moment, turns to follow, then stops and watches anxiously. I am struck by how gently her hooves touch the trail, how little sound they make as she steps, how thick the fur is on her flank and shoulder, how unfathomable her eyes look. I am consumed with a sense of her perfect elegance in the brilliant light. And then I am lost again in the whirling intensity of experience.

The doe is now ten feet from me. She never pauses or looks away. Her feet punch down mechanically into the snow, coming closer and closer, until they are less than a yard from my own. Then she stops, stretches her neck calmly toward me, and lifts her nose.

There is not the slightest question in my mind, as if this was sure to happen and I have known all along exactly what to do. I slowly raise my hand and reach out.

And my fingers touch the soft, dry, gently needling fur on top of the deer's head, and press down to the living warmth of flesh underneath.

She makes no move and shows no fear, but I can feel the flaming strength and tension that flow in her wild body as in no other animal I have touched. Time expands and I am suspended in the clear reality of the moment.

Then, by the flawed conditioning of a lifetime among fearless domesticated things, I instinctively drop my hand and let the deer smell it. Her black nose, wet and shining, touches gently against my skin at the exact instant I realize the absoluteness of my error. And a tremor runs through her entire body as she realizes hers. Her muscles seize and harden; she seems to wrench her eyes away from me but her body remains, rigid and paralyzed. Having been deceived by her other senses, she keeps her nose tight against my hand for one more moment.

Then all the energy inside her triggers in a series of exquisite bounds. She flings out over the hummocks of snow-covered moss, suspended in effortless flight like fog blown over the muskeg in a gale. Her body leaps with such power that the muscles should twang aloud like a bowstring; the earth should shudder and drum; but I hear no sound. In the center of the muskeg she stops to look back, as if to confirm what must seem impossible. The buck follows in more earthbound undulations; they dance away together; and I am left in the meeting place alone.

There is a blur of rushing feet behind me. No longer able to restrain herself, Shungnak dashes past, buries her nose in the soft tracks, and then looks back to ask if we can run after them. I had completely forgotten her, sitting near enough to watch the whole encounter, somehow resisting what must have been a prodigious urge to explode in chase. When I reach out to hug her, she smells the hand that touched the deer. And it seems as if it happened long ago.

I walk slowly from the spot, letting the whole event roll through my mind again and again, remembering the dream that began many months ago, that I might someday touch a deer. After trying and failing with the naive little fawn earlier this fall, I'd begun to think the idea was farfetched, perhaps even foolish. But now, totally unexpected and in a strange way, it has happened. Was the deer caught by some reckless twinge of curiosity? Had she never encountered a human on this wild island? Did she yield to some odd amorous confusion? Then I realize I truly do not care. I would rather accept this as pure experience and not give in to a notion that everything should be explained.

Koyukon elders simply accept what comes to them. They teach that everything in the natural world has its own spirit and awareness, and they give themselves to that other world, without expecting voices, without waiting for visions, without seeking admission to the hidden realms.

I am reminded of something that happened the last time I hunted with Grandpa William. While we sat talking at the edge of a meadow, an unusual bird started singing and chattering in a nearby treetop. At first it looked like a small hawk, but there was something different about its color and shape. When I asked what it was, he listened closely to its calls, then took my binoculars and watched it for a long while, intrigued and perplexed. "I don't know," he muttered, mostly to himself; then he suggested a difficult Koyukon name I'd never heard before. Shortly, his interest darkened to concern: was the arrival of this strange bird a sign, an omen?

Suddenly he began addressing the bird at length in the Koyukon language, speaking in a soft, gentle voice. "Who are you," he wondered, "and what are you saying to us?" He walked out into the meadow, still talking, still trying to establish that the loquacious bird was something ordinary, not an ominous stranger. "Wish us good luck, whoever you are," he said. "Wish us well, and surround us – your grandchildren – within a circle of protection." By this time I'd lost interest in identifying the bird, and my whole attention was focused on Grandpa William: a man imploring mercy and protection from a bird, addressing a feathered emissary in a treetop.

Those moments epitomized everything I had learned from Koyukon people, everything they had tried to tell me about living in a natural world filled with spirit and power. I've had few experiences that so moved me. For how many thousand generations, I wondered, have people spoken and prayed to the natural beings around them, as a customary part of daily life? At any other time in human history, this event would be as ordinary as talking to another person. To me, Grandpa William represented the universal man beseeching the powers that pervade his living world, powers so recently forgotten among my own people. More than anything else, I wished it had seemed quite unremarkable for me, wished my ancestors hadn't forsaken what Grandpa William still understood.

Neither Grandpa William nor I ever knew what that bird was, though I later concluded it must be a young northern shrike. And if the bird did carry an omen, who was it for?

I stop in the shadows along the muskeg's upper edge, and think back over the years with Koyukon people. What stands out for me at this moment is a special wisdom of their tradition – to expect nothing of nature, but to humbly receive its mystery, beauty, food, and life. In return, Koyukon people show the same respect toward nature that is shown toward humans, acknowledging that spirit and sacredness pervade all things. If I understand correctly, their behavior toward nature is ordered around a few simple principles: Move slowly, stay quiet, watch carefully, be ever humble, show no hint of arrogance or disrespect. And if they follow one overarching commandment, it is to approach all life, of which humans are a part, with humility and restraint. All things are among the chosen.

As I reflect on the experiences of yesterday and today, I find an important lesson in them, viewed in the light of wisdom taken from the earth and shaped by generations of elders. Two deer came and gave the choices to me. One deer I took and we will now share a single body. The other deer I touched and we will now share that moment. These events could be seen as opposites, but perhaps they are identical. Both are founded on the same principles, the same relationship, the same reciprocity. Both are the same kind of gift.

Koyukon elders would explain, in words quite different from my own, that I moved into two moments of grace, or what they would call luck. This is the source of success for a hunter or a watcher; not skill, not cleverness, not guile. Something is only given in nature, never taken.

Well soaked and shivering from a rough trip across the Sound, we pull into the dark waters of Anchor Bay. Sunset burns on the spindled peak of Antler Mountain. The little house is warm with lights that shimmer on the calm near shore. I see Nita looking from the window and Ethan dashes out to wait by the tide, pitching rocks at the mooring buoy. He strains to see inside the boat, knowing that a hunter who tells his news aloud might offend the animals by sounding boastful. But when he sees the deer his excited voice seems to roll up and down the mountainside.

He runs for the house with Shungnak, carrying a load of gear, and I know he'll burst inside with the news. Ethan, joyous and alive, boy made of deer.

P. V. Beck

—➤◆◄—

WILD TROUT

> I had been a man, a stag, a boar, a bird, and now I was a fish. In
> all my changes I had joy and fullness of life. But in the water joy
> lay deeper, life pulsed deeper. For on land or air there is always
> something excessive and hindering; as arms that swing at the sides
> of a man, and which the mind must remember. The stag has legs
> to be tucked away for sleep, and untucked for movement; and the
> bird has wings that must be folded and pecked and cared for. But
> the fish has but one piece from his nose to his tail. He is com-
> plete, single and unencumbered. He turns in one turn, and goes
> up and down and round in one sole movement.[5]
>
> — *The Story of Tuan Mac Cairill*

I fly fish in order to disappear, to go where there is nobody, to leave the familiar behind. It is my guide to the other world — the restless, teeming network of chaos and
order that forms the matrix of creation.

For the same reason I search out wildness I fish: for that deliberate strangeness,
that mindful twisting of fate.

Fly fishing is a way of hooking into a world, becoming the clouds, the riffle patterns on the water, the tall grasses bending towards pocket water; the chill, the sun,
the quiet or the screech of hawks. A fisherman is all of these, alone, putting a bunch
of shapeshifting elements together in a split second in order to lure a trout to a
hook. Hooking a trout lasts only a fraction of a second. Finding it may take years.

The fly fisher travels in miniature worlds — clinger nymphs on the underside of
stream bed rocks, tiny midge clusters, snowflies and vast terrains — deep basalt
canyons, alpine meadows studded with turquoise lakes like a horizon of stars. The
fly fisher spends hours squinting at an eye of a hook no bigger than a lettuce seed,
trying to thread it with almost invisible nylon gut, and climbs for days in order to
get a glimpse of a golden trout of mythical proportions only to spend the day hud-
dled in a cave waiting out a violent, sudden thunderstorm.

> They came to know me and look for me. They lay in wait at the
> waterfalls up which I leaped like a silver flash. They held out nets
> for me; they hid traps under leaves; they made cords of the color

of water, of the color of weeds ... Many a wound I got from
men, many a sorrowful scar.

— Tuan Mac Cairill

Hunting for wild trout is a never-ending quest and often a sorrowful one. The
chances of trout growing old grow scarcer. There are hints of devastation: drought-
stricken streams, irrigation-sucked rivers, and over-fished creeks.

Some people fish for profit. They use nets and weirs and spears. Some people
fish to survive. They too use lures and bait. For profit or survival the objective is to
amass the greatest number of fish with the least amount of effort. The irony is that
the fate of both subsistence fishermen and profiteers depends on the survival of
wild trout.

Fly fishing is not a test of survival, it is a journey to places where survival hangs
in the balance. Because they demand cold pristine waters for their survival, trout
are the touchstones of wildness. Finding wild trout, especially large trout, is evidence that the water is clear and running its course, that insects continue to hatch
in perennial cycles, that rocks are tumbling and crumbling into currents, creating
eddies and waterfalls, and that rivers still run into the seas and become rain again.

Fly fishing turns the notion of survival upside down. It means fishing harder,
insisting that the survival of the fish depends on our empathy with them. The
more we interact with trout (pretending we are a dragonfly, a caddie larva, an ant),
the more sensitive we become to its precarious existence, which happens also to be
our own.

This kind of fishing is harder, requiring an intimacy and attention to minutiae
which is maddeningly archaic. It is madness precisely because it makes survival
harder than it already is, and by doing so, it turns survival into an art. Fishing with
an artificial fly is a conceit: it has no usefulness. But when you catch trout on the
fly and then let them go again, it is the beginning of wisdom.

> [In order to approach the spirit powers without scaring them
> away] it is necessary to lose one's own humanness and become as
> wild as possible, as crazy as possible. Haunt lonely, desolate
> places ... climb awful mountains, climb down the rim of crater
> lakes, jump into the silent cold water, spend all night there ...[6]

Fly fishing obeys primordial laws: how to cast correctly, what a well-tied fly
should look like, how you should fish wet flies, how you should fish dries.

One learns the laws but ultimately one must leave them behind and journey into
wildness.

> How I flew through the soft element: how I joyed in the country
> where there is no harshness: in the element which upholds and
> gives way; which caresses and lets go, and will not let you fall.
>
> *— Tuan Mac Cairill*

Watery places – springs, rivers, sink holes, whirlpools, billabongs, and water-falls – are sources of healing, oracles, and mythical beginnings. In order to become a fly fisher you must ultimately enter the waters and become a fish.

What fish you become determines where your journey will take you. You may be a vulnerable native cutthroat finning for mayfly nymphs in a brushy alpine stream, a sly brown holding down deep for caddie larvae in the roiling waters of a big river, a wary brookie darting for grasshoppers in a meandering meadow creek, or an overwrought and shy rainbow rising for midges in a hidden beaver pond.

Tuan Mac Cairill passed through successive metamorphoses, stag, boar, hawk, and finally salmon, before his journey was complete. In each guise he learned some-thing about the world and about human beings.

In *The Book of Taliesin,* the Welsh poet/seer sang: "I was in many shapes before I was released, I was a slender, enchanted sword ... I was rain-drops in the air, I was stars' beam ... I was a path, I was an eagle, I was a coracle in the seas."[7]

Under the tutelage of the great wizard Merlin, the young Wart, who was later to become King Arthur, was taught specific lessons in strength, balance, and ethics by becoming an owl, a fish, a badger, an ant, a goose, and a hawk.

The concept of the transmigration of the soul appears in all shamanic mythol-ogy as well as fairy tales, which are glosses of shamanic quests.

In every quest on which the wanderer takes on different guises, each transfor-mation creates ever-expanding rings of knowledge. The rise of the trout is, for the fisherman, a metaphor for this quest.

> He had but small knowledge of the intricacies of the sport ... no instinct for it, no sense of its mysteries or feel for the way, in your spine, you canny to where a salmon is lying, patient, in the river's dark undercurrents, and how your human patience, the determi-nation in yourself and the steel of your concentration alike to the fish's wait and wiliness. That, Seamus knew naught of, nor could it ever be explained to him ...[8]

For me, the journey begins at the fly tying table. The small space in front of me where the dubbing furs, feathers, thread, and ribbing materials are spread out is the wilderness, the habitat to which I will journey. Everything around me vanishes.

I put a hook into the vice and begin to wrap the thread. The hook represents the stream in which the insect I am imitating hatches or swims, which it flies out of or falls into. The type of fly I choose to tie will choose the weather, the shoreline, the water, and ultimately the trout I go searching for. Once the fly is tied onto the tippet of my leader, it is more than an imitation insect, it is my psychopomp, the guide for my quest.

Finally, after hours of tying and a day or a week of walking, I am in the place I have desired; some faraway place, a place where I believe there might be glossy wild trout.

I look out at the world. The song begins: I am the mountainside, I am the meadow, I am the grasses, I am the mint, I am the wild garlic, I am the boulders, I am the rushes, I am the hawk, I am the soughing wind ...

I put my fly rod together and string it up. I turn over rocks to look for nymphs, watch the air for swarms of insects, feel the soft moth-like wings of caddie flies against my cheek, listen to the drone of mosquitos and gnats, the zing of dragonflies, the clicking of grasshoppers. I take a fly out of one of my fly boxes, tie it on, and walk slowly toward the water.

The song begins again: I am the brushy willows, I am the cut bank, I am the foam line, I am the riffle, I am the curling eddy, I am the bend pool, I am the beaver dam, I am the waterfall ...

I crouch and cast the fly out over the water: I am diving into the gravel current, dropping from a grassy bank, falling from a leafy branch, alighting on the glassy surface ...

A trout leaps out of the water; a hesitation after the trout strikes; the trout splashes the surface as it tugs at my line. The hush breaks, the leaves rustle again, a bird calls ...

I will keep searching for wild trout feeding in plunge pools and just after ice-out in high ponds; watch them dart out from a shadow to sip an emerging nymph or struggling mayfly. The farther out I go, the farther in, the brushier, boggier, rockier, steeper, the greater the chances are I'll be able to find a trout that will survive and grow old. This trout is my talisman.

Pam Houston

———➤●◄———

from
WOMEN ON HUNTING

When I was twenty-six years old, and just catching on to the fact that my life wasn't going to be something that came at me like opposing traffic, but something I actually had to take control of and shape, I fell in love with a man who was a hunting guide for a living. We didn't have what you would call the healthiest of relationships. He was selfish, evasive, and unfaithful. I was demanding, manipulative, and self-pitying. He was a republican, and I was a democrat. He was a Texan and I was not. I belonged to the Sierra Club and he belonged to the NRA. Yet somehow we managed to stay together for three years of our lives, and to spend two solid months of each of those three years hunting for Dall sheep in Alaska.

I was always quick, in those days, to make the distinction between a hunter and a hunting guide, for though I was indirectly responsible for the deaths of a total of five animals, I have never killed an animal myself, and never intend to. I had the opportunity once to shoot a Dall ram whose horns were so big it would have likely gotten my name into the record books. I had three decent men applying every kind of peer pressure they could come up with, and I even went so far as to raise the rifle to my eye, unsure in that moment what I would do next. But once I got it up there I couldn't think of one good reason to pull the trigger.

I learned about bullets and guns and calibers and spotting scopes, and I was a good hunting guide simply because I'm good at the outdoors. I can carry a heavy pack long distances. I can cook decent meals on a backpacker's stove. I keep my humor pretty well for weeks without a toilet and a shower. I can sleep, if I have to, on a forty-five-degree ledge of ice. I know how to move in the wilderness, and because of this I understand how the sheep move. I'm a decent tracker. I've got what they call animal sense.

When I was hunting Dall sheep in Alaska it was one on one on one. One hunter, one guide, one ram that we tracked, normally for ten days, before we got close enough to shoot it. My obvious responsibility was to the hunter. It was my job to keep him from falling into a crevasse or getting eaten by a grizzly bear, to carry his gun when he got too tired, to keep him fed and watered, to listen to his stories, to get him up at three in the morning and keep him on his feet till midnight to drag him fifteen miles and sometimes as much as four thousand vertical feet a day, and if everything went well, to get him in position to shoot a sheep to take home and put on his wall. My other job, though understated, was to protect the sheep from the hunters, to guarantee that the hunter shot only the oldest ram in the herd, and that he only fired when he was close enough to make a killing shot. A hunter can't walk down a wounded animal across the glaciers in Alaska the way he can through the trees in the Pennsylvania woods. A bad shot in Alaska almost always means a lost ram.

I describe those months in the Alaska Range now as the most conflicted time of my life. I would spend seventy days testing myself in all the ways I love, moving through the Alaska wilderness, a place of such power and vastness it is incomprehensible even to my memory. I watched a mama grizzly bear feed wild blueberries to her cubs, I woke to the footfall of a hungry-eyed silver world whispering through our campsite, I watch a bull moose rub the velvet off his bloody antlers, and a bald eagle dive for a parka squirrel. I watched the happy chaos that is a herd of caribou for hours, and the contrastingly calculated movements of the sheep for days.

I learned from the animals their wilderness survival skills, learned, of course, a few of my own. I learned, in those days, my place in the universe, learned why I need the wilderness, not why "we" need it, but why I do. That I need the opportunity to give in to something bigger than myself, like falling into love, something bigger, even, than I can define. This had to do not at all with shooting an animal (though it would have, of course, in its purest form, had we not had packages and packages of dried chicken stew), but with simpler skills: keeping warm in subzero temperatures the predominant one, avoiding the grizzly bears that were everywhere and unpredictable, and not panicking when the shale started sliding underneath my boot soles in a slide longer and steeper than anything I'd ever seen in the lower forty-eight, finally riding that shale slide out like a surfer on a giant gray wave.

I listened to the stories of the hunters, the precision and passion with which the best among them could bring the memories of past hunting camps to life. I understood that part of what we were about in hunting camp was making new stories, stories that were the closest these men ever got to something sacred, stories that would grace years, maybe even generations, of orange campfire light.

But underneath all that wonder and wildness and the telling of tales, the fact remains that in payment for my Alaskan experience I watched five of the most beautiful, smartest, and wildest animals I'd ever seen die, most of them slowly and in unspeakable pain. And regardless of the fact that it was the hunter who pulled the trigger, I was the party responsible for their deaths. And though I eat meat and wear leather, though I understand every ethical argument there is about hunting, including the one that says it is hunters who will ultimately save the animals because it is the NRA that has the money and the power to protect what is left of America's wilderness, it will never be okay with me that I led my hunters to those animals. There is no amount of learning that can, in my heart, justify their deaths.

So when I remember that time in my life, I try to think not only of the killing, but also of the hunting, which is a work of art, a feat of imagination, a flight of spirit, and a test of endless patience and skill. To hunt an animal successfully you must think like an animal, move like an animal, climb to the top of the mountain just to go down the other side, and always be watching, and waiting, and watching. To hunt well is to be at once the pursuer and the object of pursuit. The process is circular, and female somehow, like giving birth, or dancing. A hunt, at its best, ought to look from the air like a carefully choreographed ballet.

French psychoanalyst Jacques Lacan believed that men desire the object of their desire, while women desire the condition of desiring, and this gives women a greater capacity for relishing the hunt. I believe that is why, in so many ancient and contemporary societies, women have been the superior hunters. Good hunting is no more about killing an animal than good sex is about making babies or good writing is about publication. The excitement, even the fulfillment, is in the beauty of the search. While a man tends to be linear about achieving a goal, a woman can be circular and spatial. She can move in many directions at once, she can be many things at once, she can see an object from all sides, and, when it is required, she is able to wait.

Occasionally there is a man who can do these things (most of the male guides I knew were far better at them than I), and he is a pleasure to guide and to learn from. But the majority of my clients started out thinking that hunting is like war. They were impatient like a poor general, impatient like an earnest sergeant who thinks he should be the general, impatient for the sound of his own gun and impatient for the opposition to make a mistake.

But the sheep didn't often make mistakes, and they were as patient as stone. So it was my job to show the hunter that he would be required to choose a different metaphor. If hunting can be like war it can also be like opera, or like fine wine. It can be like out-of-body travel, it can be like the suspension of disbelief. Hunting can be all these things and more; like a woman, it won't sit down and be just one thing.

Susan Griffin

HIS POWER: HE TAMES WHAT IS WILD

The Hunt

Is it by its indefiniteness it shadows forth the heartless voids and immensities of the universe, and thus stabs us from behind with the thought of annihilation when beholding the milky way?

— *Herman Melville,* Moby Dick

And at last she could bear the burden of herself no more. She was to be had for the taking. To be had for the taking.

— *D. H. Lawrence,* Lady Chatterley's Lover

She has captured his heart. She has overcome him. He cannot tear his eyes away. He is burning with passion. He cannot live without her. He pursues her. She makes him pursue her. The faster she runs, the stronger his desire. He will overtake her. He will make her his own. He will have her. (The boy chases the doe and her yearling for nearly two hours. She keeps running despite her wounds. He pursues her through pastures, over fences, groves of trees, crossing the road, up hills, volleys of rifle shots sounding, until perhaps twenty bullets are embedded in her body.) She has no mercy. She has dressed to excite his desire. She has no scruples. She has painted herself for him. She makes supple movements to entice him. She is without soul. Beneath her painted face is flesh, are bones. She reveals only part of herself to him. She is wild. She flees whenever he approaches. She is teasing him. (Finally, she is defeated and falls and he sees that half of her head has been blown off, that one leg is gone, her abdomen split from her tail to her head, and her organs hang outside her body. Then four men encircle the fawn and harvest her too.) He is an easy target, he says. He says he is pierced. Love has shot him through, he says. He is a familiar mark. Riddled. Stripped to the bone. He is conquered, he says. (The boys, fond of hunting hare, search in particular for pregnant females.) He is fighting for his life. He faces annihilation in her, he says. He is losing himself to her, he says. Now, he must conquer her wildness, he says, he must tame her before she drives him wild, he says. (Once catching their prey, they step on her back, breaking it, and they call this "dancing on the hare.") Thus he goes on his knees to her. Thus he wins her over, he tells her he wants her. He makes her his own. He encloses her. He encircles her. He puts her under lock and key. He protects her. (Approaching the great mammals, the hunters make little sounds which they know will make the elephants form a defensive circle.) And once she is his, he prizes his delight. He feasts his eyes on her. He adorns her luxuriantly. He gives her ivory. He gives her perfume. (The older matriarchs stand to the outside of the circle to protect the calves and younger mothers.) He covers her with the skins of mink, beaver, muskrat, seal, raccoon, otter, ermine, fox, the feathers of ostriches, osprey, egret, ibis. (The hunters then encircle that circle and fire first into the bodies of the matriarchs. When these older elephants fall, the younger panic, yet unwilling to leave the bodies of their dead mothers, they make easy targets.) And thus he makes her soft. He makes her calm. He makes her grateful to him. He has tamed her, he says. She is content to be his, he says. (In the winter, if a single wolf has leaped over the walls of the city and terrorized the streets, the hunters go out in a band to rid the forest of the whole pack.) Her voice is now soothing to him. Her eyes no longer blaze, but look on him serenely. When he calls to her, she gives herself to him. Her ferocity lies under him. (The body of the great whale is strapped with explosives.) Now nothing of the old beast remains in her. (Eastern Bison, extinct 1825; Spectacled Cormorant, extinct 1852; Cape Lion, extinct 1865; Bonin Night Heron, extinct 1889; Barbary Lion, extinct 1922; Great Auk, extinct 1944.) And he can trust her wholly with himself. So he is blazing when he enters her, and she is consumed. (Florida Key Deer, vanishing; Wild Indian Buffalo, vanishing; Great Sable Antelope, vanishing.) Because she is his, she offers no resistance. She is a place of rest for him. A place of his making. And when his flesh begins to yield and his skin melts into her, he becomes soft, and he is without fear; he does not lose himself; though something in him gives way, he is not lost in her, because she is his now: he has captured her.

Notes

This story of the deer and her fawn being shot was taken from an account published in the *New York Times* by Ruth C. Adams, November 1, 1975. For stories such as the breaking of the back of the hare (a practice of English schoolboys), see Maureen Duffy, "Beasts for Pleasure," in *Animals, Men and Morals*. For a description of methods of hunting elephants, see Iain and Oria Douglas-Hamilton, *Among the Elephants* (New York: Viking 1975). For lists of extinct and vanishing species, see Vinzenz Ziswiler, *Extinct and Vanishing Animals* (London: English Universities Press, 1967).

Galway Kinnell

THE BEAR

1 In late winter
I sometimes glimpse bits of steam
coming up from
some fault in the old snow
and bend close and see it is lung-colored
and put down my nose
and know
the chilly, enduring odor of bear.

2 I take a wolf's rib and whittle
it sharp at both ends
and coil it up
and freeze it in blubber and place it out
on the fairway of the bears.

And when it has vanished
I move out on the bear tracks,
roaming in circles
until I come to the first, tentative, dark
splash on the earth.

And I set out
running, following the splashes
of blood wandering over the world.
At the cut, gashed resting places
I stop and rest,
at the crawl-marks
where he lay out on his belly
to overpass some stretch of bauchy ice
I lie out
dragging myself forward with bear-knives in my fists.

3 On the third day I begin to starve,
at nightfall I bend down as I knew I would
at a turd sopped in blood,

and hesitate, and pick it up,
and thrust it in my mouth, and gnash it down,
and rise
and go on running.

4 On the seventh day,
    living by now on bear blood alone,
     I can see his upturned carcass far out ahead, a scraggled,
    steamy hulk,
    the heavy fur riffling in the wind.

    I come up to him
    and stare at the narrow-spaced, petty eyes,
    the dismayed
    face laid back on the shoulder, the nostrils
    flared, catching
    perhaps the first taint of me as he
    died.

    I hack
    a ravine in his thigh, and eat and drink,
    and tear him down his whole length
    and open him and climb in
    and close him up after me, against the wind,
    and sleep.

5 And dream
    of lumbering flatfooted
    over the tundra,
    stabbed twice from within,
    splattering a trail behind me,
    splattering it out no matter which way I lurch,
    no matter which parabola of bear-transcendence,
    which dance of solitude I attempt,
    which gravity-clutched leap,
    which trudge, which groan.

6 Until one day I totter and fall —
    fall on this
    stomach that has tried so hard to keep up,
    to digest the blood as it leaked in,
    to break up
    and digest the bone itself: and now the breeze
    blows over me, blows off

the hideous belches of ill-digested bear blood
and rotted stomach
and the ordinary, wretched odor of bear,

blows across
my sore, lolled tongue a song
or screech, until I think I must rise up
and dance. And I lie still.

7 I awaken I think. Marshlights
reappear, geese
come trailing again up the flyway.
In her ravine under old snow the dam-bear
lies, licking
lumps of smeared fur
and drizzly eyes into shapes
with her tongue. And one
hairy-soled trudge stuck out before me,
the next groaned out,
the next,
the next,
the rest of my days I spend
wandering: wondering
what, anyway,
was that sticky infusion, that rank flavor of blood, that
    poetry, by which I lived?

Linda Hogan

BEAR

The bear is a dark continent
that walks upright
like a man.

It lives across the thawing river.
I have seen it
beyond the water,
beyond comfort. Last night
it left a mark at my door
that said winter
was a long and hungry night of sleep.
But I am not afraid; I have collected
other nights of fear
knowing what things walked
the edges of my sleep,

and I remember
the man who shot
a bear,
how it cried as he did
and in his own voice,
how he tracked that red song
 into the forest's lean arms
to where the bear lay weeping
on fired earth,
its black hands
covering its face from sky
where humans believe god lives
larger than death.

That man,
a madness remembers him.
It is a song in starved shadows
in nights of sleep.

It follows him.
Even the old rocks sing it.
It makes him want
to get down on his knees
and lay his own hands
across his face and turn away
from sky where god lives
larger than life.

Madness is its own country,
desperate and ruined.
It is a collector of lives.
It's a man
afraid of what he's done
and what he lives by. Safe,
we are safe
from the bear
and we have each other,
we have each other
to fear.

Robert Hedin

FROM AN INTERVIEW
WITH JOHN HAINES

You have spent a good part of your adult life living what you call "the woods life in all its fullness," attempting to retrieve something "of that native ground, the original and hardly comprehended thing under our feet." In retrospect, can you point to any single moment or occurrence when you realized your life at the Richardson homestead had suddenly opened beyond its dailiness to take on greater resonance, some sort of historical or esthetic significance?

I suppose there may have been such a moment, but what I remember now is more like a sequence of such moments, half-conscious intuitions that the life I was living extended far beyond that moment and that immediate activity, whatever it may have been. I think this feeling can be particularly acute when we are living close to the ancient life of people — in hunting, tilling the soil, tending to animals, and so forth. At any moment, a sudden clarity, and we are, so to speak, *returned*, or it may be, reconciled, to something forgotten in our natures. I think it is, in part, in the nature of the artist, the poet, and the novelist, to encourage these moments, and to record them, to keep the continuity of things alive. But, in fact, many trades and activities in their own way do this. I recall one cool morning in Madrid years ago when I stepped out onto the street and saw the shopkeepers washing down the sidewalks and opening their shops. Here was something that had been going on for centuries and was part of the life of people. The fact that I was in Spain, in a much older country, heightened my impression. Whether a modern office or factory job retains much of this feeling for things, I doubt. And if not, then I wonder what the consequences will be for humanity cut off from even these rather tentative urban roots.

Japanese

from
RYOJIN-HISHO

To make a living
   in this world of dreams,
I fished in the seas
   and hunted in the hills,
so all the Buddhas now have fled from me.

Now how am I supposed to live
   the next life?

translated by Yasuhiko Moriguchi
and David Jenkins

CULTIVATION

Claude Monet, Grainstacks

Few images of modern art are more familiar to us than Monet's *Grainstacks.* In them, we've been taught, Monet and Impressionism brought to the fore a passionate interest in light and color – apparently to the exclusion of everything else.

The appearance, however, misleads. As Paul Hayes Tucker has wonderfully demonstrated (in the catalogue to *Monet in the Nineties*):

> These paintings are as replete with associations as they are rich in visual incident.... The early morning light glistens on the frozen earth, filling the scene with the aura of potential.... Though isolated and erect like weighty monuments, the stacks are literal extensions of the town. They are the farmer's source of income and the town's most substantial product. They are also the tangible evidence of the prosperity of the place and of the countryside's fertile soil and benevolent climate.[1]

The *Grainstacks,* Tucker concludes, suggest not so simply the labor itself but rather the rewards of good labor: "this is the countryside that fulfills all promises."

These paintings speak about painting itself, of course, but they also suggest, along with much else in this book, that what we call the work of art – *culture* – involves a relationship with the land and everything connected to it. The English words *culture* and *cultivation* derive from the latin *cultus,* from *colere,* meaning to till or cultivate the land, which in turn goes back to Indo-European origins in *kwel,* which meant both "to move around" and "to dwell" (as in the derivative *colony,* a word that suggests both movement and stasis: a group that separates from the "mother country" in order to dwell elsewhere, and yet remains in relationship to her).

This is why Tucker can conclude that Monet's paintings in these years "are not only about light and color, instantaneity, and agrarian phenomena. They are also about nurturing and growth, commitment and community, concerns that Monet believes can be found in the countryside."

Monet of course is not alone in his belief. The work of Wendell Berry among many others is ample testimony to such a faith. But the underlying point here has to do – once again – with relationship. The *Grainstacks* stand alone in one sense, and it has certainly been possible to view them aesthetically as isolated objects – as pure color and form. But in another, and I would suggest truer sense, their existence as art objects is possible *only* through their original and true (natural) existence *as* grainstacks. And to see this is to see them in relationship to the land, to the distant houses, and to the invisible workers.

Cultivation – and the culture that derives from it – is both individual and communal. Why else should schooling be a matter of public concern? It is clearly not just a matter of interest to the child and her parents, but to all of us, for the education of that child – the way she learns to see and understand her place in relationship to the world – matters deeply to how we all go on.

Berry writes, in a recent collection of essays, that "in October of 1993, the *New York Times* announced that the United States Census Bureau would 'no longer count the number of Americans who live on farms.'" Between 1910 and 1920, he continues, "we had thirty-two million farmers living on farms – about a third of our population.... By 1991, the number was only 4.6 million, less than 2 percent of the national population."[2] Farmers, he concludes, no longer count.

John Berger, writing about peasants in Europe, notes that in 1789 "the population [of France] was twenty-seven million, of whom twenty-two million were rural."

> The revolution and the scientific progress of the nineteenth century offered the peasant land and physical protection such as he had not known before; at the same time they exposed him to capital and the market economy; by 1848 the great peasant exodus to the cities had begun and by 1900 there were only eight million French peasants. The deserted village has probably almost always been – and certainly is again today – a feature of the countryside: it represents a site of no survivors.[3]

While there are powerful ways in which the newest revolution – the digital one – has created what some call a "global village," it is also true that this term is at best a kind of euphemism, disguising the fact that we have lost the village.

Of course there is also the argument that with the move to agriculture we had already left one kind of paradise behind. Paul Shepard sums up one aspect of this early revolution:

> The care of crops, stock, and children fixed the daily routine and increased the amount of work. Like casual gathering or preambles to the chase, the work was probably light in the earliest centuries of planting, but in time it would take everything. The world of drudgery would eventually seem normal, the savage would be scorned for his indolence and lack of expectant suspense, and the only escape for tillage or bureaucratic time-serving would be death.[4]

"Early farming," he concludes, "represents a 'state of surrender,' . . . and the farmer was a defeated captive."

Much follows from the development of culture, and much of it destructive. An alienation from what we now call "the wild," for example, is one common consequence; a sundering of relationship. With greater control over the food supply comes (as Shepard notes) the accumulation of "belongings." At our best we learn through cultivation that we belong to the land, and not the other way around. At our worst, however, we gain our sense of security not from belonging but from our belongings, including above all our ownership of the land and what we build upon it. The home becomes a castle that in turns becomes a prison: we build walls to protect our investments (whether in grain, in gold, or in Monet canvases) finding that what we wall out also walls us in. It also walls us away from the very land that supports and roots us.

John Haines quotes from Ortega y Gasset a passage that, as Haines comments, "sums up very well how things may be with us":

> The man in the forest reacts to his problems by creating culture. To that end he manages to retreat from the forest and withdraw into himself. There is no creation without withdrawing into oneself. Well then; the man who is too cultivated and socialized, who is living on top of a culture which is already false, is in urgent need of another culture, that is to say a culture which is genuine. But this can only start in the sincere and naked depths of his own personal self. There he must go back to make contact with himself. But this cultivated self, the culture which he has received from without, and which is now decrepit and devoid of evidence, prevents him from doing this.... Thanks to culture, man has gotten away from himself.... So he has no other course than to rise up against that culture, to shake himself free of it, so that he may once more face the universe in the live flesh and return to living in very truth. Hence, those periods of a "return to nature," that is to say to what is natural in man, in contrast to what is cultivated in him.[5]

One could suggest that the dialectic here – between forest and farm, between wilderness and cultivation – is beautifully played out in the conversations between writers such as Wendell Berry and Wes Jackson on the one hand and Edward Abbey and – to an extent – Gary Snyder on the other. One could suggest this, except that to do so ignores the balance that already exists in much of their work; Berry, for example, always acknowledges the necessity of the wild and uncultivated, whether in the land, an animal, a work of art or in a human being. In "Setting Out" he writes:

> Even love must pass through loneliness,
> the husbandman become again
> the Long Hunter, and set out
> not to the familiar woods of home
> but to the forest of the night,
> the true wilderness, where renewal
> is found.[6]

This poem beautifully marks the tension between ways of being in the world, and especially between the ancient place of the hunter and that of the farmer. As well as anyone I know Berry understands, lives, and writes within this tension. Cultivation only appears to eliminate the wild; instead, the farm – its soil especially – depends upon the wild. "An enduring agriculture must never cease to consider and respect and preserve wildness," he writes. "The farm can exist only within the wilderness of mystery and natural force. And if the farm is to last and remain in health, the wilderness must survive within the farm. This is what agricultural fertility is: the survival of natural process in the human order."[7]

Culture is rooted: It is particular to a people and a place. This is both its glory and its danger. But the glory is truly there. Consider the domestication of animals, which for some critics is a perfect example of the enslavement of the wild for human ends. Such is not the conclusion of Vicki Hearne; a poet, philosopher, and professional animal trainer, she suggests in *Adam's Task* that the training of a horse or dog has everything to do with the creature's own deeper sense of freedom and self – ownership: ultimately the horse belongs to her *self*. And at the heart of this sense of belonging – like a guide or thread – lies the beauty of form. Here's the glory, and it's one that not only humans may experience.

One example. Hearne is training a "crazy" horse named Drummer Girl, and one day attempts to mount her. The horse's response is to flip her head back and break open Hearne's eyebrow. She writes, without a pause, "I asked her to perform a volte at trot, instead of gingerly moving off at a walk." And the horse does the difficult movement beautifully – shocked, the writer suggests, by this "outrageous, unorthodox response on my part." But the trick of course *was* to startle her, to shock her into the unexpected and the difficult. And in performing it, however briefly, in moving into a "trot that was just about classically pure for just those few moments ... she achieved under saddle what horsemen call 'self-carriage,' and those moments of congruence and contact with her own splendor accomplished more than years of people babbling about her sweetness and prettiness had. She was in any event neither sweet nor pretty. She was, however, beautiful."[8]

This moment of "congruence and contact with her own splendor" – this is what cultivation teaches. The form that is true to one's essence is not imposed, but found through work, just as Chuang Tzu's woodcarver finds the form in the tree that is true and just. Such work *is* work, whatever the form we work upon. But mastery of the craft comes not with a sense of power over anything, but through a kind of attunement, or even an *atonement:* we atone through the work we do, and through that struggle – *by means of* that struggle – we seek to return to the radical One that we know we are. At-one-ment: such is the root, and such is the goal.

This approaches the Navajo sense of *hózhǫ́,* where a return to harmony and beauty – the true sense of being cultivated – has everything to do with *tuning in* to what lies around us.[9] Sin in this sense is a failure to *hear,* and atonement requires again a going out of ourselves, a dying to ourselves as we attend to each other. As the hunter must listen, so too must the farmer, the crafts-person, the teacher, the parent.

We too are noble animals, Hearne writes. "I mean that we are born to it, born to the demands of the heroic, of a pleasure earlier than love and nearer to heaven, the pleasure of the heroic approach to knowledge of form." This is to redefine what we mean by heroic: It is their skill, their *techne,* we might even conclude, that make both Odysseus and Penelope heroic in *The Odyssey;* it is for this that Athena – from whom we get *techne* – loves them.[10] So too does Hearne conclude:

> In false romances that oppose the quest and the hearth, safety and the heroic, safety becomes in this way "degeneration," but the great literature of the heroic tells us that the quest and the hearth are the same thing, that genuine safety demands the genuinely heroic, or at least that they must be mated if life is to be fecund of meaning.

Penobscot

CORN MOTHER

When Kloskurbeh, the All-maker, lived on earth, there were no people yet. But one day when the sun was high, a youth appeared and called him "Uncle, brother of my mother." This young man was born from the foam of the waves, foam quickened by the wind and warmed by the sun. It was the motion of the wind, the moistness of water, and the sun's warmth which gave him life — warmth above all, because warmth is life. And the young man lived with Kloskurbeh and became his chief helper.

Now, after these two powerful beings had created all manner of things, there came to them, as the sun was shining at high noon, a beautiful girl. She was born of the wonderful earth plant, and of the dew, and of warmth. Because a drop of dew fell on a leaf and was warmed by the sun, and the warming sun is life, this girl came into being — from the green living plant, from moisture, and from warmth.

"I am love," said the maiden. "I am a strength giver, I am the nourisher, I am the provider of men and animals. They all love me."

Then Kloskurbeh thanked the Great Mystery Above for having sent them the maiden. The youth, the Great Nephew, married her, and the girl conceived and thus became First Mother. And Kloskurbeh, the Great Uncle, who teaches humans all they need to know, taught their children how to live. Then he went away to dwell in the north, from which he will return sometime when he is needed.

Now people increased and became numerous. They lived by hunting, and the more people there were, the less game they found. They were hunting it out, and as the animals decreased, starvation came upon the people. And First Mother pitied them.

The little children came to First Mother and said: "We are hungry. Feed us." But she had nothing to give them, and she wept. She told them: "Be patient. I will make some food. Then your little bellies will be full." But she kept weeping.

Her husband asked: "How can I make you smile? How can I make you happy?"

"There is only one thing that will stop my tears."

"What is it?" asked her husband.

"It is this: you must kill me."

"I could never do that."

"You must, or I will go on weeping and grieving forever."

Then the husband traveled far, to the end of the earth, to the north he went, to ask the Great Instructor, his uncle Kloskurbeh, what he should do.

"You must do what she wants. You must kill her," said Kloskurbeh. Then the young man went back to his home, and it was his turn to weep. But First Mother said: "Tomorrow at high noon you must do it. After you have killed me, let two of our sons take hold of my hair and drag my body over that empty patch of earth. Let them drag me back and forth, back and forth, over every part of the patch, until all my flesh had been torn from my body. Afterwards, take my bones, gather them up, and bury them in the middle of this clearing. Then leave that place."

She smiled and said, "Wait seven moons and then come back, and you will find my flesh there, flesh given out of love, and it will nourish and strengthen you forever and ever."

So it was done. The husband slew his wife and her sons, praying, dragged her body to and fro as she had commanded, until her flesh covered all the earth. Then they took up her bones and buried them in the middle of it. Weeping loudly, they went away.

When the husband and his children and his children's children came back to that place after seven moons had passed, they found the earth covered with tall, green, tasseled plants. The plants' fruit – corn – was First Mother's flesh, given so that the people might live and flourish. And they partook of First Mother's flesh and found it sweet beyond words. Following her instructions, they didn't eat all, but put many kernels back into the earth. In this way her flesh and spirit renewed themselves every seven months, generation after generation.

And at the spot where they had burned First Mother's bones, there grew another plant, broad-leafed and fragrant. It was First Mother's breath, and they heard her spirit talking: "Burn this up and smoke it. It is sacred. It will clear your minds, help your prayers, and gladden your hearts."

And First Mother's husband called the first plant *Skarmunal*, corn, and the second plant *utarmur-wayeh*, tobacco.

"Remember," he told the people, "and take good care of First Mother's flesh, because it is her goodness become substance. Take good care of her breath, because it is her love turned into smoke. Remember her and think of her whenever you eat, whenever you smoke this sacred plant, because she has given her life so that you might live. Yet she is not dead, she lives: in undying love she renews herself again and again."

— A Penobscot (New England Algonquian) tale,
retold from three nineteenth-century sources, including Joseph Nicolar

Hebrew

---

from
THE BOOK OF GENESIS

Now Adam knew Eve his wife, and she conceived and bore Cain, saying, "I have gotten a man with the help of the Lord." And again, she bore his brother Abel. Now Abel was a keeper of sheep, and Cain a tiller of the ground. In the course of time Cain brought to the Lord an offering of the fruit of the ground, and Abel brought of the firstlings of his flock and of their fat portions. And the Lord had regard for Abel and his offering, but for Cain and his offering he had not regard. So Cain was very angry, and his countenance fell. The Lord said to Cain, "Why are you angry, and why has your countenance fallen? If you do well, will you not be accepted? And if you do not well, sin is crouching at the door; its desire is for you, but you must master it."

Cain said to Abel his brother, "Let us go out to the field." And when they were in the field, Cain rose up against his brother Abel, and killed him. The Lord said to Cain, "Where is Abel your brother?" He said, "I do not know; am I my brother's keeper?" And the Lord said, "What have you done? The voice of your brother's blood is crying to me from the ground. And now you are cursed from the ground, which has opened its mouth to receive your brother's blood from your hand. When you till the ground, it shall no longer yield to you its strength; you shall be a fugitive and a wanderer on the earth." Cain said to the Lord, "My punishment is greater than I can bear. Behold, thou hast driven me this day away from the ground; and from thy face I shall be hidden; and I shall be a fugitive and a wanderer on the earth, whoever finds me will slay me." Then the Lord said to him, "Not so! If any one slays Cain, vengeance shall be taken on him sevenfold." And the Lord put a mark on Cain, lest any who came upon him should kill him. Then Cain went away from the presence of the Lord, and dwelt in the land of Nod, east of Eden.

Cain knew his wife, and she conceived and bore Enoch; and he built a city, and called the name of the city after the name of his son, Enoch. To Enoch was born Irad; and Irad was the father of Me-hu´ja-el, and Me-hu´ja-el the father of Me-thu´sha-el, and Me-thu´sha-el the father of Lamech. And Lamech took two wives; the name of the one was Adah, and the name of the other Zillah. Adah bore Jabal; he was the father of those who dwell in tents and have cattle. His brother's name was Jubal; he was the father of all those who play the lyre and pipe. Zillah bore Tubal-cain; he was the forger of all instruments of bronze and iron.

Homer

from
THE ODYSSEY

In the next land we found were Kyklopês,
giants, louts, without a law to bless them.
In ignorance leaving the fruitage of the earth in mystery
to the immortal gods, they neither plow
nor sow by hand, nor till the ground, though grain –
wild wheat and barley – grows untended, and
wine-grapes, in clusters, ripen in heaven's rain.
Kyklopês have no muster and no meeting,
no consultation or old tribal ways,
but each one dwells in his own mountain cave
dealing out rough justice to wife and child,
indifferent to what the others do.
                                        Well, then:
across the wide bay from the mainland
there lies a desert island, not far out,
but still not close inshore. Wild goats in hundreds
breed there; and no human being comes
upon the isle to startle them – no hunter
of all who ever tracked with hounds through forests
or had rough going over mountain trails.
The isle, unplanted and untilled, a wilderness,
pastures goats alone. And this is why:
good ships like ours with cheekpaint at the bows
are far beyond the Kyklopês. No shipwright
toils among them, shaping and building up
symmetrical trim hulls to cross the sea
and visit all the seaboard towns, as men do
who go and come in commerce over water.
This isle – seagoing folk would have annexed it
and built their homesteads on it: all good land,
fertile for every crop in season: lush
well-watered meads along the shore, vines in profusion,
prairie, clear for the plow, where grain would grow
chin high by harvest time, and rich sub-soil.

translated by Robert Fitzgerald

Kalapuya

A KALAPUYA PROPHECY

In the old time, by the forks of the Santiam,
a Kalapuya man lay down in an alder-grove
and dreamed his farthest dream. When he woke in the night
he told the people, "This earth beneath us
was all black, all black in my dream!"
No man could say what it meant,
that dream of our greening earth.
We forgot. But then the white men came,
those iron farmers, and we saw them plow up the ground,
the camas meadow, the little prairies by the Santiam,
and we knew we would enter their dream
of the earth plowed black forever.

version by Jarold Ramsey

Henry David Thoreau

THE BEAN-FIELD

Meanwhile my beans, the length of whose rows, added together, was seven miles already planted, were impatient to be hoed, for the earliest had grown considerably before the latest were in the ground; indeed they were not easily to be put off. What was the meaning of this so steady and self-respecting, this small Herculean labor, I knew not. I came to love my rows, my beans, though so many more than I wanted. They attached me to the earth, and so I got strength like Antaeus. But why should I raise them? Only Heaven knows. This was my curious labor all summer, – to make this portion of the earth's surface, which had yielded only cinquefoil, blackberries, johnswort, and the like, before, sweet wild fruits and pleasant flowers, produce instead this pulse. What shall I learn of beans or beans of me? I cherish them, I hoe them, early and late I have an eye to them; and this is my day's work. It is a fine broad leaf to look on. My auxiliaries are the dews and rains which water this dry soil, and what fertility is in the soil itself, which for the most part is lean and effete. My enemies are worms, cool days, and most of all woodchucks. The last have nibbled for me a quarter of an acre clean. But what right had I to oust johnswort and the rest, and break up their ancient herb garden? Soon, however, the remaining beans will be too tough for them, and go forward to meet new foes.

When I was four years old, as I well remember, I was brought from Boston to this my native town, through these very woods and this field, to the pond. It is one of the oldest scenes stamped on my memory. And now to-night my flute has waked the echoes over that very water. The pines still stand here older than I, or, if some have fallen, I have cooled my supper with their stumps, and a new growth is rising all around, preparing another aspect for new infant eyes. Almost the same johnswort springs from the same perennial root in this pasture, and even I have at length helped to clothe that fabulous landscape of my infant dreams and one of the results of my presence and influence is seen in these bean leaves, corn blades, and potato vines.

I planted about two acres and a half of upland; and as it was only about fifteen years since the land was cleared, and I myself had got out two or three cords of stumps, I did not give it any manure; but in the course of the summer it appeared by the arrow-heads which I turned up in hoeing, that an extinct nation had anciently dwelt here and planted corn and beans ere white men came to clear the land, and so, to some extent, had exhausted the soil for this very crop.

Before yet any woodchuck or squirrel had run across the road, or the sun had got above the shrub-oaks, while all the dew was on, though the farmers warned me against it, – I would advise you to do all your work; if possible while the dew is on, – I began to level the ranks of haughty weeds in my bean-field and throw dust upon their heads. Early in the morning I worked barefooted, dabbling like a plastic artist in the dewy and crumbling sand, but later in the day the sun blistered my feet. There the sun lighted me to hoe beans, pacing slowly backward and forward over that yellow gravelly upland, between the long green rows, fifteen rods, the one end terminating in a shrub oak copse where I could rest in the shade, the other in a blackberry field where the green berries deepened their tints by the time I had made another bout. Removing the weeds, putting fresh soil about the bean stems, and encouraging this weed which I had sown, making the yellow soil express its summer thought in bean leaves and blossoms rather than in wormwood and piper and millet grass, making the earth say beans instead of grass, – this was my daily work. As I had little aid from horses or cattle, or hired men or boys, or improved implements of husbandry, I was much slower, and became much more intimate with my beans than usual. But labor of the hands, even when pursued to the verge of drudgery, is perhaps never the worst form of idleness. It has a constant and imperishable moral, and to the scholar it yields a classic result. A very *agricola laboriosus* was I to travellers bound westward through Lincoln and Wayland to nobody knows where; they sitting at their ease in gigs, with elbows on knees, and reins loosely hanging in festoons; I the home-staying, laborious native of the soil. But soon my homestead was out of their sight and thought. It was the only open and cultivated field for a great distance on either side of the road; so they made the most of it; and sometimes the man in the field heard more of travellers' gossip and comment than was meant for his ear: "Beans so late! peas so late!" – for I continued to plant when others had began to hoe, – the ministerial husbandman had not suspected it. "Corn, my boy, for fodder; corn for fodder." "Does he live there?" asks the black bonnet of the gray coat; and the hard-featured farmer reins up his grateful dobbin to inquire what you are doing where he sees no manure in the furrow, and recommends a little chip dirt, or any little waste stuff, or it may be ashes or plaster. But here were two acres and a half of furrows, and only a hoe for cart and two hands to draw it, – there being an aversion to other carts and horses, – and chip dirt far away. Fellow-travellers as they rattled by compared it aloud with the fields which they had passed, so that I came to know how I stood in the agricultural world. This was one field not in Mr. Coleman's report. And, by the way, who estimates the value of the crop which Nature yields in the still wilder fields unimproved by man? The crop of *English* hay is carefully weighed, the moisture calculated, the silicates and the potash; but in all dells and pond holes in the woods and pastures and swamps grows a rich and various crop only unreaped by man. Mine was, as it were, the connecting link between wild and cultivated fields; as some states are civilized, and others half-civilized, and others savage or barbarous, so my field was, though not in a bad sense, a half-cultivated field. They were beans cheerfully returning to their wild and primitive state that I cultivated, and my hoe played the *Rans des Vaches* for them.

Near at hand, upon the topmost spray of a birch, sings the brown-thrasher – or red mavis, as some love to call him – all the morning, glad of your society, that would find out another farmer's field if yours were not here. While you are planting the seed, he cries, – "Drop it, drop it, – cover it up, cover it up, – pull it up, pull it up, pull it up." But this was not corn, and so it was safe from such enemies as he. You may wonder what his rigmarole, his amateur Paganini performances on one string or on twenty, have to do with your planting, and yet prefer it to leached ashes or plaster. It was a cheap sort of top dressing in which I had entire faith.

As I drew a still fresher soil about the rows with my hoe, I disturbed the ashes of unchronicled nations who in primeval years lived under these heavens, and their small implements of war and hunting were brought to the light of this modern day. They lay mingled with other natural stones, some of which bore the marks of having been burned by Indian fires, and some by the sun, and also bits of pottery and glass brought hither by the recent cultivators of the soil. When my hoe tinkled against the stones, that music echoed to the woods and the sky, and was an accompaniment to my labor which yielded an instant and immeasurable crop. It was no longer beans that I hoed, nor I that hoed beans; and I remembered with as much pity as pride, if I remembered at all, my acquaintances who had gone to the city to attend the oratorios. The night-hawk circled overhead in the sunny afternoons – for I sometimes made a day of it – like a mote in the eye, or in heaven's eye, falling from time to time with a swoop and a sound as if the heavens were rent, torn at last to very rags and tatters, and yet a seamless cope remained; small imps that fill the air and lay their eggs on the ground on bare sand or rocks on the tops of hills, where few have found them; graceful and slender like ripples caught up from the pond, as leaves are raised by the wind to float in the heavens; such kindredship is in Nature. The hawk is aerial brother of the wave which he sails over and surveys, those his perfect air-inflated wings answering to the elemental unfledged pinions of the sea. Or sometimes I watched a pair of hen-hawks circling high in the sky, alternately soaring and descending, approaching and leaving one another, as if they were the embodiment of my own thoughts. Or I was attracted by the passage of wild pigeons from this wood to that, with a slight quivering winnowing sound and carrier haste; or from under a rotten stump my hoe turned up a sluggish portentous and outlandish spotted salamander, a trace of Egypt and the Nile, yet our contemporary. When I paused to lean on my hoe, these sounds and sights I heard and saw any where in the row, a part of the inexhaustible entertainment which the country offers.

On gala days the town fires its great guns, which echo like popguns to these woods, and some waifs of martial music occasionally penetrate thus far. To me, away there in my bean-field at the other end of the town, the big guns sounded as if a puff ball had burst; and when there was a military turnout of which I was ignorant, I have sometimes had a vague sense all the day of some sort of itching and disease in the horizon, as if some eruption would break out there soon, either scarlatina or canker-rash, until at length some more favorable puff of wind, making haste over the fields and up the Wayland road, brought me information of the "trainers." It seemed by the distant hum as if somebody's bees had swarmed, and that the neighbors, according to Virgil's advice, by a faint tintinnabulum upon the most sonorous of their domestic utensils, were endeavoring to call them down into the hive again. And when the sound died quite away, and the hum had ceased, and the most favorable breezes told no tale, I knew that they had got the last drone of them all safely into the Middlesex hive, and that now their minds were bent on the honey with which it was smeared.

I felt proud to know that the liberties of Massachussets and of our fatherland were in such safe keeping; and as I turned to my hoeing again I was filled with an inexpressible confidence, and pursued my labor cheerfully with a calm trust in the future.

When there were several bands of musicians, it sounded as if all the village was a vast bellows, and all the buildings expanded and collapsed alternately with a din. But sometimes it was a really noble and inspiring strain that reached these woods, and the trumpet that sings of fame, and I felt as if I could spit a Mexican with a good relish, — for why should we always stand for trifles? — and looked round for a woodchuck or a skunk to exercise my chivalry upon. These martial strains seemed as far away as Palestine, and reminded me of a march of crusaders in the horizon, with a slight tantivy and tremulous motion of the elm-tree tops which overhang the village. This was one of the *great* days; though the sky had from my clearing only the same everlastingly great look that it wears daily, and I saw no difference in it.

It was a singular experience that long acquaintance which I cultivated with beans, what with planting, and hoeing, and harvesting, and threshing, and picking over, and selling them, — the last was the hardest of all, — I might add eating, for I did taste. I was determined to know beans. When they were growing, I used to hoe from five o'clock in the morning till noon, and commonly spent the rest of the day about other affairs. Consider the intimate and curious acquaintance one makes with various kinds of weeds, — it will bear some iteration in the account, for there was no little iteration in the labor, — disturbing their delicate organizations so ruthlessly, and making such invidious distinctions with his hoe, levelling whole ranks of one species, and sedulously cultivating another. That's Roman wormwood, — that's pigweed, — that's sorrel, — that's pipergrass, — have at him, chop him up, turn his roots upward to the sun, don't let him have a fibre in the shade, if you do he'll turn himself t'other side up and be as green as a leek in two days. A long war, not with cranes, but with weeds, those Trojans who had sun and rain and dews on their side. Daily the beans saw me come to their rescue armed with a hoe, and thin the ranks of their enemies, filling up the trenches with weedy dead. Many a lusty crest-waving Hector, that towered a whole foot above his crowding comrades, fell before my weapon and rolled in the dust.

Those summer days which some of my contemporaries devoted to the fine arts in Boston or Rome, and others to contemplation in India, and others to trade in London or New York, I thus, with the other farmers of New England, devoted to husbandry. Not that I wanted beans to eat, for I am by nature a Pythagorean, so far as beans are concerned, whether they mean porridge or voting, and exchanged them for rice; but, perchance, as some must work in fields if only for the sake of tropes and expression, to serve a parable-maker one day. It was on the whole a rare amusement, which continued too long, might have become a dissipation. Though I gave them no manure, and did not hoe them all once, I hoed them unusually well as far as I went, and was paid for it in the end, "there being in truth," as Evelyn says, "no compost or laetation whatsoever comparable to this continual motion, repastination, and turning of the mould with the spade." "The earth," he adds elsewhere, "especially if fresh, has a certain magnetism in it, by which it attracts the salt, power, or virtue (call it either) which gives it life, and is the logic of all the labor and stir we keep about it, to sustain us; all dungings and other sordid temperings being but the vicars succedaneous to this improvement." Moreover, this being one of those "worn-out and exhausted lay fields which enjoy their sabbath," had perchance, as Sir Kenelm Digby thinks likely, attracted "vital spirits" from the air. I harvested twelve bushels of beans.

But to be more particular, for it is complained that Mr. Coleman has reported chiefly the expensive experiments of gentlemen farmers, my outgoes were, —

For a hoe,	$ 0 54
Ploughing, harrowing, and furrowing,	7 50, Too much.
Beans for seed,	3 12 ½
Potatoes " ,	1 33
Peas " ,	0 40
Turnip seed,	0 06
White line for crow fence,	0 02
Horse cultivator and boy three hours,	1 00
horse and cart to get crop,	0 75
In all,	$14 72 ½

My income was, (*patrem familias vendacem, non emacem oportet,*) from

Nine bushels and twelve quarts of beans sold,	$16 94
Five " large potatoes,	2 50
Nine " small,	2 25
Grass,	1 00
Stalks,	0 75
In all,	$23 44

Leaving a pecuniary profit, as I have elsewhere said, of $8 71 ½.

This is the result of my experience in raising beans. Plant the common small white bush bean about the first of June, in rows three feet by eighteen inches apart, being careful to select fresh round and unmixed seed. First look out for worms, and supply vacancies by planting anew. Then look out for woodchucks, if it is an exposed place, for they will nibble off the earliest tender leaves almost clean as they go; and again, when the young tendrils make their appearance, they have notice of it, and will shear them off with both buds and young pods, sitting erect like a squirrel. But above all harvest as early as possible, if you would escape frosts and have a fair and salable crop; you may save much loss by this means.

This further experience also I gained. I said to myself, I will not plant beans and corn with so much industry another summer, but such seeds, if the seed is not lost, as sincerity, truth, simplicity, faith, innocence, and the like, and see if they will not grow in this soil, even with less toil and manurance, and sustain me, for surely it has not been exhausted for these crops. Alas! I said this to myself; but now another summer is gone, and another, and another, and I am obliged to say to you, Reader, that the seeds which I planted, if indeed they *were* the seeds of those virtues, were wormeaten or had lost their vitality, and so did not come up. Commonly men will only be brave as their fathers were brave, or timid. This generation is very sure to plant corn and beans each new year precisely as the Indians did centuries ago and taught the first settlers to do, as if there were a fate in it. I saw an old man the other day, to my astonishment, making the holes with a hoe for the seventieth time at least, and not for himself to lie down in! But why should not the New Englander try new adventures, and not lay so much stress on his grain, his potato and grass crop, and his orchards, – raise other crops than these? Why concern ourselves so much about our beans for seed, and not be concerned at all about a new generation of men? We should really be fed and cheered if when we met a man we were sure to see that some of the qualities which I have named, which we all prize more than those other productions, but which are for the most part broadcast and floating in the air, had taken root and grown in him. Here comes such a subtile and ineffable quality, for instance, as truth or justice, though the slightest amount or new variety of it, along the road. Our ambassadors should be instructed to send home such seeds as these, and Congress help to distribute them over the land. We should never stand upon ceremony with sincerity. We should never cheat and insult and banish one another by our meanness, if there were present the kernel of worth and friendliness. We should not meet thus in haste. Most men I do not meet at all, for they seem not to have time; they are busy about their beans. We should not deal with a man thus plodding ever, leaning on a hoe or a spade as a staff between his work, not as a mushroom, but partially risen out of the earth, something more than erect, like swallows alighted and walking on the ground: –

> "And as he spake, his wings would now and then
> Spread, as he meant to fly, then close again."

so that we should suspect that we might be conversing with an angel. Bread may not always nourish us; but it always does us good, it even takes stiffness out of our joints, and makes us supple and buoyant, when we knew not what ailed us, to recognize any generosity in man or Nature, to share any unmixed and heroic joy.

Ancient poetry and mythology suggest, at least, that husbandry was once a sacred art; but it is pursued with irreverent haste and heedlessness by us, our object being to have large farms and large crops merely. We have no festival, nor procession, nor ceremony, not excepting our Cattle-shows and so called Thanksgivings, by which the farmer expresses a sense of the sacredness of his calling, or is reminded of its sacred origin. It is the premium and the feast which tempt him. He sacrifices not to Ceres and the terrestrial Jove, but to the infernal Plutus rather. By avarice and selfishness, and a grovelling habit, from which none of us is free, of regarding the soil as property, or the means of acquiring property chiefly, the landscape is deformed, husbandry is degraded with us, and the farmer leads the meanest of lives. He knows Nature but as a robber. Cato says that the profits of agriculture are particularly pious or just, (*maximeque pius quaestus*,) and according to Varro the old Romans "called the same earth Mother and Ceres, and thought that they who cultivated it led a pious and useful life, and that they alone were left of the race of King Saturn."

We are wont to forget that the sun looks on our cultivated fields and on the prairies and forests without distinction. They all reflect and absorb his rays alike, and the former make but a small part of the glorious picture which he beholds in his daily course. In his view the earth is all equally cultivated like a garden. Therefore we should receive the benefit of his light and heat with a corresponding trust and magnanimity. What though I value the seed of these beans, and harvest that in the fall of the year? This broad field which I have looked at so long looks not to me as the principal cultivator, but away from me to influences more genial to it, which water and make it green. These beans have results which are not harvested by me. Do they not grow for woodchucks partly? The ear of wheat, (in Latin *spica*, obsoletely *speca*, from *spe*, hope,) should not be the only hope of the husbandman; its kernel or grain (*granum*, from *gerendo*, bearing,) is not all that it bears. How, then, can our harvest fail? Shall I not rejoice also at the abundance of the weeds whose seeds are the granary of birds? It matters little comparatively whether the fields fill the farmer's barns. The true husbandman will cease from anxiety, as the squirrels manifest no concern whether the woods will bear chestnuts this year or not, and finish his labor with every day, relinquishing all claim to the produce of his fields, and sacrificing in his mind not only his first but his last fruits also.

Wendell Berry

THE MAKING OF A MARGINAL FARM

One day in the summer of 1956, leaving home for school, I stopped on the side of the road directly above the house where I now live. From there you could see a mile or so across the Kentucky River Valley, and perhaps six miles along the length of it. The valley was a green trough full of sunlight, blue in its distances. I often stopped here in my comings and goings, just to look, for it was all familiar to me from before the time my memory began: woodlands and pastures on the hillsides; fields and croplands, wooded slew-edges and hollows in the bottoms; and through the midst of it the tree-lined river passing down from its headwaters near the Virginia line toward its mouth at Carrollton on the Ohio.

Standing there, I was looking at land where one of my great-great-great-grand-fathers settled in 1803, and at the scene of some of the happiest times of my own life, where in my growing-up years I camped, hunted, fished, boated, swam, and wandered — where, in short, I did whatever escaping I felt called upon to do. It was a place where I had happily been, and where I always wanted to be. And I remember gesturing toward the valley that day and saying to the friend who was with me: "That's all I need."

I meant it. It was an honest enough response to my recognition of its beauty, the abundance of its lives and possibilities, and of my own love for it and interest in it. And in the sense that I continue to recognize all that, and feel that what I most need is here, I can still say the same thing.

And yet I am aware that I must necessarily mean differently — or at least a great deal more — when I say it now. Then I was speaking mostly from affection, and did not know, by half, what I was talking about. I was speaking of a place that in some ways I knew and in some ways cared for, but did not live in. The differences between knowing a place and living in it, between cherishing a place and living responsibly in it, had not begun to occur to me. But they are critical differences, and understanding them has been perhaps the chief necessity of my experience since then.

I married in the following summer, and in the next seven years lived in a number of distant places. But, largely because I continued to feel that what I needed was here, I could never bring myself to want to live in any other place. And so we returned to live in Kentucky in the summer of 1964, and that autumn bought the house whose roof my friend and I had looked down on eight years before, and with it "twelve acres more or less." Thus I began a profound change in my life. Before, I had lived according to expectation rooted in ambition. Now I began to live according to a kind of destiny rooted in my origins and in my life. One should not speak too confidently of one's "destiny"; I use the word to refer to causes that lie deeper in history and character than mere intention or desire. In buying the little place known as Lanes Landing, it seems to me, I began to obey the deeper causes.

We had returned so that I could take a job at the University of Kentucky in Lexington. And we expected to live pretty much the usual academic life: I would teach and write; my "subject matter" would be, as it had been, the few square miles in Henry County where I grew up. We bought the tiny farm at Lanes Landing, thinking that we would use it as a "summer place," and on that understanding I began, with the help of two carpenter friends, to make some necessary repairs on the house. I no longer remember exactly how it was decided, but that work had hardly begun when it became a full-scale overhaul.

By so little our minds had been changed: this was not going to be a house to visit, but a house to live in. It was as though, having put our hand to the plow, we not only did not look back, but could not. We renewed the old house, equipped it with plumbing, bathroom, and oil furnace, and moved in on July 4, 1965.

Once the house was whole again, we came under the influence of the "twelve acres more or less." This acreage included a steep hillside pasture, two small pastures by the river, and a "garden spot" of less than half an acre. We had, besides the house, a small barn in bad shape, a good large building that once had been a general store, and a small garage also in usable condition. This was hardly a farm by modern standards, but it was land that could be used, and it was unthinkable that we would not use it. The land was not good enough to afford the possibility of a cash income, but it would allow us to grow our food – or most of it. And that is what we set out to do.

In the early spring of 1965 I had planted a small orchard; the next spring we planted our first garden. Within the following six or seven years we reclaimed the pastures, converted the garage into a henhouse, rebuilt the barn, greatly improved the garden soil, planted berry bushes, acquired a milk cow – and were producing, except for hay and grain for our animals, nearly everything that we ate: fruit, vegetables, eggs, meat, milk, cream, and butter. We built an outbuilding with a meat room and a food-storage cellar. Because we did not want to pollute our land and water with sewage, and in the process waste nutrients that should be returned to the soil, we built a composting privy. And so we began to attempt a life that, in addition to whatever else it was, would be responsibly agricultural. We used no chemical fertilizers. Except for a little rotenone, we used no insecticides. As our land and our food became healthier, so did we. And our food was of better quality than any that we could have bought.

We were not, of course, living an idyll. What we had done could not have been accomplished without difficulty and a great deal of work. And we had made some mistakes and false starts. But there was great satisfaction, too, in restoring the neglected land, and in feeding ourselves from it.

Meanwhile, the forty-acre place adjoining ours on the downriver side had been sold to a "developer," who planned to divide it into lots for "second homes." This project was probably doomed by the steepness of the ground and the difficulty of access, but a lot of bulldozing – and a lot of damage – was done before it was given up. In the fall of 1972, the place was offered for sale and we were able to buy it.

We now began to deal with larger agricultural problems. Some of this new land was usable; some would have to be left in trees. There were perhaps fifteen acres of hillside that could be reclaimed for pasture, and about two and a half acres of excellent bottomland on which we would grow alfalfa for hay. But it was a mess, all of it badly neglected, and a considerable portion of it badly abused by the developer's bulldozers. The hillsides were covered with thicket growth; the bottom was shoulder high in weeds; the diversion ditches had to be restored; a bulldozed gash meant for "building sites" had to be mended; the barn needed a new foundation, and the cistern a new top; there were no fences. What we had bought was less a farm than a reclamation project – which has now, with a later purchase, grown to seventy-five acres.

While we had only the small place, I had got along very well with a Gravely "walking tractor" that I owned, and an old Farmall A that I occasionally borrowed from my Uncle Jimmy. But now that we had increased our acreage, it was clear that I could not continue to depend on a borrowed tractor. For a while I assumed that I would buy a tractor of my own. But because our land was steep, and there was already talk of a fuel shortage – and because I liked the idea – I finally decided to buy a team of horses instead. By the spring of 1973, after a lot of inquiring and looking, I had found and bought a team of five-year-old sorrel mares. And – again by the generosity of my Uncle Jimmy, who has never thrown any good thing away – I had enough equipment to make a start.

Though I had worked horses and mules during the time I was growing up, I had never worked over ground so steep and problematical as this, and it had been twenty years since I had worked a team over ground of any kind. Getting started again, I anticipated every new task with uneasiness, and sometimes with dread. But to my relief and delight, the team and I did all that needed to be done that year, getting better as we went along. And over the years since then, with that team and others, my son and I have carried on our farming the way it was carried on in my boyhood, doing everything with our horses except baling the hay. And we have done work in places and in weather in which a tractor would have been useless. Experience has shown us – or re-shown us – that horses are not only a satisfactory and economical means of power, especially on such small places as ours, but are probably necessary to the most conservative use of steep land. Our farm, in fact, is surrounded by potentially excellent hillsides that were maintained in pasture until tractors replaced the teams.

Another change in our economy (and our lives) was accomplished in the fall of 1973 with the purchase of our first wood-burning stove. Again the petroleum shortage was on our minds, but we also knew that from the pasture-clearing we had ahead of us we would have an abundance of wood that otherwise would go to waste – and when that was gone we would still have our permanent wood lots. We thus expanded our subsistence income to include heating fuel, and since then have used our furnace only as a "backup system" in the coldest weather and in our absences from home. The horses also contribute significantly to the work of fuel-gathering; they will go easily into difficult places and over soft ground or snow where a truck or a tractor could not move.

As we have continued to live on and from our place, we have slowly begun its restoration and healing. Most of the scars have now been mended and grassed over, most of the washes stopped, most of the buildings made sound; many loads of rocks have been hauled out of the fields and used to pave entrances or fill hollows; we have done perhaps half of the necessary fencing. A great deal of work is still left to do, and some of it – the rebuilding of fertility in the depleted hillsides – will take longer than we will live. But in doing these things we have begun a restoration and a healing in ourselves.

I should say plainly that this has not been a "paying proposition." As a reclamation project, it has been costly both in money and in effort. It seems at least possible that, in any other place, I might have had little interest in doing any such thing. The reason I have been interested in doing it here, I think, is that I have felt implicated in the history, the uses, and the attitudes that have depleted such places as ours and made them "marginal."

I had not worked long on our "twelve acres more or less" before I saw that such places were explained almost as much by their human history as by their nature. I saw that they were not "marginal" because they ever were unfit for human use, but because in both culture and character we had been unfit to use them. Originally, even such steep slopes as these along the lower Kentucky River Valley were deep-soiled and abundantly fertile; "jumper" plows and generations of carelessness impoverished them. Where yellow clay is at the surface now, five feet of good soil may be gone. I once wrote that on some of the nearby uplands one walks as if "knee-deep" in the absence of the original soil. On these steeper slopes, I now know, that absence is shoulder-deep.

That is a loss that is horrifying as soon as it is imagined. It happened easily, by ignorance, indifference, "a little folding of the hands to sleep." It cannot be remedied in human time; to build five feet of soil takes perhaps fifty or sixty thousand years. This loss, once imagined, is potent with despair. If a people in adding a hundred and fifty years to itself subtracts fifty thousand from its land, what is there to hope?

And so our reclamation project has been, for me, less a matter of idealism or morality than a kind of self-preservation. A destructive history, once it is understood as such, is a nearly insupportable burden. Understanding it is a disease of understanding, depleting the sense of efficacy and paralyzing effort, unless it finds healing work. For me that work has been partly of the mind, in what I have written, but that seems to have depended inescapably on work of the body and of the ground. In order to affirm the values most native and necessary to me – indeed, to affirm my own life as a thing decent in possibility – I needed to know in my own experience that this place did not have to be abused in the past, and that it can be kindly and conservingly used now.

With certain reservations that must be strictly borne in mind, our work here has begun to offer some of the needed proofs.

Bountiful as the vanished original soil of the hillsides may have been, what remains is good. It responds well – sometimes astonishingly well – to good treatment. It never should have been plowed (some of it never should have been cleared), and it never should be plowed again. But it can be put in pasture without plowing, and it will support an excellent grass sod that will in turn protect it from erosion, if properly managed and not overgrazed.

Land so steep as this cannot be preserved in row crop cultivation. To subject it to such an expectation is simply to ruin it, as its history shows. Our rule, generally, has been to plow no steep ground, to maintain in pasture only such slopes as can be safely mowed with a horse-drawn mower, and to leave the rest in trees. We have increased the numbers of livestock on our pastures gradually, and have carefully rotated the animals from field to field, in order to avoid overgrazing. Under this use and care, our hillsides have mended and they produce more and better pasturage every year.

As a child I always intended to be a farmer. As a young man, I gave up that intention, assuming that I could not farm and do the other things I wanted to do. And then I became a farmer almost unintentionally and by a kind of necessity. That wayward and necessary becoming – along with my marriage, which has been intimately a part of it – is the major event of my life. It has changed me profoundly from the man and the writer I would otherwise have been.

There was a time, after I had left home and before I came back, when this place was my "subject matter." I meant that too, I think, on the day in 1956 when I told my friend, "That's all I need." I was regarding it, in a way too easy for a writer, as a mirror in which I saw myself. There was obviously a sort of narcissism in that – and an inevitable superficiality, for only the surface can reflect.

In coming home and settling on this place, I began to *live* in my subject, and to learn that living in one's subject is not at all the same as "having" a subject. To live in the place that is one's subject is to pass through the surface. The simplifications of distance and mere observation are thus destroyed. The obsessively regarded reflection is broken and dissolved. One sees that the mirror was a blinder; one can now begin to see where one is. One's relation to one's subject ceases to be merely emotional or esthetical, or even merely critical, and becomes problematical, practical, and responsible as well. Because it must. It is like marrying your sweetheart.

Though our farm has not been an economic success, as such success is usually reckoned, it is nevertheless beginning to make a kind of economic sense that is consoling and hopeful. Now that the largest expenses of purchase and repair are behind us, our income from the place is beginning to run ahead of expenses. As income I am counting the value of shelter, subsistence, heating fuel, and money earned by the sale of livestock. As expenses I am counting maintenance, newly purchased equipment, extra livestock feed, newly purchased animals, reclamation work, fencing materials, taxes, and insurance.

If our land had been in better shape when we bought it, our expenses would obviously be much smaller. As it is, once we have completed its restoration, our farm will provide us a home, produce our subsistence, keep us warm in winter, and earn a modest cash income. The significance of this becomes apparent when one considers that most of this land is "unfarmable" by the standards of conventional agriculture, and that most of it was producing nothing at the time we bought it.

And so, contrary to some people's opinion, it *is* possible for a family to live on such "marginal" land, to take a bountiful subsistence and some cash income from it, and, in doing so, to improve both the land and themselves. (I believe, however, that, at least in the present economy, this should not be attempted without a source of income other than the farm. It is now extremely difficult to pay for the best of farmland by farming it, and even "marginal" land has become unreasonably expensive. To attempt to make a living from such land is to impose a severe strain on land and people alike.)

I said earlier that the success of our work here is subject to reservations. There are only two of these, but both are serious.

The first is that land like ours — and there are many acres of such land in this country — can be conserved in use only by competent knowledge, by a great deal more work than is required by leveler land, by a devotion more particular and disciplined than patriotism, and by ceaseless watchfulness and care. All these are cultural values and resources, never sufficiently abundant in this country, and now almost obliterated by the contrary values of the so-called "affluent society."

One of my own mistakes will suggest the difficulty. In 1974 I dug a small pond on a wooded hillside that I wanted to pasture occasionally. The excavation for that pond — as I should have anticipated, for I had better reason than I used — caused the hillside to slump both above and below. After six years the slope has not stabilized, and more expense and trouble will be required to stabilize it. A small hillside farm will not survive many mistakes of that order. Nor will a modest income.

The true remedy for mistakes is to keep from making them. It is not in the piece-meal technological solutions that our society now offers, but in a change of cultural (and economic) values that will encourage in the whole population the necessary respect, restraint, and care. Even more important, it is in the possibility of settled families and local communities, in which the knowledge of proper means and methods, proper moderations and restraints, can be handed down, and so accumulate in place and stay alive; the experience of one generation is not adequate to inform and control its actions. Such possibilities are not now in sight in this country.

The second reservation is that we live at the lower end of the Kentucky River watershed, which has long been intensively used, and is increasingly abused. Strip mining, logging, extractive farming, and the digging, draining, roofing, and paving that go with industrial and urban "development," all have seriously depleted the capacity of the watershed to retain water. This means not only that floods are higher and more frequent than they would be if the watershed were healthy, but that the floods subside too quickly, the watershed being far less a sponge, now, than it is a roof. The floodwater drops suddenly out of the river, leaving the steep banks soggy, heavy, and soft. As a result, great strips and blocks of land crack loose and slump, or they give way entirely and disappear into the river in what people here call "slips."

The flood of December 1978, which was unusually high, also went down extremely fast, falling from banktop almost to pool stage within a couple of days. In the aftermath of this rapid "drawdown," we lost a block of bottomland an acre square. This slip, which is still crumbling, severely damaged our place, and may eventually undermine two buildings. The same flood started a slip in another place, which threatens a third building. We have yet another building situated on a huge (but, so far, very gradual) slide that starts at the river and, aggravated by two state highway cuts, goes almost to the hilltop. And we have serious river bank erosion the whole length of our place.

What this means is that, no matter how successfully we may control erosion on our hillsides, our land remains susceptible to a more serious cause of erosion that we cannot control. Our river bank stands literally at the cutting edge of our nation's consumptive economy. This, I think, is true of many "marginal" places – it is true, in fact, of many places that are not marginal. In its consciousness, ours is an upland society; the ruin of watersheds, and what that involves and means, is little considered. And so the land is heavily taxed to subsidize an "affluence" that consists, in reality, of health and goods stolen from the unborn.

Living at the lower end of the Kentucky River watershed is what is now known as "an educational experience" – and not an easy one. A lot of information comes with it that is severely damaging to the reputation of our people and our time. From where I live and work, I never have to look far to see that the earth does indeed pass away. But however that is taught, and however bitterly learned, it is something that should be known, and there is a certain good strength in knowing it. To spend one's life farming a piece of the earth so passing is, as many would say, a hard lot. But it is, in an ancient sense, the human lot. What saves it is to love the farming.

Edward Deming Andrews and Faith Andrews

from
WORK AND WORSHIP
The Economic Order of the Shakers

What made the Shaker agriculture distinctive was its diversity, the neatness of the tillage, the experimental attitude toward farming methods, the democratic manner in which labor was allocated, and the spirit pervading all farm operations.

The careful study of agriculture was exalted by the Shakers into a kind of religious ritual. They looked upon the soil as something to be redeemed from "rugged barrenness into smiling fertility and beauty." This thought is expressed in many ways. Shaker land "is easily known," wrote one visitor, "by its superior cultivation, and by its substantial stone-wall fences." Hepworth Dixon found the Shakers believing that "if you would have a lovely garden, you should live a lovely life," and in the introduction to the *Gardener's Manual*, published in 1843, the writer insists that the garden is "an index of the owner's mind." Dixon's conversation with Elder Frederick Evans illuminates this attitude of spiritual devotion to husbandry.

> This morning [he writes] I have spent an hour with Frederick in the new orchard, listening to the story of how he planted it, as to a tale by some Arabian poet. "A tree has its wants and wishes," said the Elder; "and a man should study them as a teacher watches a child, to see what he can do. If you love the plant, and take heed of what it likes, you will be well repaid by it. I don't know if a tree ever comes to know you; and I think it may; but I am sure it feels when you care for it and tend it; as a child does, as a woman does. Now, when we planted this orchard, we first got the very best cuttings in our reach; we then built a house for every plant to live in, that is to say, we dug a deep hole for each; we drained it well; we laid down tiles and rubble, and then filled in a bed of suitable manure and mould; we put the plant into its nest gently, and pressed up the earth about it, and protected the infant tree by this metal fence."
>
> "You take a world of pains," I said.
>
> "Ah, Brother Hepworth," he rejoined, "Thee sees we love our garden."

William Carlos Williams

THE CORN HARVEST

Pieter Breughel (the elder), The Harvesters

Summer!
The painting is organized
about a young

reaper enjoying his
noonday rest
completely

relaxed
from his morning labors
sprawled

in fact sleeping
unbuttoned
on his back

the women
have brought him his lunch
perhaps

a spot of wine
they gather gossiping
under a tree

whose shade
carelessly
he does not share the

resting
center of
their workaday world

HOME-WORK

Jan Vermeer, Woman Pouring Milk

The Egyptians do practically everything backwards from other people, in their customs and laws – among which the women go to market and make deals, whereas the men stay at home and weave; and other folk weave by pushing the weft upwards, but the Egyptians push it down. Men carry burdens on their heads, whereas women do so on their shoulders. The women piss standing up, and the men sitting down.[1]

– *Herodotus,* Histories 2.35–36

In the old days, strong, sturdy women were most admired. One of my most vivid preschool memories is of the crew of Laguna women, in their forties and fifties, who came to cover our house with adobe plaster. They handled the ladders with great ease, and while two women ground the adobe mud on stones and added straw, another woman loaded the hod with mud and passed it up to the two women on ladders, who were smoothing the plaster on the wall with their hands. Since women owned the houses, they did the plastering. At Laguna, men did the basket making and the weaving of fine textiles; men helped a great deal with the child care too. Because the Creator is female, there is no stigma on being female; gender is not used to control behavior. No job was a man's job or a woman's job; the most able person did the work.[2]

— *Leslie Marmon Silko*

Home-work. At one end, the image of Jan Vermeer's *Woman Pouring Milk*, light suffusing the space, which is enriched with earth tones, browns and yellows and oranges — harvest colors — while the woman gives her attention not to us but to the act of pouring, so that our attention too travels down her body, her arms, to the clay pitcher, to the stream of milk and to the dark hole inside brown clay.

And at the other end? "Sumangala's Mother," "Stained and squalid by the cooking pots," desperate to get out of the kitchen, desperate for silence, for solitude. Or in the honest recollections of Louise Erdrich:

> We have a baby: our sixth child, our third birth. During that year, our older adopted children hit adolescence like runaway trucks. Dear grandparents weaken and die. My husband, Michael, and I both work full time. He rises at four in the morning, hardly seems to sleep at all, juggles schedules, his own work, and day-care trips. To keep the door to the other self, the writing self, open, I scratch messages on the envelopes of letters I can't answer, in the margins of books I'm too tired to review. On pharmacy prescription bags, dime store notebooks, children's construction paper, I keep writing. The fragments accumulate, the jotted scraps become a journal.[3]

The finished book (*The Blue Jay's Dance: A Birth Year*) can belie its very subject: it looks too neat, too finished. But such is the miracle of perfected form: like Vermeer's exquisite *Woman*, it's *supposed* to look effortless. Recall Yeats, in the aptly named "Adam's Curse." He is here, as a fairly young man, speaking with his beloved Maud Gonne:

> We sat together at one summer's end,
> That beautiful mild woman, your close friend,
> And you and I, and talked of poetry.
> I said: "A line will take us hours maybe;
> Yet if it does not seem a moment's thought,
> Our stitching and unstitching has been naught.
> Better go down upon your marrow bones
> And scrub a kitchen pavement, or break stones
> Like an old pauper, in all kinds of weather;
> For to articulate sweet sounds together
> Is to work harder than all these, and yet
> Be thought an idler by the noisy set
> Of bankers, schoolmasters, and clergymen
> The martyrs call the world."[4]

Well, my friends who clean houses for a living might say – Let him just *try* it for a while. And indeed one wonders: Did Yeats *ever* in his long life scrub a kitchen floor?

As Brenda Peterson suggests (in "The Sacredness of Chores"), there is – here too – some connection between the outer and inner work. Cleaning up one's office, bedroom, or bathroom can go a long way toward restoring mental sanity (from *sanus*, "health"). Clutter – like what I'm living in today, as I work at finishing this book – can be draining. The kitchen counter fills up with dirty dishes and food, the living room is scattered with papers and magazines, a child's shoes and socks, books and games – one either ignores it or slowly becomes insane. And to ignore seems like ignoring my environment, as if I were saying that all of this stuff of the body is inconsequential, surmountable. It is a failure to take care.

And yet: there is also the great pleasure in making a mess, in letting things *be.* Who knows what forms might bubble up, spontaneously generated? It's the lovely muck of life itself. Yeats knew this, too; as an old man he wrote:

> Those masterful images because complete
> Grew in pure mind, but out of what began?
> A mound of refuse or the sweepings of a street,
> Old kettles, old bottles, old rags, that raving slut
> Who keeps the till. Now that my ladder's gone,
> I must lie down where all the ladders start,
> In the foul rag and bone shop of the heart.[5]

The beauty of final form has its origins – as do we all – in the mud. The lotus as truly as the Madonna arises out of the fluids, the wetness of a messy love and life.

Home-work. Childbirth. The daily labor that we know we shall have to do again tomorrow, and then again the day after. It is, for many of us, the stuff of life that – so we feel and so we are taught – keeps us from our *real* work. And this, of course, is an illusion. As Thich Nhat Hanh suggests, if we are washing the dishes in order to get on to a pleasant cup of tea, "we are not alive during the time we are washing the dishes. In fact we are completely incapable of realizing the miracle of life while standing at the sink. If we can't wash the dishes, the chances are we won't be able to drink our tea either. While drinking the cup of tea, we will only be thinking of other things, barely aware of the cup in our hands."[6]

As with so much in this book, what might sound sentimental or simply absurd is in fact just simple. And I'm reminded that there's a reason that we think of fools as "simple," and that in many cultures such fools have the adjective "holy" in front of them. Or "silly" – from the Middle English *seely*, meaning happy, blessed.

Often when I'm putting away cups and glasses my twelve-year-old daughter will assist me by standing by the cupboard to receive them from my hands, saving me from walking back and forth. She's old enough to resist this chore, but the truth is

– music is on as I clean, Springsteen, an old Phil Spector tape, or Garrison Keillor – and we weave together a dance out of the dishes. The work goes more slowly, and with a certain risk of breakage, but there we are, perfecting a life.

Is this "mindfulness" in Thich Nhat Hanh's sense? Perhaps not. But transformation's the game. When alone in the winter I sometimes do dishes by moonlight, willing to risk missing a few spots for the aesthetics of the thing. I like to wash to Van Morrison or Duke Ellington, gazing out the window, out beyond the laurel to the trees and sky in the distance. I like to watch the sparrows. I like to dance and chant. I do not easily stay put. It's how I clean.

I admire deeply those who do so well the everyday things of life. I admire the rooted ones, the ones who stay put and help others stay put: the gardeners, like my wife, Judy, who is also a fine lawyer, and who knows the value of details, of getting things right. I admire the fathers and mothers who give themselves so deeply to their kids, not as an act of martyrdom but out of difficult and timely love. These are the true alchemists of our lives, the ones whose hands know the mess of impure metals, the ones with the patience to sit with it and let it be, just let it be – imagining gold, *seeing* it when no one else has a clue.

Above all with the children – those parents and day-care workers and teachers in the pre-schools and kindergartens, primary and secondary schools – all of them living with those growing and fermenting lives. A parent myself, I know a little of what it takes, and stand amazed at those with the gift.

Layman P'ang

MY DAILY AFFAIRS ARE QUITE ORDINARY . . .

My daily affairs are quite ordinary;
but I'm in total harmony with them.
I don't hold on to anything, don't reject anything;
nowhere an obstacle or conflict.
Who cares about wealth and honor?
Even the poorest thing shines.
My miraculous power and spiritual activity:
drawing water and carrying wood.

translated by Stephen Mitchell

Saint Teresa of Avila

---

from
THE LETTERS

The other thing for which I have often asked our Father is that he should prescribe some manual labour, were it only basket-making, to be done during recreation if there is no other time. It is most important, except during study time, that such work should be done. You must understand, my Father, that I wish the virtues to be insisted on, not austerities, as you will see in our convents. It must be because I am not much given to penance myself.

Brother Lawrence

GATHERED THOUGHTS

It matters not to me what I do, or what I suffer, so long as I abide lovingly united to GOD's will, – that is my whole *business*.

I am in the hands of GOD, and He has His own good purposes regarding me; therefore I trouble not myself for aught that man can do to me. If I cannot serve GOD here, elsewhere I shall find a place wherein to serve Him.

The practice of the Presence of GOD is the shortest and easiest *Way* to attain to *Christian perfection:* it is *the Form and Life of Virtue,* it is the great *Preservative from Sin.* The practice will become easy, if we have but courage and a good will.

The whole world seems to me to be no longer real; all that my outward eyes behold pass like fantasies and dreams. That which I see with the eyes of the soul is what alone I long for, and to be not yet in the possession of my heart's desire brings to me sorrow and drooping of spirit. On the one hand dazzled by the brightness of the Sun of Righteousness, the Scatterer of the shades of night, and, on the other, with eyes dimmed by my own sin, I feel at times as if I were beside myself. And yet, I make it my ordinary business to abide in the Presence of GOD with the humility of a useless, though a faithful servant.

Since I first entered on the religious life, I have looked on GOD as the *Goal* and *End* of all the thoughts and affections of the soul. As a novice, during the hours appointed for prayer I labored to arrive at a conviction of the truth of the Divine Being, rather by the light of faith than by the deductions of the intellect, and by this short and certain method I grew in the knowledge of this *Object* of Love, in Whose Presence I resolved evermore to abide. Possessed thus entirely with the greatness and the majesty of this INFINITE BEING, I went straightway to the place which duty had marked out for me – the kitchen. There, when I had carried out all that called for me, I gave to prayer whatever time remained, as well before my work as after. Before beginning any task I would say to GOD, with childlike trust: "O GOD, since Thou art with me, and it is Thy will that I must now apply myself to these outward duties, I beseech Thee, assist me with Thy grace that I may continue in Thy Presence; and to this end, O LORD, be with me in this my work, accept the labor of my hands, and dwell within my heart with all Thy Fulness." Moreover, as I wrought, I would continue to hold familiar converse, offering to Him my little acts of service, entreating the unfailing succor of His grace. When I had finished, I would examine how I had performed my duty: if I found well, I gave Him thanks;

if ill, I besought His pardon, and without losing heart I set my spirit right, and returned anew unto His Presence, as though I had never wandered from Him. Thus, by rising after every fall, and by doing all in faith and love, without wearying, I have come to a state in which it would be as little possible for me not to think of GOD, as it was hard to discipline myself thereto at the beginning.

O LORD, enlarge the chambers of my heart that I may find room for Thy love. Sustain me by Thy power, lest the fire of Thy love consume me.

The practice of the Presence of GOD is of very great service in helping us to pray in truth; it restrains the mind from wandering throughout the day and holds it fixed steadfastly on GOD; thus it will more easily remain tranquil in the hour of prayer.

Life is full of perils and of hidden reefs, on which we shall make shipwreck without the continual succor of the grace of GOD. Yet how can we ask for it, unless we are with Him? How can we be with Him, unless our thoughts are ever of Him? How can He be in our thoughts, unless we form a holy habit of abiding in His Presence, there asking for the grace we need each moment of our life?

If you would go forward in the spiritual life, you must avoid relying on the subtle conclusions and fine reasonings of the unaided intellect. Unhappy they who seek to satisfy their desire therein! The Creator is the great teacher of Truth. We can reason laboriously for many years, but fuller far and deeper is the knowledge of the hidden things of faith and of Himself, which He flashes as light into the *heart* of the *humble.*

Nothing can give us so great relief in the trials and sorrows of life, as a loving intercourse with GOD; when such is faithfully practiced, the evils that assail the body will prove light to us. GOD often ordains that we should suffer in the body to purify the soul, and to constrain us to abide with Him. How can anyone whose life is hid with GOD, and whose only desire is GOD, be capable of feeling pain? Let us then worship Him in our infirmities, offering to Him our sorrows, just when they press upon us, asking Him lovingly, as a child his dear father, to give us strength, and mold our will to His. Brief prayers as these are very proper for all sick persons, and prove a wonderful charm against sorrow.

Ah, did I know that my heart loved not GOD, this very instant I would pluck it out.

O Loving-Kindness so old and still so new, I have been too late of loving Thee. You are young, my brethren; profit therefore I beseech you from my confession, that I cared too little to employ my early years for GOD. Consecrate all yours to His Love. If I had only known Him sooner, if I had only had some one to tell me then what I am telling you, I should not have so long delayed in loving Him. Believe me, count as lost each day you have not used in loving GOD.

Denise Levertov

THE CONVERSION OF BROTHER LAWRENCE

> Let us enter into ourselves. Time presses.
> — *Brother Lawrence, 1611–1691*

1 What leafless tree plunging
  into what pent sky was it
  convinced you Spring, bound to return
  in all its unlikelihood, was a word
  of God, a Divine message?
  Custom, natural reason, are everyone's assurance;
  we take the daylight for granted, the moon,
  the measured tides. A particular tree, though,
  one day in your eighteenth winter,
  said more, an oracle. Clumsy footman,
  apt to drop the ornate objects handed to you,
  cursed and cuffed by butlers and grooms,
  your inner life unsuspected,
  you heard, that day, a more-than-green
  voice from the stripped branches.
  Wooden lace, a celestial geometry, uttered
  more than familiar rhythms of growth.
  It said *By the Grace of God.*
  Midsummer rustled around you that wintry moment.
  Was it elm, ash, poplar, a fruit-tree, your rooted
  twig-winged angel of annunciation?

2 Out from the chateau park it sent you
  (by some back lane, no doubt,
  not through the wide gates of curled iron),
  by ways untold, by soldier's marches, to the obscure
  clatter and heat of a monastery kitchen,
  a broom's rhythmic whisper for music,
  your torment the drudgery of household ledgers. Destiny

without visible glory. "Time pressed." Among pots and pans,
heart-still through the bustle of chores,
your labors, hard as the pain in your lame leg,
grew slowly easier over the years, the years
when, though your soul felt darkened, heavy, worthless,
yet God, you discovered, never abandoned you but walked
at your side keeping pace as comrades had
on the long hard roads of war. You entered then
the unending "silent secret conversation,"
the life of steadfast attention.
Not work transformed you; work, even drudgery,
was transformed: that discourse
pierced through its monotones, infused them
with streams of sparkling color.
What needed doing, you did; journeyed if need be
on rocking boats, lame though you were,
to the vineyard country to purchase the year's wine
for a hundred Brothers, laughably rolling yourself
over the deck-stacked barrels when you couldn't
keep your footing; and managed deals with the vintners
to your own surprise, though business was nothing to you.
Your secret was not the craftsman's delight in process,
which doesn't distinguish work from pleasure –
your way was not to exalt nor avoid
the Adamic legacy, you simply made it irrelevant:
everything faded, thinned to nothing, beside
the light which bathed and warmed, the Presence
your being had opened to. Where it shone,
there life was, and abundantly; it touched
your dullest task, and the task was easy.
                    Joyful, absorbed,
you "practiced the presence of God" as a musician
practices hour after hour his art:
"A stone before the carver,"
you "entered into yourself."

Chuang Tzu

THE SECRET OF
CARING FOR LIFE
(Cutting Up an Ox)

Your life has a limit but knowledge has none. If you use what is limited to pursue what has no limit, you will be in danger. If you understand this and still strive for knowledge, you will be in danger for certain! If you do good, stay away from fame. If you do evil, stay away from punishments. Follow the middle; go by what is constant, and you can stay in one piece, keep yourself alive, look after your parents, and live out your years.

Cook Ting was cutting up an ox for Lord Wen-hui. At every touch of his hand, every heave of his shoulder, every move of his feet, every thrust of his knee – *zip! zoop!* He slithered the knife along with a *zing*, and all was in perfect rhythm, as though he were performing the dance of the Mulberry Grove or keeping time to the Ching-shou music.

"Ah, this is marvelous!" said Lord Wen-hui. "Imagine skill reaching such heights!"

Cook Ting laid down his knife and replied, "What I care about is the Way, which goes beyond skill. When I first began cutting up oxen, all I could see was the ox itself. After three years I no longer saw the whole ox. And now – now I go at it by spirit and don't look with my eyes. Perception and understanding have come to a stop and spirit moves where it wants. I go along with the natural makeup, strike in the big hollows, guide the knife through the big openings, and follow things as they are. So I never touch the smallest ligament or tendon, much less a main joint.

"A good cook changes his knife once a year – because he cuts. A mediocre cook changes his knife once a month – because he hacks. I've had this knife of mine for nineteen years and I've cut up thousands of oxen with it, and yet the blade is as good as though it had just come from the grindstone. There are spaces between the joints, and the blade of the knife has really no thickness. If you insert what has no thickness into such spaces, then there's plenty of room – more than enough for the blade to play about in. That's why after nineteen years the blade of my knife is still as good as when it first came from the grindstone.

"However, whenever I come to a complicated place, I size up the difficulties, tell myself to watch out and be careful, keep my eyes on what I'm doing, work very slowly, and move the knife with the greatest subtlety, until — *flop!* The whole thing comes apart like a clod of earth crumbling to the ground. I stand there holding the knife and look all around me, completely satisfied and reluctant to move on, and then I wipe off the knife and put it away."7

"Excellent!" said Lord Wen-hui. "I have heard the words of Cook Ting and learned how to care for life!"

translated by Burton Watson

Stonehouse

from
THE ZEN WORKS
OF STONEHOUSE

a hoe supplies a living
the water and wood last all year
mountains soothe my eyes
no troubles burden my mind
swirling mist soaks through hatch
a trail of moss climbs dirt steps
accepting saves my strength
no need to arrange a thing

lunch in my mountain kitchen
the spring provides the perfect sauce
behold a stew of preserved bamboo
a pot of fragrant hard-grain rice
blue-cap mushrooms fried in oil
purple-bud ginger pickles
none of them heavenly dishes
but why should I cater to gods

perfect emptiness is a transparent sea
where the faintest breath makes foam
as soon as we have a body
we have worries about food and clothes
runaway racehorse perceptions
uncaged monkey delusions
until you understand the Lord of Emptiness
the Wheel of Rebirth rolls on

the Eighth Month in the mountains
the perennial fruits are all at hand
pea pods hang on terraced banks
rice-flower perfume fills the fields

I cut tall grass to patch my hut
I chop bamboo to channel the spring
I wonder if anyone knows
how much I enjoy old age ...

Translator's Notes
The Chinese hoe is more like a mattock, with a bladed end somewhat longer than the Western hoe. In the mountains, thatch is the most common roof covering, although hermits who can afford them use earthenware tiles. If there is one element of Chinese culture that most Westerners find incomprehensible, if not exasperating, it's the Chinese glorification of acceptance. But acceptance provides the basis for transcendence, while struggle keeps us enslaved to the dialectic of opposites. At the end of his *Taoteching,* Lao-tzu says, "The Way of the sage / is to act without struggling."

The spring was next to Stonehouse's hut. In stews, long thin bamboo shoots that have been preserved in salt are preferred over the larger, fresh shoots. *Hard-grain rice* refers to a nonglutinous variety and not the softer rice the Chinese prefer. I'm not sure what kind of mushroom Stonehouse had in mind. The violet *cortinarius* and the indigo *lactarius* are both edible. Meanwhile, some editions have "clear-cap" in place of "blue-cap."

Perfect emptiness isn't empty. And the Lord of Emptiness is the Buddha. At the end of the *Diamond Sutra,* the Buddha says, "All composite things / are like a dream, an illusion, a bubble, a shadow / like dew or like lightning / thus should we regard them" (32). And Lao-tzu says, "The reason we have disaster / is because we have a body / if we didn't have a body / we wouldn't have disaster" (13). The Buddhist Wheel of Rebirth encompasses six varieties of existence: gods, asuras (demi-gods who make war on gods), humans, beasts, hungry ghosts (beings with large stomachs and small mouths), and creatures consigned to the various hells. In the middle and turning the Wheel are the Three Poisons: Delusion, Desire, and Anger.

The eighth month of China's lunar calendar is roughly equivalent to September in the Gregorian calendar. Farmers often take advantage of the hiatus that occurs during this period when weeding and watering are no longer necessary and harvesting has not yet begun so that they can make repairs to their homes as well as to their fields and irrigation systems. In areas where fields are terraced, farmers often grow beans and melons on the banks separating levels. Bamboo canes are prepared for use as water pipes by dropping hot coals into one end and allowing them to burn through the various junctures.

translated by Red Pine

Brenda Peterson

THE SACREDNESS
OF CHORES
for C.H.

One bright May morning, my arms piled high with clean, freshly folded laundry, I walked up to my housemate and dear friend's room and discovered that she'd taken her life. B.J. lay on that pale green carpet as if fallen from a great height, one hand outstretched. I did not see the gun gleaming like a dark fist at her temple as I knelt down to grab her wrist. Not dead, I thought, teeth chattering, just hurt. I had never seen anyone so hurt. Fumbling with her wrist, I finally felt a thready pulse against my forefinger – but it was only my own heart beating. I was so cold. Never have I felt that bone-deep shiver and chill. Her body was warm with sunlight, even though its own inner warmth was gone.

Then I saw her face, the eyelids darkly swollen, shut. From her nose and mouth ran congealed rushes of blood, a red so brilliant and dense that I remembered my sister saying that she'd once watched a heart explode on the operating table as she assisted a surgery, that it bloomed upward from the body like a rose bursting open. For a moment I jumped up, then fell right down, legs buckling. I again took B.J.'s hand, thinking somehow my touch might spare her the sight of herself.

But it was I who needed sparing. Alongside B.J.'s dead body, I knelt on all fours and howled until suddenly I heard a far-off accompaniment. It was a *thud-thud*, not of footsteps up the stairs but of something from deep within the bowels of the house itself. I listened, head cocked like an animal, listening with my eyes. And only after a time did I recognize the spin of the dryer. Then the thumping stopped and a piercing buzz began. It summoned me, this shrill signal, to stand upright, to leave the dead, to go downstairs and open the dryer door. More clean clothes tumbled into my arms, and I buried my face in the warm, fragrant cotton and colorful flannel. And because I could not carry B.J.'s body alone, because she no longer carried herself, I bunched her clean laundry against my chest and called for help. Then I carefully folded every sock and cotton camisole, every blouse and nightgown until the sirens stopped at my door.

It was so breathtakingly swift, so complete, B.J.'s leave-taking of her body, of her son and family and friends; and, though in my mind some part of me will always be howling on all fours in fury and grief over her brutal abandonment, there also lingers with me these six years later the exact weight and clean smell of her laundry.

After sharing domestic chores for six months, B.J. and I had struck a bargain: I did laundry and vacuumed; she did dishes and dusting. We shared scouring bathrooms, cooking, and the yard work, which was a kind of desultory dance between dandelions and an ancient push mower that mangled more than it trimmed. On the afternoon of B.J.'s death, I found myself sitting absolutely still in the kitchen. I stared at the bright haze of sunlight off Lake Washington, the silly burble of my coffee cheerful on the stove, the whir of the fridge, its rhythm loud and labored. I thought of the food inside this stupid, square, and noisy box — *Let it all rot and die!* At the same moment I remembered dully, *I should defrost that fridge.* It had been on my list of chores for the day, right after the laundry.

My morning list for that May day had read:

1) Finish Chapter 10
2) Laundry
3) Defrost fridge
4) Meet P.N. in the market (check for rhubarb)

I gazed at the little list, and it seemed so earnest, so busy, so foolish. What did defrosting fridges, making a strawberry-rhubarb pie, or even finishing a chapter have to do with anything when all the while I'd scribbled that list my friend had been dead upstairs? The coroner said she'd died deep in the night while I lay down the hall sleeping, practicing for my own death.

I looked despairingly down at my clothes and realized I was still in my pajamas, the ones I'd bought in imitation of Lauren Bacall, the ones I'd rolled up at wrist and ankle, the ones, I realized now, that must also be washed clean. It was only when I threw my pajamas in the washer, slathered Cheer on the load, and turned on the churning machine that I found myself crying, kneeling on the cold cement floor and at last lamenting. It was safe enough to sob — the world had not stopped spinning, just as this washing machine spun and spun its little load through all its warm, delicate cycles.

This is how my friends found me. First, Paula, who arrived and busied herself during all the unexpected official paperwork of death by mowing the lawn furiously, up and down outside as if her precise patterns in the scraggly grass could bring order back to my little yard, my small world. Two days later, when I decided to leave this house, my friends Laura and Susan came heroically armed with buckets, Fantastik, and huge, brightly colored sponges to scrub and scour and spend hours on their hands and knees, a final cleansing of B.J.'s room, a kind of womanly worship. I put Alberta Hunter on the stereo, and we all got down on the floor, crying and cleaning. As we left the house for the last time, it shone in the sun, welcoming. Others would live here and wake up to the lapping lake, the coffee, fresh laundry. This house was again ready for life, life abundant.

Those mundane tasks that sunny May ten years ago have forever changed my sense of daily life. Those simple chores, both solitary and in the company of other women, were my first comfort in what was also my first death. The smell of Comet is forever linked with consolation, the spin of a dryer with survival, the syncopated chant of women scrubbing with the racial memory of reverence.

"Cleaning is incantation, physical prayer," says a friend who is an artist. "You create a small and ordered sacred place that has been touched a thousand times by your hands. It's a ritual of caring."

"The actual cleaning is sometimes secondary to the mental housekeeping that takes place," adds my friend Rebecca, who has always made her living with her hands, either gardening or massaging. "Cleaning your house is like pruning a tree. The house and the tree are both alive. You take care of the debris first, then stand back to look at the true form — and that clarity, that original vision is what happens in the mind."

Stevie Smith, the British poet, commented that she dreamt up some of her best poems while "Hoovering." I have also opted for the vacuuming chores in my own household because the *rush* and *whoosh* of the Kirby, its solid paths on the thick carpet tell me where I've been, where I am, and exactly where I want to go.

All of us claim territory. Traditionally, the masculine way is to mark territory by scent, by song, by a boast, a show of power, a pile of weapons: "This is mine, do not enter or you'll reckon with me!" The feminine claiming is perhaps a fierce physical possessing of the space by adorning home with spells, magic, or brightly waving scarves in trees, as do the aborigines, who put powerful altars near their hearths both for worship and to summon protective guardian spirits.

In my current household, upon hearing that our rental home was to be scrutinized by potential buyers, my two housemates and I broke all real estate rules by staying home and doing our Saturday morning chores. While the house buyers perused, I maneuvered the noisiest vacuum this side of Seattle; one housemate ran the dishwasher and slung wet laundry everywhere, like so many volunteer scarecrow troops; my other housemate followed the harried home buyers from room to room wielding a defending dust mop. She actually sprayed the real estate agent with her lemon Pledge. Such was the territorial claiming of womanly warriors — and no prospective buyers have yet to make an offer these five months later.

Cleaning has long been women's work. For years women have borne the archetype of body, darkness, the erotic, the unclean, the Earth. This association has often imprisoned women in the home and trapped men in the world. Thus, leaving the home is traditionally associated with the heroic explorer, the powerful "man of the world," while the housework is seen as trivial, timid, uninspired, menial labor left to servants. But we are all in service to our homes, as well as our homeland of Earth.

For years environmentalists have been educating us to recognize that the whole wide world *is* our home; we cannot leave the world, or transcend it, or truly throw anything away. We must learn to be here. If women claim the world the way they already have their homes and if men claim their homes as fervently as they have the world, what might we create?

But instead of men and women creating their own homes, more and more people are leaving the home chores and ritual cleanings to hired hands. Are there some deep losses we all might incur from not cleaning up after ourselves? I suspect that doing our own chores is everyone's calling, no matter what our other important jobs. There is some sacredness in this daily, thoughtful, and very grounding housework that we cannot afford to lose if we are to be whole, integrated.

"Just getting down on my hands and knees and scouring the bathroom is like cleaning my soul," says a male friend. He adds with a laugh, "it shines – not necessarily my soul – but that white porcelain. And I feel new, like I've forgiven myself something."

Another of my men friends tells of his mother's death. When she, a meticulous cleaner, died, he stayed on alone in her house for three days and put everything right and tidy. "I felt very close to my mother then," he says. "After all, she had taught me how to clean."

Chores are a child's first work, though they are often presented in the form of play. Girls play house, and boys spend hours running toy trucks over miniature mud mountains. Before we even teach children to speak, we instruct them in their separate chores, and so we shape the world, the future. Somewhere along the line, society quit expecting boys to clean up their rooms, insisting they order the outside world instead. If I were a man, I would feel this as a loss, a wisdom and honor denied me and my home.

Among my friends, no matter their living situation, cleaning is a crucial issue. Perhaps it is simply the symbol of how we treat what we love. Some people clean like Lady Macbeth – "Out, damned spot!" Others clean haphazardly, or methodically, earnestly or devotedly. One of my housemates, Lynettie Sue, cleans as a way of understanding and organizing her life. From room to room she goes, sighing with satisfaction, as under her broom and dust rag and window-washing squeegee the world must give way to her scrutiny, her vision of a higher order suggested by perfectly folded sheets and a piano that looks spit shined. She is particularly imperious in the bathroom, being a microbiologist and knowing well that those telltale bits of black mold on the shower ceiling are unhealthy organisms. I teasingly beg her, "Don't take me to Comet-witz," when she suggests my upstairs bathroom looks like a biologist's field trip, "*not* cleaning concentration camp!" But I have found, under her diligence, a luxury that nothing except lounging in a hot, sparkling clean bathtub can give me.

Cleaning can be an art. I've often spent a Saturday morning dancing on the freeway of love right in the middle of my living room with Aretha and a vacuum. I admit to practicing arcane rites of exorcism as deep as psychoanalysis by simply cutting up ex-lovers' clothes to use as rags for those deep-down, won't-go-away cleaning jobs like stains on a rug, on a heart. Most recently cleaning came to my rescue when I received the final galley proofs for my novel in the mail with the dire red rubber stamp: RETURN: 36-HOUR PROOF. What did I do with only three days to read and correct my entire book? I spent the first day and a half in a frenzy of old-fashioned, whirlwind spring cleaning that shook the spiders from the rafters and my soul. The book was a breeze after my walk-in winter closet.

When we clean up after ourselves, whether it's a spilled jar, a broken chair, a dis-organized study, or a death, we can see and reflect upon our own life and perhaps envision a new way that won't be so broken, so violent, so unconscious. By clean-ing up our own homes we take responsibility for ourselves and for preserving what we love. But if our attitude is "my kingdom is not of this world," then there is a disturbing possibility that we'll finally do away with the world rather than clean it or ourselves. The feminine attitude of getting down on our hands and knees to scour — and at the most primitive level look at what needs cleaning — deserves our attention. For in this gesture of bended knees is some humility, some meditation, some time to recognize the first foundation of our homes.

It was a simple washing machine and dryer that got me to my knees that day my friend died — in horror, in mourning, in surrender not to death but to survival. It was a homing instinct that grounded me and made me want to stay on. To this day I have a ritual of running the washer and dryer while I am in my study at work. There is no more comforting sound to me than the spinning of that washer or dryer. It is the whole world spinning in there, cleansing itself and me.

As long as the washer and dryer spin, I tell myself, I am safe and those I love may choose to keep living alongside me. For there is laundry to be done and so many chores — chores of the living. There is so much to be remembered under the dust of our old contempt for cleaning up after ourselves, picking up our own socks. There is much to be swept away and shined bright and scrubbed down to its deep-est, most illuminating level. Think of all the chores we have yet to do, quietly and on our knees — because home is holy.

Henry David Thoreau

from
WALDEN

I had this advantage, at least, in my mode of life, over those who were obliged to look abroad for amusement, to society and the theatre, that my life itself was become my amusement and never ceased to be novel. It was a drama of many scenes and without an end. If we were always indeed getting our living, and regulating our lives according to the last and best mode we had learned, we should never be troubled with ennui. Follow your genius closely enough, and it will not fail to show you a fresh prospect every hour. Housework was a pleasant pastime. When my floor was dirty, I rose early, and, setting all my furniture out of doors on the grass, bed and bedstead making but one budget, dashed water on the floor, and sprinkled white sand from the pond on it, and then with a broom scrubbed it clean and white; and by the time the villagers had broken their fast the morning sun had dried my house sufficiently to allow me to move in again, and my meditations were almost uninterrupted. It was pleasant to see my whole household effects on the grass, making a little pile like a gipsy's pack, and my three-legged table, from which I did not remove the books and pen and ink, standing amid the pines and hickories. They seemed glad to get out themselves, and as if unwilling to be brought in. I was sometimes tempted to stretch an awning over them and take my seat there. It was worth the while to see the sun shine on these things, and hear the free wind blow on them; so much more interesting most familiar objects look out of doors than in the house. A bird sits on the next bough, life-everlasting grows under the table, and blackberry vines run round its legs; pine cones, chestnut burs, and strawberry leaves are strewn about. It looked as if this was the way these forms came to be transferred to our furniture, to tables, chairs, and bedsteads — because they once stood in their midst.

Linda Hogan

WAKING UP THE RAKE

In the still dark mornings, my grandmother would rise up from her bed and put wood in the stove. When the fire began to burn, she would sit in front of its warmth and let down her hair. It had never been cut and it knotted down in two long braids. When I was fortunate enough to be there, in those red Oklahoma mornings, I would wake up with her, stand behind her chair, and pull the brush through the long strands of her hair. It cascaded down her back, down over the chair, and touched the floor.

We were the old and the new, bound together in front of the snapping fire, woven like a lifetime's tangled growth of hair. I saw my future in her body and face, and her past was alive in me. We were morning people, and in all of earth's mornings the new intertwines with the old. Even new, a day itself is ancient, old with earth's habit of turning over and over again.

Years later, I was sick, and I went to a traditional healer. The healer was dark and thin and radiant. The first night I was there, she also lit a fire. We sat before it, smelling the juniper smoke. She asked me to tell her everything, my life spoken in words, a case history of living, with its dreams and losses, the scars and wounds we all bear from being in the world. She smoked me with cedar smoke, wrapped a sheet around me, and put me to bed, gently, like a mother caring for her child.

The next morning she nudged me awake and took me outside to pray. We faced east where the sun was beginning its journey on our side of earth.

The following morning in red dawn, we went outside and prayed. The sun was a full orange eye rising up the air. The morning after that we did the same, and on Sunday we did likewise.

The next time I visited her it was a year later, and again we went through the same prayers, standing outside facing the early sun. On the last morning I was there, she left for her job in town. Before leaving, she said, "Our work is our altar."

Those words have remained with me.

Now I am a disciple of birds. The birds that I mean are eagles, owls, and hawks. I clean cages at the Birds of Prey Rehabilitation Foundation. It is the work I wanted to do, in order to spend time inside the gentle presence of the birds.

There is a Sufi saying that goes something like this: "Yes, worship God, go to church, sing praises, but first tie your camel to the post." This cleaning is the work of tying the camel to a post.

I pick up the carcasses and skin of rats, mice, and of rabbits. Some of them have been turned inside out by the sharp-beaked eaters, so that the leathery flesh becomes a delicately veined coat for the inner fur. It is a boneyard. I rake the smooth fragments of bones. Sometimes there is a leg or shank of deer to be picked up.

In this boneyard, the still-red vertebrae lie on the ground beside an open rib cage. The remains of a rabbit, a small intestinal casing, holds excrement like beads in a necklace. And there are the clean, oval pellets the birds spit out, filled with fur, bone fragments, and, now and then, a delicate sharp claw that looks as if it were woven inside. A feather, light and soft, floats down a current of air, and it is also picked up.

Over time, the narrow human perspective from which we view things expands. A deer carcass begins to look beautiful and rich in its torn redness, the muscle and bone exposed in the shape life took on for a while as it walked through meadows and drank at creeks.

And the bone fragments have their own stark beauty, the clean white jaw bones with ivory teeth small as the head of a pin still in them. I think of medieval physicians trying to learn about our private, hidden bodies by cutting open the stolen dead and finding the splendor inside, the grace of every red organ, and the smooth, gleaming bone.

This work is an apprenticeship, and the birds are the teachers. Sweet-eyed barn owls, such taskmasters, asking us to be still and slow and to move in time with their rhythms, not our own. The short-eared owls with their startling yellow eyes require the full presence of a human. The marsh hawks, behind their branches, watch our every move.

There is a silence needed here before a person enters the bordered world the birds inhabit, so we stop and compose ourselves before entering their doors, and we listen to the musical calls of the eagles, the sound of wings in air, the way their feet with sharp claws, many larger than our own hands, grab hold of a perch. Then we know we are ready to enter, and they are ready for us.

The most difficult task the birds demand is that we learn to be equal to them, to feel our way into an intelligence that is different from our own. A friend, awed at the thought of working with eagles, said, "Imagine knowing an eagle." I answered her honestly, "It isn't so much that we know the eagles. It's that they know us."

And they know that we are apart from them, that as humans we have somehow fallen from our animal grace, and because of that we maintain a distance from them, though it is not always a distance of heart. The places we inhabit, even sharing a common earth, must remain distinct and separate. It was our presence that brought most of them here in the first place, nearly all of them injured in a clash with the human world. They have been shot, or hit by cars, trapped in leg hold traps, poisoned, ensnared in wire fences. To ensure their survival, they must remember us as the enemies that we are. We are the embodiment of a paradox; we are the wounders and we are the healers.

There are human lessons to be learned here, in the work. Fritjof Capra wrote:

"Doing work that has to be done over and over again helps us recognize the natural cycles of growth and decay, of birth and death, and thus become aware of the dynamic order of the universe." And it is true, in whatever we do, the brushing of hair, the cleaning of cages, we begin to see the larger order of things. In this place, there is a constant coming to terms with both the sacred place life occupies, and with death. Like one of those early physicians who discovered the strange, inner secrets of our human bodies, I'm filled with awe at the very presence of life, not just the birds, but a horse contained in its living fur, a dog alive and running. What a marvel it is, the fine shape life takes in all of us. It is equally marvelous that life is quickly turned back to the earth-colored ants and the soft white maggots that are time's best and closest companions. To sit with the eagles and their flute-like songs, listening to the longer flute of wind sweep through the lush grasslands, is to begin to know the natural laws that exist apart from our own written ones.

One of those laws, that we carry deep inside us, is intuition. It is lodged in a place even the grave-robbing doctors could not discover. It's a blood-written code that directs us through life. The founder of this healing center, Sigrid Ueblacker, depends on this inner knowing. She watches, listens, and feels her way to an understanding of each eagle and owl. This vision, as I call it, directs her own daily work at healing the injured birds and returning them to the wild.

"Sweep the snow away," she tells me. "The Swainson's hawks should be in Argentina this time of year and should not have to stand in the snow."

I sweep.

And that is in the winter when the hands ache from the cold, and the water freezes solid and has to be broken out for the birds, fresh buckets carried over icy earth from the well. In summer, it's another story. After only a few hours the food begins to move again, as if resurrected to life. A rabbit shifts a bit. A mouse turns. You could say that they have been resurrected, only with a life other than the one that left them. The moving skin swarms with flies and their offspring, ants, and a few wasps, busy at their own daily labor.

Even aside from the expected rewards for this work, such as seeing an eagle healed and winging across the sky it fell from, there are others. An occasional snake, beautiful and sleek, finds its way into the cage one day, eats a mouse and is too fat to leave, so we watch its long muscular life stretched out in the tall grasses. Or, another summer day, taking branches to be burned with a pile of wood near the little creek, a large turtle with a dark and shining shell slips soundlessly into the water, its presence a reminder of all the lives beyond these that occupy us.

One green morning, an orphaned owl perches nervously above me while I clean. Its downy feathers are roughed out. It appears to be twice its size as it clacks its beak at me, warning me: stay back. Then, fearing me the way we want it to, it bolts off the perch and flies, landing by accident onto the wooden end of my rake, before it sees that a human is an extension of the tool, and it flies again to a safer place, while I return to raking.

The word *rake* means to gather or heap up, to smooth the broken ground. And that's what this work is, all of it, the smoothing over of broken ground, the heal-ing of the severed trust we humans hold with earth. We gather it back together again with great care, take the broken pieces and fragments and return them to the sky. It is work at the borderland between species, at the boundary between injury and healing.

There is an art to raking, a very fine art, one with rhythm in it, and life. On the days I do it well, the rake wakes up. Wood that came from dark dense forests seems to return to life. The water that rose up through the rings of that wood, the min-erals of earth mined upward by the burrowing tree roots, all come alive. My own fragile hand touches the wood, a hand full of my own life, including that which rose each morning early to watch the sun return from the other side of the planet. Over time, these hands will smooth the rake's wooden handle down to a sheen.

Raking. It is a labor round and complete, smooth and new as an egg, and the rounding seasons of the world revolving in time and space. All things, even our own heartbeats and sweat, are in it, part of it. And that work, that watching the turning over of life, becomes a road into what is essential. Work is the country of hands, and they want to live there in the dailiness of it, the repetition that is time's lan-guage of prayer, a common tongue. Everything is there, in that language, in the humblest of labor. The rake wakes up and the healing is in it. The shadows of leaves that once fell beneath the tree the handle came from are in that labor, and the rab-bits that passed this way, on the altar of our work. And when the rake wakes up, all earth's gods are reborn and they dance and sing in the dusty air around us.

Marc Hudson

IAN

At first glance, to the noninitiate, it must seem pretty much like hard labor – lifting him out of bed, laying him carefully on the floor making sure his head doesn't flop back and strike the carpet too hard, unfastening the tabs of his urine-heavy diaper and putting on a fresh one, stretching his arms and legs (his leg abductors are very tight, his arms tend to pull tightly to his chest), holding his arms straight while you put on his T-shirt, then his shirt, holding that long board of his body pressing against your chest while you try to reach down to pull his jeans up, then put on his socks, his AFOs, his tennis shoes. You could be serving time, but the term of the sentence is not definite but looks to extend into your fifties and sixties – as long as your body holds up. For there is no possibility of change. People ask, "But he will walk some day … ?" And you feel, ridiculously, that you must put the painful news gently to them, to protect them from the naked truth a little, when you reply, "I am afraid there's not much chance of improvement at this stage of the game. Right now, the big thing is to find a muscle group that Ian can reliably control to link up with a computer. Even that seems a bit of a long shot." They look at you curiously, wondering how a father can live with such diminished expectations.

I would tell them that it's best to live without expectations, that expectations can get you into trouble. I would tell them not to pray for my son's healing, for I exhausted that route years ago. If you want, give me a hand, or better, help some single mom struggling to raise her disabled child on a small paycheck and too little sleep. Life, I've learned, is not theoretical, but a practicum. It's a hands-on affair in which the heart counts a good deal more than the intellect.

I am suspicious of generalizations, but not the one above. Likewise, I would add that a disabled child is a curriculum. I would never have chosen to wear sackcloth in this life or to go about like a Jain with a small broom to keep from treading on insects. But you learn a certain humility when a long-haired streetperson in Louisville wearing a torn Chicago Bulls T-shirt comes up to you and offers you and your son sixty-three cents. (This happens so frequently you wonder if you should get a beggar's bowl.) And surely you must acquire some compassion for all creatures when you look down at your son who is pinioned to the floor by a one-g force and his own dysfunctional body and can scarcely lift his head. In my judgment, there's no great leap from this realization and becoming a vegetarian. Aren't we all one body?

This is the work that isn't hard labor, the work of the heart, the soul, if you prefer. This is the work that takes place in the cell of your solitude, and makes every mother's son of us a desert father. When Ian was born almost thirteen years ago now, I had yet to learn my catechism. I was a poet who wanted to speak for the American wilderness, I was a scholar of Old English who had translated *Beowulf* and fancied he knew something of "the bitter ale of mortality." I was a husband, but a reluctant father. I worried about how a baby would distract me from my life's work.

It seems like one of those too-obvious parables now that in the early summer of 1983 I was awaiting both the arrival of my first child and my first book of poems. One was the spontaneous accomplishment of my wife's and my wedded life energies, the creative zeal of our genes, if you will, the work of a mere nine months, and the other was the result of an arduous ten-year labor with language. Ian, my son, arrived first, delivered unto Omak, Washington, via a crash C-section, born post-term, stippled with meconium and wheezing. His Apgar was 2; Ian was a blue, anoxic neonate, but to us, astonishingly beautiful, with eyes that seemed preternaturally luminous and wise.

He was flown by Life-Bird helicopter to Sacred Heart Hospital in Spokane, to its well-equipped NICU, from which we received various intelligences via telephone of his seizure-racked body and hemorrhaging brain. Pure nightmare, a full draft of grief and then some. When, a week later, the box of spanking-new books arrived from the University of Massachusetts Press (*Afterlight* in flowing red uncials on a gray-green background) it lay unopened several days while we went to fetch Ian home from the hospital. First things first.

Thereby was the new-born father taught that life weighed infinitely more than art in the balance of his affections. (Or, in Marxist terms, the biological preceded the cultural.) Often, in those first months of his compromised life, I chafed mightily against that knowledge, but that baby who couldn't grip my hand held my heart in a hammerlock.

That knowledge was absolute, instantaneous gnosis. As soon as I heard that baby's stifled birth-cry and willed him with all my might to live, I knew he was my fate. I was his, he was mine: fatherhood. An Aristotelian anagnorisis. But other, correlative knowledge came slowly, reluctantly.

Despite the anoxia, the seizures and hemorrhages, Ian came home to us after two weeks. Dr. Bodenstein, the intense young neonatologist who had labored over Ian that first long night, professed he was leery. Ian had made an all but miraculous recovery but the "neurological insult" he'd suffered could manifest itself at any time.

Despite all expectations, Ian throve those first few months. He sucked lustily, he grew, he smiled, the P.T. gave us a thumbs up at his three-month check-up. For a brief while we lived in a beautiful dream of normalcy. Our "bear's son," our little "coal-biter," had beaten the odds! He'd fought death and come out the stronger! What was the kid going to do when he grew up? He'd show Bodenstein, that's what! Ha!

Then, on our visit to my parents at Christmastime, he developed an implacable seizure disorder. On Christmas Day, 1983, he was admitted to Tallahassee Memorial Hospital as "status epilepticus." "Infantile spasms" was the eventual diagnosis. The disorder is associated with "salaam seizures" – the baby drops its head, its face sags into a sorrow's mask, and the child jackknifes repeatedly (Ian's record was forty-one times). It has a very high correlation with profound mental retardation.

We flew back to Seattle, drove back to our trailer in eastern Washington near Nespelem, all the while those seizures laying siege to our baby's body. Phenolbarb, dilantin, clonapin – we tried a varied menu of depressants with imperfect results. Ian's eyes remained clouded, as did his future. Now came for me the most difficult soul-work. Bodenstein's dismal prognostication that first night over the phone – "cerebral palsy plus or minus mental retardation" – was coming true. Helen seemed to have reserves of courage and love that I lacked. All I saw was three stunted lives. Away and away before us stretched the endless Sisyphusean labor of parenting a dependent who could never grow up or so much as lift a spoon to his lips. I lived in a torment of grief and self-pity. Only a few months before my life had seemed so full of possibility. I'd had a plan of writing a birth-poem, something in the vein of Whitman's "There Was a Child Went Forth" – an open-ended catalogue of all the glories my child might discover there in his natal country of the Okanogan – sage and yarrow and the great yellow balsamroot, the azure flash of the magpie, the red-tailed hawk, yellow-crested kingbirds – the joy of consciousness encountering light and all its dependents for the first time.

What to make of a diminished thing?

Tight-lipped, I set down a journal of spare little poems marking the progress of winter:

February 14

After Ian's shot this morning
I drove to the head of Panama Canyon,
poured coffee from my blue
thermos, watched mist
rising off scree.

Two starlings
warbling harshly
tseer tseeer
perched in the near ponderosa
and I noticed
a sprig of yarrow
under the ice.

Valentine's Day
and my wife bathes our son
careful of his sore thigh.

It's true
the world wounds us
in our most tender parts.

But the journal also marked moments of light, of comprehension. Ian was far from an insensate lump of flesh – whatever his intellectual gifts or physical abilities, he appeared deeply sensitive to me. He watched things carefully with his eyes, he smiled, he chortled with pleasure – he responded lovingly to the world. More than once, I thought of that precocious boy, John Keats, and one of his more famous letters – *whereby this Chamber of Maiden Though becomes gradually darkened and at the same time on all sides of it many doors are set open –but all dark – all leading to dark passages. . . . We are in a Mist –We are now in that state – We feel the "burden of the Mystery."*

The room was darkening, no question, but it had also seemed that before Ian's birth I had been a somewhat untested creature, my soul, at best, half-made, "an unlicked bear" as the Dutch might say. An alchemist might say that my soul hadn't been placed in the crucible yet. Whatever, I began to push against the depression, and the poems helped me to clarify and consolidate whatever small gains I made:

April 5

At 37, I no longer write
of wounded ridges,
the sea's autism. I've exhausted
the reticence of stones, my cormorants,
the clumsy symbols, take wing.
The man obsessed
with a broken world
may himself need some healing.
I leave off combing the hills
for the blue flower, hybrid
of the iris and camas root.
Now I drive to Sacred Heart
with my wife and injured son.
I count the marsh hawks
along a hundred miles of windy
plateau. It is enough
to pray well for one child.

Somewhere Theodore Roethke wrote that the spirit's progress is glacially slow, akin to that frog in the math conundrum that makes its way up the slippery well, three up and two back. In those early days, it seemed to me that I was backsliding rather than making any progress. My grief was a kind of stupor from which I would erupt occasionally with histrionic gestures.

It amazes me now that we survived Ian's first year, Helen and Ian and I, Ian with his seizures, his ACTH injections that raised his blood pressure to perilously high levels, Helen and I, who had to deal too often with the more noisy infant of my developing soul.

There is a gender difference, which I am sure has been investigated and duly subjected to statistical analysis, between how men and women typically respond to their child's disability. Mothers often sacrifice themselves on the altars of their children's broken bodies, while fathers, like as not, bail out. I know of many mothers who are raising their brain-injured children alone; I don't know one father in a similar predicament. In some cases, there is violence. Sometime in early 1984, I heard Paul Harvey relate a story about a young veterinarian attending his son's birth. The child was delivered obviously deformed. Before the doctor or nurse could respond, the father picked up his new-born and dashed him to the floor. The terrible irony that Harvey fastened on was that child's deformity was a cleft lip, which could be corrected by surgery. But that raw, ungovernable impulse is probably shared by most parents of profoundly injured children. They are feelings as deep as instinct and human DNA. They too were part of the grief-bundle fate handed me with Ian. I had always believed myself a kind person, and now there were monstrous longings in me that made me seem a stranger to my own self. How could I civilize this stranger and recover that gentle self I knew was me?

Alone I couldn't do it. This same event which demolished my frail belief in a personal, caring deity has slowly developed my faith in human community and its spiritual resources. In the communities where we have lived since Ian's birth – in Nespelem, Washington, in Green Bay, Wisconsin, and now in Crawfordsville, Indiana, there are tremendous reserves of kindness and consideration for families such as ours.

Perhaps the most remarkable story of this sort happened in the Spring of '84 while Ian was still undergoing ACTH injections to control his infantile spasms. We were by this time the sole caretakers of several trailers of an abandoned archaeology camp. We had no neighbors, no callers. But on this particular evening in early April, someone knocked at our door.

A slender, fortyish, dark-haired man in a clerical collar, Father Dick Mercy, introduced himself. He had come from Spokane, from the Rineharts, some folks we'd met over the phone who had gone through the ACTH routine with their toddler son. We had talked about their loaning us a sphygmomanometer, a blood pressure cuff, to monitor Ian's blood pressure. And here was Father Dick Mercy, S.J., whose parish was the Colville Indian Reservation, come to give us some solace and say a healing prayer for Ian. As Helen held Ian before her, Dick lay his hands on Ian's head and said these words –

And I joined him, asking for the logos-light to enter Ian and repair the damaged neurons.

I often think of the power of priestly office because of Dick Mercy's visit. He came to our army surplus trailer there in the empty archaeology camp, a stranger stepping out of the twilight and laying his hands on our sick infant. He took us by surprise, and caught us, therefore, more credulous. For those moments, I was one of the faithful.

It almost seemed too much, too strident a proof of the power of prayer that the next day we saw no evidence of the salaam seizures, and that they never, ever returned again.

Over the next few months, I visited Dick several times in his quarters at St. Mary's in Nespelem. During one conversation, he told me of a young tribal woman, Peggy Disautel, who wanted to get together with us. She had a Down's child, a boy of nine, and knew something of what we were going through.

Peggy had us over to her house, a small ranch house just north of town. She was a sturdily built young woman with a quiet, intent manner. While Dick played ball out in the street with her son, she served us coffee and we talked. Talked of our children, our fears and uncertainties. Peggy was maybe twenty-seven, younger than we by several years, but our senior in parenthood. In addition to Dallas, she had two younger daughters who would peek out at us now and again and then return to their yelps and giggles in their bedroom. She told us her story – of the original diagnosis of Dallas's condition and how she didn't know what it meant. Perhaps he seemed a little slow, but she denied there was anything wrong with him. Slowly he taught her what Down's meant, the difficulty with learning language, the awkwardness, but not the frailty – for Dallas was a strong, healthy child. She feared obsessively for him and tried to protect him as much as possible. Then one day, going to fetch him at the playground, she saw that a group of children were surrounding him, taunting his slowness. He stood there, red-faced, unable to speak, while the children jeered at him. She wanted to rush to him and scoop him up in her arms, but something made her hold back, watching. Then a small boy who had been silent spoke up. He said that there was nothing wrong with Dallas, that they were the ones with a problem. It was their turn to fall silent and be ashamed. The anxious young mother watched all this and was comforted. With such unlooked-for kindness, her son, she felt, could negotiate the tough moments he would face.

Throughout our conversation, Ian had remained fretful. Peggy asked if she might hold him. When he didn't settle down, Peggy asked, "Do you bind him?" She meant, in a bundling cloth.

"No," Helen replied.

"May I bind him then? It often helps the little ones relax."

Helen smiled and nodded.

So Peggy fetched a purple bundling cloth and carefully laced Ian into it. As she did so, she observed how big his shoulders were and how well he was made. Soon he quieted and we went on talking, sharing our lives.

As we got into our car, she suddenly came forward and stood by my window and peered in at us, urgently, as if to protect us from the brunt of our anxieties. She said with quiet conviction, "He is going to have a good life. Not half your fears for him will come true. I am sure he will surprise you with his accomplishments." And she handed me the bundling cloth. "Please. I want you to have this. He may sleep better, if you lace him into it." The gift unlooked for, the unexpected kindness, the bundling cloth, the cup of coffee, a young woman's wisdom words – these balance the harsh contingencies, the irresistible connivances of chance.

Some have found in God that moderation of immoderate loss. In Nespelem, on the Rez in 1984, I found it in Father Mercy and Peggy Disautel. Perhaps they were agents of providence. I suppose the clarified soul has a marked propensity to align itself with the divine will. I lack the authority to speak with insight of these mysteries. But their acts did possess for Helen and me that "quality of mercy" which as Portia avers, "droppeth as the gentle rain from heaven / Upon the place beneath." We were consoled.

I still have an Anglo-Saxon's sense of the obdurate nature of things. Fate will exact its pound of flesh. But the hard work the heart has is not to harden with those inevitable blows; but, rather, to soften, to grow tender.

For me, it all comes back to my son. He is my soul's curriculum vita, the most challenging employment I have had in this life. And what I have learned in my line of work is wonderfully simple: to stay in this moment with a kind and clear attention. Grief is useless, expectation is useless. Only the clear, compassionate eye focused on this world with all its griefs and joys. The great teachers teach this – Gautama Buddha smiling, holding up the flower, Jesus washing the feet of his disciples. Dick Mercy and Peggy Disautel were for me the local teachers of this knowledge that bitter spring of '84. And, always, now each day my wife and children.

Louise Erdrich

from
THE BLUE JAY'S DANCE:
A BIRTH YEAR

Most of the instruction given to pregnant women is as chirpy and condescending as the usual run of maternity clothes – the wide tops with droopy bows slung beneath the neck, the T-shirts with arrows pointing to what can't be missed, the childish sailor collars, puffed sleeves, and pastels. It is cute advice: what to pack in the hospital bag (don't forget a toothbrush, deodorant, comb, or hair dryer). Or it's worse: pseudo-spiritual, misleading, silly, and even cruel. In giving birth to my daughters, I have found it impossible to eliminate the pain through breathing by focusing on a soothing photograph. It is true *pain* one is attempting to endure in drugless labor, not discomfort, and the way to deal with pain is not to call it something else but to increase in strength, to prepare the will. Women are strong, strong, terribly strong. We don't know how strong we are until we're pushing out our babies. We are too often treated like babies having babies when we should be in training, like acolytes, novices to high priestess-hood, like serious applicants for the space program.

Pali

SUMANGALA'S MOTHER

A free woman. At last free!
Free from slavery in the kitchen
where I walked back and forth stained
and squalid among cooking pots.
My brutal husband ranked me lower
than the shade he sat in.
Purged of anger and the body's hunger,
I live in meditation
in my own shade from a broad tree.
I am at ease.

translated by Willis Barnstone

ARTS, CRAFTS &
HANDWORK

Mimbres Pot

Craft "is not just a representation," D.M. Dooling says, "but an actual rearrangement of the flow and order of energy."[1] This means, of course, that what we work at makes a difference, changing, however slightly, the balance of our world. No matter that we may never get it quite right; the smallest glint of beauty in what we compose tells us that there *is* a right, and that our craft is our struggle to embody it.

Perhaps we also realize that even as we haltingly tend to our work something in it is tending to us. *Vocation,* I'm thinking: In every such moment the Master is there, calling out from inside of our labor. Jesus' call to Peter and Andrew, for example: "Follow me, and I will make you fishers of men." This is a call not to abandon craft but to deepen it, to go to its source.

When I teach poetry these days I sometimes end with Adrienne Rich's poem "Transcendental Étude," a poem about (among many other things) craft. The craft's gift, the poem says, does not concern performance, brilliance, competitiveness. "We aren't virtuosi / or child prodigies, there are no prodigies / in this realm, only a half-blind stubborn / cleaving to the timbre, the tones of what we are / —

even when all the texts describe it differently." The craft is about "[t]he woman who sits watching, listening, / eyes moving in the darkness."[2] It is about attending, *ad-tendere*, a steady stretching toward, paying attention to a stillness in the air, something deep under the water. We become like deer, head up, alert to the slightest movement. But what we are attending to is not visible. There is, apparently, nothing there: a girl jumping rope. A slight wind rustling the leaves.

Perhaps this steady listening is the beginning of craft, as it is of the arts in general. (The *Oxford English Dictionary* confirms the ancient kinship between craft and art, which for a time were essentially synonymous, both of them suggesting human – as opposed to natural – skill, and both of them thereby becoming associated with magic: witchcraft, the black arts.) Listening is itself the greatest of disciplines. It is that taut line of attention practiced most purely in the craft of prayer or meditation, where one's entire being becomes the instrument, and you know you are there for no other reason but to attend. Contemplation is the womb of craft; each of us has our moment as Mary, startled out of the silence by the Word suddenly leaping within us, salmon-like.

I read these lines from "Transcendental Étude" aloud, usually twice:

> But there come times – perhaps this is one of them –
> when we have to take ourselves more seriously or die;
> when we have to pull back from the incantations,
> rhythms we've moved to thoughtlessly,
> and disenthrall ourselves, bestow
> ourselves to silence, or a severer listening.

Of course, the poet reminds us, craft is not black magic; the truth is just the reverse. If the craft weaves a spell it does so to break the charm of those everyday rhythms. We must "disenthrall ourselves" by moving back to silence.

"Craftsmanship begins with disillusion," potter Carla Needleman writes. Perhaps we are first drawn to crafts looking for an easier, simpler life, seeking to reconnect body and mind, outside and inside. Instead, Needleman says, what comes is "a shattering self-discovery." The craft "may bring upon me the weighty knowledge that the inner life I am striving to express isn't there – that I have no access to an expressible inner life."[3]

This realization is shattering indeed: *I have, it seems, no way of getting there.* I believe something's there, can feel it as the deepest thing about me, but am at a loss as to how to reach it. Here, as Rich knows, is a tremendous solitude, "the pitch of utter loneliness" that comes with the "cutting away of an old force that held her / rooted to an old ground." Paradoxically, it is my faithfulness to the craft that has brought me to this rift.

Yet, Needleman continues, disillusion "is a sacred state" because through it I begin to see who I am. Even the flaws – perhaps especially the flaws – in my craftsmanship are revelatory: they speak loudly, boldly of me. This work "contradicts my ideas, my illusions of what I should be producing ... it wounds my self-love to see it. I think it should be better and so I suffer from it. But it is me. It *could* not be better – I have worked as well as I could, not very well but as well as I could, and this object is the only possible truthful representation of that work."4

Craft is not, Needleman and Rich suggest, simply an issue of technique; it is also a matter of attention. How well do I listen? How courageous am I? How *long* can I go on listening?

To see myself honestly is, under normal circumstances, the last thing in the world I want, and is certainly the last thing society teaches me to want. And yet the work itself pulls me in like a lover. Beauty does it to me – something in the sound of words, the sound of the world tonight that I want to manifest in the words. I go back over these pages, revising the lines, listening to my words and to the silence from which they came, trying to stay in touch with something, or trying to grow towards it, grow *into* it. A new seriousness enters, a commitment. And if it continues long enough I shall find that I have truly become married to this work. I discover that I want this way of being more than anything else in the world. Indeed I could almost say that without it I would die.

Disillusion begins by dividing me from my tendency to identify with a dream, that elusive image of myself that usually gets dispelled as soon as I settle down to work. The image, the mood, is as easy and light as air. It sets me going – and then the going gets tough. I fall in love, but soon enough I begin to suffer from the discrepancy between what I imagined and what I actually do every day. And disillusion quickly grows into despair. I cannot endure how poorly my work compares with that glory I thought I'd wedded. I begin to think that I'm not worthy enough, talented enough, courageous – or crazy enough – to continue.

It's the difference between imagining the view from the mountaintop, and even imagining the climb – clear skies, a picnic lunch, and Mt. Adams, Mt. Hood, Mt. St. Helens all in the distance – and the actual climb itself, one long step after another.

I must, it seems, learn to attend even to my own suffering. Rather than fleeing, I must wait upon it, believe in its significance in spite of everything, because it alone is now the connection to my own depths. The suffering I endure is precisely the distance I feel between me and this Beloved. If I cease to feel this pain it does not mean that the distance is gone; more likely it means I have stopped paying attention to it. In the loss of pain I will have lost the thread that leads me out of my pain.

In a sense it doesn't matter how "good" my work is in the eyes of others, or even to myself, because in working I have reached the place where I know I must be – which, of course, isn't a place at all; it's more like a *way*. How I know this I cannot explain, except to say that my suffering – and my joy – tells me this is so. It is certainly not because of the greatness of my work; more likely it is due to what is still missing. In fact the importance of the work lies in its ability to remind me again and again how far from finished I am. It is often my one thin line home.

Or, as the Sufis say: hunger itself is my food.

And so I work and I wait, and my work is my waiting. In attending to my work

I remain connected invisibly to what I know mostly by its absence. It is my faith-fulness to something I cannot see, cannot name, but nevertheless believe has claimed me for its own. I keep the lamp filled with oil as I await the return of the Bridegroom. I become Penelope, weaving by day and unweaving by night, year after year covering and uncovering the same empty space on the page as a way to remain faithful to the one who's missing. And of course every morning the despair returns; it whispers in my ear *you're going nowhere with this, and you're not getting any younger . . .*

Failure stretches us, Needleman writes. I am brought low, humbled, and yet para-doxically find myself more intact than before. "And," she adds, "I find a new strength in myself coming from an unsuspected place, a new and very different sin-cerity that makes it possible to go on. It feels like the sensation of obedience, al-though I couldn't say what it is I am beginning to feel obedient to. It may be that what I perceive as obedience . . . is the first thread of real connectedness, relation-ship with the movement of energies both within me and in the world."[5]

Annie Kahn, a Navaho medicine woman, similarly speaks of her attention to her craft as a kind of obedience to the world around her. "Know what you are doing," she tells her interviewers. "You came here, *zooom*, you know. But the trees were looking for you because I told them to. Because they are of me. The moun-tains were looking for you. The flowers . . . They knew you were coming. But you did not relate to them. *Those* are the ones that do the healing."[6]

"We cut the wires," Rich writes, "find ourselves in free-fall." But what we cut is our enchantment to the "rhythms we've moved to thoughtlessly." We cut away our old sense of who we are, and our old sense of a world as unrelated to us. In thrall to the everyday I might endlessly wonder where the real magic in my life could be. But – fortunately, gracefully – I'm always called back. It's there even in writing these lines, as I skim through a few pages in Soetsu Yanagi's *The Unknown Craftsman*, where I read that "the Sung dynasty pottery of China reveals a beauty that is forever new. . . . It is like a fountainhead from which one may draw water a thousand times and still find fresh water springing forth. Its beauty belongs, in the words of Jesus, to the realm of 'I am,' not to that of 'I have been,' 'I was,' or 'I shall be.'"[7] In this and a thousand other places I hear the voices whispering from the silence: *Just what do you think you're doing?*

There come times . . . when we have to take ourselves more seriously or die. This is not hy-perbole. Listen to Blake: "If you who are organized by Divine Providence for Spiritual communion. Refuse & bury your Talent in the Earth even tho you should want Natural Bread. Sorrow & Desperation pursues you thro life! & after death shame & confusion of face to eternity."[8]

Just what do you think you're doing?

It's another day. I'm home alone for a few hours, stretching myself in the unex-pected solitude. For a few more minutes I stray from my revisions while I make myself a cup of tea and carry it outside to the warm steps. As I move away from the cool shelter of the house hundreds of songs seem ready to burst forth from the air around me, all conjured up by the power of sunlight and the smell of dry pine. Something's clamoring again to fly, to dive deep. I listen to the noon bells from St. Joseph's, remembering some familiar, if ironic words from Lao-tzu: He who knows doesn't speak; he who speaks doesn't know. Perhaps, I'm thinking, I speak in order to know.

We must choose, Yeats claimed, between perfection of the life and perfection of the craft. Since so little in life seems clear to me it's pleasant to feel how certain I am about my disagreement with this statement. Yeats's desire to divorce his work from his life reminds me too much of a model from which I'm trying to break away, a model created by a society that sent men (and increasingly women) out from their homes and communities to do "work" that involved the individual hardly at all. Work for many ceased to involve craft, and at that moment, I suspect, ceased to make possible the transformation of the individual. Instead, in the separation of our deeper selves from our work we end up creating little more than a professional persona. And if, God forbid, you *have* no such work, or your work is deemed trivial, then you cease to *be* much of a person. Without this mask of a profession you become invisible.

"Yeats" for me has been the heroic persona of the poems. But what of the man who suffered these poems, who lived them into birth, who died? What has the craft done for this man?

"Vision begins to happen," Rich concludes, "as if a woman quietly walked away / from the argument and jargon in a room / and sitting down in the kitchen, began turning in her lap / bits of yarn, calico, and velvet scraps, / laying them out absently on the scrubbed boards." There in the kitchen she attends to the small, neglected details of life, "the finest findings," out of which she will make something of herself, something composed from the bits and pieces of her home, her neighborhood. "Such a composition," the poet continues, "has nothing to do with eternity, / the striving for greatness, brilliance —"

> only with the musings of a mind
> one with her body, experienced fingers quietly pushing
> dark against bright, silk against roughness,
> pulling the tenets of a life together
> with no mere will to mastery,
> only care for the many-lived, unending
> forms in which she finds herself,
> becoming now the shard of broken glass
> slicing light in a corner, dangerous
> to flesh, now the plentiful, soft leaf
> that wrapped around the throbbing finger, soothes the wound;
> and now the stone foundation, rockshelf further
> forming underneath everything that grows.

"Vision begins to happen." With a final glance at the summer day I duck back inside, back out of the light, back to work again.

Navajo

---

from
DINÉ BAHANE
The Navajo Creation Story

The descendants of *Áłtsé hastiin* the First Man and *Áłtsé asdzą́ą́* the First Woman established a great farm. They built a dam and dug a wide irrigation canal. They feared that the *Kiis'áanii* might destroy their dam, though, or that they might injure the crops. So they put one of the nonchildbearing *nádleeh* in charge of the dam. And they bid the other twin guard the lower end of the field.

With nothing else to do, the hermaphrodite twin who watched the dam invented pottery. First he made a plate. Then he made a bowl. Then he made a ladle. And the people all admired the work he had done. They knew at once how useful those implements would be.

As for the twin who stood guard over the lower field, he too had time enough and skill enough to design something useful. So he invented the wicker bottle. The people all admired what he had done, too, for they could see immediately how useful that implement would be.

Others among the people made scythes out of split cottonwood boards which they used to clear the land. Still others made hoes from the shoulder blades of deer. And others made axes out of stone. From the *Kiis'áanii* the people got seeds. And so they flourished as people who farmed the earth.

Lao-tzu

TAOTECHING #11

Thirty spokes converge on a hub
but it's the emptiness
that makes a wheel work
pots are fashioned from clay
but it's the hollow
that makes a pot work
windows and doors are carved for a house
but it's the spaces
that make a house work
existence makes something useful
nonexistence makes it work

translated by Red Pine

M. C. Richards

CENTERING AS DIALOGUE
from *Centering in Pottery, Poetry and the Person*

CENTERING: that act which precedes all others on the potter's wheel. The bringing of the clay into a spinning, unwobbling pivot, which will then be free to take innumerable shapes as potter and clay press against each other. The firm, tender, sensitive pressure which yields as much as it asserts. It is like a handclasp between two living hands, receiving the greeting at the very moment that they give it. It is this speech between the hand and the clay that makes me think of dialogue. And it is a language far more interesting than the spoken vocabulary which tries to describe it, for it is spoken not by the tongue and lips but by the whole body, by the whole person, speaking and listening. And with listening too, it seems to me, it is not the ear that hears, it is not the physical organ that performs that act of inner receptivity. It is the total person who hears. Sometimes the skin seems to be the best listener, as it prickles and thrills, say to a sound or a silence; or the fantasy, the imagination: how it bursts into inner pictures as it listens and then responds by pressing its language, its forms, into the listening clay. To be open to what we hear, to be open in what we say ...

There is a joke that always amuses me whenever I think of it. You may know it too. A man and woman have stayed happily married for years. Nobody can understand how they do it. Everybody else is getting divorced or separated – suffering the agonies of marital estrangement. A friend asks the husband of the lucky pair how they have been able to make a go of it. What's the secret of their success? "Oh," answers the husband, "it's very simple. We simply divide up the household problems. My wife makes all the minor decisions and I make all the major decisions. No friction!" "I see," says the friend, "and what are the minor decisions your wife makes, for example; and the major decisions, which are they?" "Well," answers the husband, "my wife makes all the little decisions like where shall we send our son to college, shall we sell the house, should we renew our medical insurance, and, uh ... and then I take the big ones: like Should Red China Join the United Nations, Should the United States Disarm Unilaterally, Is Peace Possible ...?"

I think this is a good joke because it takes a warm and humorous view of what is exactly the task of a marriage: a marriage of one person with another, or a marriage within one person of what seem to be separate concerns, and yet unless both are managed well, one's life or one's marriage tends to be wobbly indeed. Craftsmen live with a special immediacy in the double realms of these concerns: the questions of technique and the questions of meaning. Where shall I attach the handle to this pitcher? Shall I decorate this surface or let the clay stand clean? How thin? How thick? as well as What is a potter? What is the relation of pottery to poetry? What is the meaning of impermanence? When is a pot not a pot? What is freedom? What is originality? Are there rules?

I will now act as husband and wife to these dilemmas. I will answer these questions:

Where should I attach the handle to this pitcher? The question here lies in the "should." What does it mean, "should"? What kind of handle do I *want?* I don't know, I don't know. What does it mean, "I don't know"? It means that there are many different kinds of considerations, and I don't know how to satisfy them all. I want the handle to be strong enough to support the weight of the pitcher when it is filled. I want to be able to get my hand through it. I want it to be placed so that it does not weaken the wall and crack the pot, and so that the balance of the pitcher is good in pouring. I want it to make a beautiful total shape. I want it to be my handle at the same time that I want to please my customer, my friends, my critics, whomever. And in another impulse I don't care about any of these things: I want it to be a complete surprise. Poetry often enters through the window of irrelevance. So if the handle does not satisfy any of the above requirements, the pot may have a certain marvelous charm, an original image: a cracked pitcher that carries in it the magic of the self-forgetful impulse which in a rage of joy and irreverence stuck the handle on in something of the spirit in which we pin the tail on the donkey blindfolded. A glee, an energy, that escapes from all those questions-and-answers, thumbs its nose, stands on the ridgepole, and crows like a cock for its own dawning.

What is it all about? These different moods sweep through us. How much authority should we give them? To be solemn to be merry to be chaste to be voluptuous to be reserved to be prodigal to be elegant to be vulgar to be tasteful to be tasteless to be useful to be useless to be something to be nothing to be alive is to live in this weather.

A pot should this, and a pot should that — I have little patience with these prescriptions. I cannot escape paradox when I look deep into things, in the crafts as well as in poetry in metaphysics or in physics. In physics, matter is immaterial. The physical world, it turns out, is invisible, inaudible, immeasurable; supersensible and unpredictable. Law exists; and yet freedom is possible. In metaphysics, life and death in the commonplace sense collaborate in rhythms which sustain life. The birth of the new entails the death of the old, change; and yet the old does not literally die, it lives on, transformed. In ancient mystery religions, initiation for life required a ritual death. In poetry, in metaphor which is its instrument, the opposites also fuse: for example, I once wrote a very short poem, in the style of the Japanese haiku. It was entitled "Snow." And it went like this:

> White moths in crazy mobs
> hunt everywhere
> the flame of the winter sun.

Why do I write about moths and call the poem "Snow"? Snow is crystalline mineral inert. Moths are alive, fluttering, impelled. The snow melts in the sun, dies. Turns to water, symbol of life. In the swirling snow I see the realm of life, not with my senses but with what you might call my supersenses: supersensible life. Life seeking life, the sun. Seeking light. The cold seeking the warm. The instinct seeking its transformation. Physical weather as the image of the dance of life; the quest, even in the heart of winter, the glorious sun making us ecstatic to burn ourselves alive in its energy, to worship at the center.

At the center. Pottery as metaphysics. Centering. How all these thoughts and experiences create a sense of an enormous cosmic unity, a sense of a quiet inner unity, a unity within me, child of that vast single god-sea, that unity, wherein we swim. In pottery, as my first teacher Robert Turner said, the toughest thing to learn comes at the very beginning, if you are learning to throw on the potter's wheel. The centering of the clay. It took me seven years before I could, with certainty, center any given piece of clay. Another person might center the clay the first time he sat down to it. His task then might be to allow the centered clay to live into a form which it would itself declare. My task was to learn how to bring in the flying images, how to keep from falling in love with a mistake, how to bring the images in, down, up, smoothly, centered, and then to allow them the kind of breath they cannot have if all they know how to be is passionate or repressed.

But of course we have to be passionate. That is to say, when we are, we must be able to be. We must be able to let the intensity – the Dionysian rapture and disorder and the celebration of chaos, of potentiality, the experience of surrender – we must be able to let it live in our bodies, in our hands, through our hands into the materials we work with. I sense this: that we must be steady enough in ourselves, to be open and to let the winds of life blow through us, to be our breath, our inspiration; to breathe with them, mobile and soft in the limberness of our bodies, in our agility, our ability, as it were, to dance, and yet to stand upright, to be intact, to be persons. We come to know ourselves, and others, through the images we create in such moods. These images are disclosures of ourselves to ourselves. They are life-revelations. If we can stay "on center" and look with clear-seeing eyes and compassionate hearts at what we have done, we may advance in self-knowledge and in knowledge of our materials and of the world in its larger concerns.

The creative spirit creates with whatever materials are present. With food, with children, with building blocks, with speech, with thoughts, with pigment, with an umbrella, or a wineglass, or a torch. We are not craftsmen only during studio hours. Any more than a man is wise only in his library. Or devout only in church. The material is not the sign of the creative feeling for life: of the warmth and sympathy and reverence which foster being; techniques are not the sign; "art" is not the sign. The sign is the light that dwells within the act, whatever its nature or its medium.

Craft, as you may know, comes from the German word *Kraft,* meaning "power" or "strength." As Emerson said, the law is: "Do the thing, and you shall have the power. But they who do not the thing, have not the powers." We can't fake craft. It lies in the act. The strains we have put in the clay break open in the fire. We do not have the craft, or craftsmanship, if we do not speak to the light that lives within the earthly materials; this means ALL earthly materials, including men themselves.

There is a wonderful legend in Jewish Hasidism that in the beginning when God poured out his grace, man was not able to stand firm before the fullness and the vessels broke and sparks fell out of them into all things. And shells formed around them. By our hallowing, we may help to free these sparks. They lie everywhere, in our tools, in our food, in our clothes ... A kind of radiance, an emanation, a freedom, something that fills our hearts with joy and gratitude no matter how it may strike our judgment! There is something within man that seeks this joy. That knows this joy. Joy is different from happiness. I am not talking about happiness. I am talking about joy. How, when the mind stops its circling, we say YES, YES to what we behold.

Another picture from which I draw inspiration: Robert Turner, sitting at the potter's wheel in our shop at Black Mountain College, giving a demonstration. He was centering the clay, and then he was opening it and pulling up the walls of the cylinder. He was not looking at the clay. He had his ear to it. He was listening. "It is breathing," he said; and then he filled it with air.

There are many marvelous stories of potters in ancient China. In one of them a noble is riding through a town and he passes a potter at work. He admires the pots the man is making: their grace and a kind of rude strength in them. He dismounts from his horse and speaks with the potter. "How are you able to form these vessels so that they possess such convincing beauty?" "Oh," answers the potter, "you are looking at the mere outward shape. What I am forming lies within. I am interested only in what remains after the pot has been broken."

It is not the pots we are forming, but ourselves. That is the husband's concern. The wife's: Will it hold water? Can I cook in it?

In a book entitled *Zen Flesh Zen Bones,* there is a section called "Centering." The editor, Paul Reps, tells us it is a transcription of ancient Sanskrit manuscripts. It presents teaching, still alive in Kashmir and parts of India after more than four thousand years, that may well be the roots of Zen Buddhism. The editor, plainly reserving for himself the major questions, ends his introduction with these words: "The problem of our mind, relating conscious to preconscious awareness, takes us deep into everyday living. Dare we open our doors to the source of our being? What are flesh and bones for?"

I am a question-asker and a truth-seeker. I do not have much in the way of status in my life, nor security. I have been on quest, as it were, from the beginning. For a long time I thought there was something wrong with me: no ambition, no interest in tenure, always on the march, changing every seven years, from landscape to landscape. Certain elements were constant: the poetry, the desire for relationship, the sense of voyage. But lately I have developed also a sense of destination, or destiny. And a sense that if I am to be on quest, I must expect to live like a pilgrim; I must keep to the inner path. I must be able to be whoever I am.

For example, it seemed strange to me, as to others, that, having taken my Ph.D. in English, I should then in the middle of my life, instead of taking up a college professorship, turn to the art of pottery. During one period, when people asked me what I did, I was uncertain what to answer; I guessed I could say I taught English, wrote poetry, and made pottery. What was my occupation? I finally gave up and said "Person."

Having been imbued with the ordinary superstitions of American higher education, among which is the belief that something known as the life of the mind is more apt to take you where you want to go than any other kind of life, I busied myself with learning to practice logic, grammar, analysis, summary, generalization; I learned to make distinctions, to speculate, to purvey information. I was educated to be an intellectual of the verbal type. I might have been a philosophy major, a literature major, a language major. I was always a kind of oddball even in undergraduate circles, as I played kick-goal on the Reed College campus with President Dexter Keezer. And in graduate school, even more so. Examinations tended to make me merry, often seeming to me to be some kind of private game, some secret ritual compulsively played by the professors and the institution. I invariably became facetious in all the critical hours. All that solemnity for a few facts! I couldn't believe they were serious. But they were. I never quite understood it. But I loved the dream and the reality that lay behind those texts and in the souls of my teachers. I often felt like a kind of fraud, because I suspected that the knowledge I was acquiring and being rewarded for by academic diploma was wide wide of the truth I sensed to live somewhere, somewhere. I felt that I knew little of real importance; and when would the day come that others would realize it too, and I would be exposed? I have had dream after dream in which it turns out that I have not really completed my examinations for the doctorate and have them still to pass. And I sweat with anxiety. A sense of occupying a certain position without possessing the real thing: the deeper qualifications of wisdom and prophecy. But of course it was not the world who exposed me, it was my dreams. I do not know if I am a philosopher, but if philosophy is the love of wisdom, then I am a philosopher, because I love wisdom and that is why I love the crafts, because they are wise....

I took up pottery..., in a sense, by chance. Unforeseen opportunity joined with interest and readiness. Like teaching, not a consciously sought but surely a destined union. For the materials and processes of pottery spoke to me of cosmic presences and transformations quite as surely as the pots themselves enchanted me. Experiences of the plastic clay and the firing of the ware carried more than commonplace values. Joy resonated deep within me, and it has stirred these thoughts only slowly to the surface. I have come to feel that we live in a universe of spirit, which materializes and dematerializes grandly; all things seem to me to live, and all acts to contain meaning deeper than matter-of-fact; and the things we do with deepest love and interest compel us by the spiritual forces which dwell in them. This seems to me to be a dialogue of the visible and the invisible to which our ears are attuned.

There was, first of all, something in the nature of the clay itself. You can do very many things with it, push this way and pull that, squeeze and roll and attach and pinch and hollow and pile. But you can't do everything with it. You can go only so far and then the clay resists. To know ourselves by our resistances – this is a thought first expressed to me by the poet Charles Olson.

And so it is with persons. You can do very many things with us: push us together and pull us apart and squeeze us and roll us flat, empty us out and fill us up. You can surround us with influences, but there comes a point when you can do no more. The person resists, in one way or another (if it is only by collapsing, like the clay). His own will becomes active.

This is a wonderful moment, when one feels his will become active, come as a force into the total assemblage and dynamic intercourse and interpenetration of will impulses. When one stands like a natural substance, plastic but with one's own character written into the formula, ah, then one feels oneself part of the world, taking one's shape with its help – but a shape only one's own freedom can create.

And the centering of the clay, of which I have spoken. The opening of the form. And the firing of the pot. This experience has deep psychic reverberations: how the pot, which was originally plastic, sets into dry clay, brittle and fragile, and then by being heated to a certain temperature hardens into stone. By natural law as it were, it takes its final form. Ordeal by fire. Then, the form once taken, the pot may not last, the body may perish; but the inner form has been taken, and it cannot break in the same sense.

I, like everyone I know, am instinctively motivated toward symbols of wholeness. What is a simpler, more natural one than the pot fired? Wholeness may be thought of as a kind of inner equilibrium, in which all our capacities have been brought into functioning as an organism. The potencies of the whole organism flow into the gestures of any part. And the sensation in any part reverberates throughout the soul. The unconscious and conscious levels of being can work together at the tasks of life, conveying messages to each other, assimilating one another. In wholeness I sense an integration of those characteristics which are uniquely ME and those interests which I share with the rest of mankind. As for example any bowl is symbolic of an archetypal circular form which I share with all, but which *I* make and which therefore contains those very qualities of myself which are active in the making. I believe that pots have the smell of the person who makes them: a smell of tenderness, of vanity or ambition, of ease and naturalness, of petulance, uncertainty, callousness, fussiness, playfulness, solemnity, exuberance, absentmindedness. The pot gives off something. It gives off its innerness, that which it holds but which cannot be seen.

In pottery, by developing sensitivity in manipulating natural materials by hand, I found a wisdom which had died out of the concepts I learned in the university: abstractions, mineralized and dead; while the minerals themselves were alive with energy and meaning. The life I found in the craft helped to bring to a new birth my ideals in education. Some secret center became vitalized in those hours of silent practice in the arts of transformation.

The experience of centering was one I particularly sought because I thought of myself as dispersed, interested in too many things. I envied people who were "single-minded," who had one powerful talent and who knew when they got up in the morning what it was they had to do. Whereas I, wherever I turned, felt the enchantment: to the window for the sweetness of the air; to the door for the passing figures; to the teapot, the typewriter, the knitting needles, the pets, the pottery, the newspaper, the telephone. Wherever I looked, I could have lived.

It took me half my life to come to believe I was okay even if I did love experience in a loose and undiscriminating way and did not know for sure the difference between good and bad. My struggles to accept my nature were the struggles of centering. I found myself at odds with the propaganda of our times. One is supposed to be either an artist or a homemaker, by one popular superstition. Either a teacher or a poet, by a theory which says that poetry must not sermonize. Either a craftsman or an intellectual, by a snobbism which claims either hand or head as the seat of true power. One is supposed to concentrate and not to spread oneself thin, as the jargon goes. And this is a jargon spoken by a cultural leadership from which it takes time to win one's freedom, if one is not lucky enough to have been born free. Finally, I hit upon an image: a seed-sower. Not to worry about which seeds sprout. But to give them as my gift in good faith.

But in spite of my self-acceptance, I still clung to a concept of purity which was chaste and aloof from the fellowship of man, and had yet to center the image of a pure heart in whose bright warm streams the world is invited to bathe. A heart who can be touched and who stirs in response, bringing the whole body into an act of greeting.

Well then, I became a potter.

And I found that the mute arts of the craftsman's world combine fruitfully with the verbal arts of the teacher or poet. For what is poetry anyway, and teaching? In order to teach, you must be able to listen. You must be able to hear what the person before you means. You cannot assume the meanings and be a teacher; you must enter again into a dialogue – with all senses alert to the human meanings expressed, however implicitly. The experience of the potter listening to his clay strengthens this capacity. One must be able to hear the inner questions, the unspoken ones; the inner hopes and misgivings and dreams and timidities and potentialities and stupidities. One must listen carefully in order to serve as a proper midwife to the birth of consciousness in the student. The world is always bigger than one's own focus. And as we bring ourselves into center wherever we are, the more of that world we can bring into service, the larger will be the capacity of our action and our understanding. The more sensitivity and courage I develop working with clay and water and mineral pigments and fire, the more helpful I can be to my Negro student from Panama who is taking freshman composition. All teachers should, as part of their class preparation, practice an art.

And the poetry. What is poetry: poetry is truth; and what is truth: truth is reality; and what is reality: reality is nature; and what is nature (you see what a good husband I am, asking all these Important Questions and answering them!): nature is life; and what is life: life is a death-dance; and what is a death-dance: a death-dance is the casting off of the corpse and the eating of the flame: the flame enters the womb, the green flame flickers in the seed, the new being is born, the next moment, the unfolding mystery. All the forces of the mineral world, in our skeleton as it were, all that salt and calcium and whatever it all is, want to grow rigid, want to congeal; all our habits and learned ignorance weigh us down; the death-dance burns away the bone, burns away, and lets the living impulses rise, the vision rise. Poetry tells the truth. But it doesn't invent the truth. It too must listen, to the poetry that flows inaudibly beneath all speech. So it is difficult to use words and yet to invoke the sense of life which is unspoken, unspeakable, what is left after the books are all decayed, lost, burned, forgotten. What remains after the pot has disappeared.

Pottery has helped my poetry because I was less instructed in the handcraft and therefore less inhibited. I permitted myself a kind of freedom in the use of clay which I would not have known how to find in the verbal world. The freedom I experienced in my studio began to drift into my study.

Well, and what is freedom? First of all, freedom seems to mean the absence of external restraint, the freedom to play. When we are free from external tyrannies, we seek freedom from our inner limitations. We find that in order to play we must be nimble and flexible and imaginative, we must be able to have fun, we must feel enjoyment, and sometimes long imprisonment has made us numb and sluggish. And then we find out that there are, paradoxically, disciplines which create in us capacities which allow us to seek our freedom. We learn how to rid ourselves of our boredom, our stiffness, our repressed anger, our anxiety. We become brighter, more energy flows through us, our limbs rise, our spirit comes alive in our tissues. And our gratitude is immeasurable for all the hours of labor that carry us forward.

As I grow quiet, the clay centers. For example, I used to grieve because I could not make reliably a close-fitting lid for a canister, a teapot, a casserole. Sometimes the lid fitted, sometimes it didn't. But I wanted it to fit. And I was full of aggravation. Then a GI friend of mine who was stationed in Korea sent me an ancient Korean pot, about a thousand years old. I loved it at once, and then he wrote that he thought I might like it because it looked like something I might have made. Its lid didn't fit at all! Yet it was a museum piece, so to speak. Why, I mused, do I require of myself what I do not require of this pot? Its lid does not fit, but it inspires my spirit when I look at it and handle it. So I stopped worrying. Now I have very little trouble making lids that fit.

What I want to say is that as our personal universes expand, if we keep drawing ourselves into center again and again, everything seems to enhance everything else. It becomes unnecessary to choose which person to be as we open and close the same ball of clay. We will make pots for our English classes. Read poems to our pottery classes. Write on the clay, print from the clay. The activity seems to spring out of the same source: poem or pot, loaf of bread, letter to a friend, a morning's meditation, a walk in the woods, turning the compost pile, knitting a pair of shoes, weeping with pain, fainting with discouragement, burning with shame, trembling with indecision: what's the difference. I like especially two famous Zen stories: the one about the great Japanese master of the art of archery who had never in his life hit the bull's eye. And the other about the monk who said, "Now that I'm enlightened, I'm just as miserable as ever."

What I mean here is that in poetry, in pottery, in the life of the mind, it seems to me that one must be able to picture before oneself the opposite of what one has just declared in order to keep alive the possibility of freedom, of mobility, of growth. As soon as we find ourselves spellbound by order and our ability to control our medium and our tools, to do exactly what we want, we must do the opposite as well. As soon as we feel drunk with the sport of building and destroying, of forming in order to deform, of working unconsciously, with risk (with poetry, if poetry is saying hello to whoever-whatever is there): with danger, and disrespect for the canons of taste, do the opposite. One does not decide between craft and art, pottery and sculpture, tradition and the individual talent. One is in a perpetual dialogue and performs the act one performs.

Life leads us at a certain moment to step beyond the dualisms to which we have been educated: primitive and civilized, chaos and order, abnormal and normal, private and public, verbal and nonverbal, conventional and far-out, good and bad. To transform our tuitions, as Emerson called our learning, into the body of our intuitions so that we may use this body as in pottery we use our clay. By an act of centering we resolve the oppositions in a single experience. The surrealists in France called it *le point suprême* and found it also at the center: *le foyer central*. When the sense of life in the individual is in touch with the life-power in the universe, is turning with it, he senses himself as potentially whole. And he senses all his struggles as efforts toward that wholeness. And he senses that wholeness as implicit in every part. When we are working on the potter's wheel, we are touching the clay at only one point; and yet as the pot turns through our fingers, the whole is being affected, and we have an experience of this wholeness. "The still point of the turning world."

Most of the separations we make need to be looked at very carefully: weakness and strength, sickness and health, not-knowing and knowing, play and seriousness. Human beings are an odd breed. We find it so difficult to give in to possibility – to envision what is not visible. For example, we tend to think that strength is all-important, and yet we have a very shallow notion of what strength consists of. For unless our weaknesses play into our strengths we are not as supple as we should be. And with our fixation upon health, we would do well to listen to the story that sickness is telling, as it brings its truth into our work. We must fill our devotion with the spirit of play, of celebration and holiday. Love-play. The rhythms of work seem to be the natural rhythms of life: they seem to go by polarities which swing around that unmoving center: the very rhythms of our breathing are the dialogue of inner and outer. The single craftsman finding his own way, and the same craftsman seeking fellowship with others. Working by preliminary design is answered by a desire to improvise. The joy of producing a well-made pot, beautiful in its physical balance and grace and accurate in its usefulness, is answered by a kinship with the ambiguous: some image which fills us with wonder or mirth or which leads us into continuous exercise of our faculties in an effort to fathom it, to grasp it, to embrace it. For we must surely embrace our world. Unless our ideals of peace and of love are so much cant, we must surely embrace our world in all its daily happenings and details.

What is the purpose of thinking about it in this way? Well, lots of folks worry about what things are called. Is it craft? is it art? is it sculpture? is it Dada? is it music? is it noise? is it poetry? *what is it?* The words people use won't change anything (I'm not absolutely sure of this). Certainly these words of mine won't change anything. And the worrying has its own function to perform. Life changes things. If there are life and truth in anybody's words, okay. Then they will correspond with nature. And if we are going along with nature, we will not need to be told anything. The Buddha, you may recall, came to speak to a gathering, and he used no words. He held a flower up before the people.

"Poetry," said Wallace Stevens, "is a process of the personality of the poet." Creative work is a training of each individual's perception according to the level on which he is alive and awake; that is why it is so difficult to evaluate. And it should be difficult. In art, perception is embodied: in dust, in pigment, in sounds, in movements of the body, in metals and stone, in threads and stuffs. Each product, each goal, is an intermediate moment in a much longer journey of the person. Once when I was asked to write something about art, I wrote: "Art is an intuitive act of the spirit in its evolution toward divine nature." Because it is an act of self-education in this sense, it cannot be evaluated apart from its maker, the one whose vision it represents. That is why judging is such a ticklish business. To judge prematurely is often to cripple. To refrain from judging is sometimes to impoverish. One must, again, listen with one's total faculties before one speaks. For answers to questions of technique are, at another level, answers to questions of personal growth. The "minor" questions: How shall I make this lid, what kind of a handle shall I pull, how high a foot shall I throw on this pot, how small an opening should this bottle have, how much iron oxide shall I apply to this surface? – all these minor questions are the echoes and small ripples from the deeper questions: What am I doing? what do I know? what do I want to learn? how shall I bring myself into ripeness? Teachers of ourselves, we over and over again ask, "How do I want this to look?" And what we mean is, "What do I want to bring to birth in the world? In myself?" Our pots do bear our spirits into the world. We may then, it seems to me, let them grow like wild flowers, in all their varieties. But in our own gardens we may foster those which bring into our lives the influences we long for. We may also judge according to standards derived from the highest development we have observed.

My answer to the question, What shall I do about this handle or this lid? is – and I quote from that ancient text on "Centering" – Wherever your attention alights, at this very point, *experience."* Make dozens, now this way, now that; putting them now here, now there. The *should* enters only when the goal is fixed, the standards formulated, and the techniques refined. Few of our moments have this character.

In teaching pottery, I am continually aware of how the learning of a handcraft reverberates throughout the spiritual organism, and it is this sense of personal destiny at stake which makes teaching such a serious and stimulating endeavor. I wish now to speak of two friends whom I taught only briefly but whose experiences were especially meaningful to me in the terms I have been using here: two people in whose personal transformation craft played its part. One, an English teacher who had never before in her life touched a piece of raw clay with any hope of forming it, was imprisoned by fear and striving. The other, a college art teacher, more skillful than I on the potter's wheel, was impotent with ambition and conceit.

The beginner, a person of deep culture and intuition, did indeed listen, but with such tension that she could hardly hear; and she was tongue-tied in her own behalf. "Is that all right?" she would ask quaveringly. She touched each hunk of clay as if at any moment she might plunge through the bottom into the abyss. Everything seemed alarming, and delicious. Her body sought the contact, but her taste reproved the appearance. Finally I asked her to work with her eyes closed so that her hands could be liberated from the censure of her critically trained eyes. To let the pleasure and search and sinew for making grow a little bit before chastising their immaturity. To do all the things that hands can do: tear and swat and push and pinch and squeeze and caress and scratch and model and beat. She sat like a blind woman with her clay, and she made a bowl this way, and when she opened her eyes, delight preceded doubt, and she was that much stronger in herself to do it again. She began to understand how it was for her to say if it was all right, not for me. I encouraged her to buy a can of workable clay and take it to her apartment. Her eyes are tired from reading. Let the hands carry forward the education.

Now the other potter had the opposite agony. He worked well, and produced in the beginning a regular storm of pots. But the more he did, the more he drooped. I heard he was going to drop pottery and take up weaving. One night I stood beside him at the wedging board while he morosely kneaded and slapped his clay. Suddenly he spoke. "What is a potter?" His accomplishment meant nothing to him. He did not LIKE his pots. They bore no individual stamp, he said. They did not speak to him. (Perhaps he had not spoken to them?) "What should a potter do?" he asked me. What should he make? Who should a potter be? (You see these are real questions that men do ask!) Well, I don't remember what I said, probably something about how a potter is a person; what should a person do? who should a person be? I suggested that he take a vacation from these thoughts of "should" – make some clay balloons and take them down to the granite sea shore and roll them on the lichen-textured boulders, and have some fun. He did that, and made a charming little stoneware garden. Although he didn't know exactly what to think about it, he liked it. But his troubles were by no means over. He did for a while give up pottery and take up weaving. I heard later that during the rest of the summer he gradually came back to center and worked with the clay in a way that brought more and more of himself into it, so that he felt good.

We have to trust these feelings. We have to trust the invisible gauges we carry within us. We have to realize that a creative being lives within ourselves, whether we like it or not, and that we must get out of its way, for it will give us no peace until we do. Certain kinds of egotism and ambition as well as certain kinds of ignorance and timidity have to be overcome or they will stand in the way of that creator. And though we are well thought of by others, we will feel cross and frustrated and envious and petulant, as if we had been cheated, somehow, by life.

I cannot talk about the crafts without appealing to the evolving spirit of man. We grow and change and develop capacities for centering and for dialogue throughout our lives.

Part of the training we enjoy as craftsmen is to bring into our bodies the imagination and the will. We enact. The handcrafts stand to perpetuate the living experience of contact with natural elements – something primal, immediate, personal, material, a dialogue between our dreams and the forces of nature.

In pottery it is perhaps because of the fire that the sense of collaboration is so strong. The potter does everything he can do. But he cannot burst into flame and reach a temperature of 2300 degrees Fahrenheit for a period varying from eight hours to a week and harden plastic clay into rigid stone, and transform particles of silica and spar into flowing glaze. He cannot transmute the dull red powder that lies upon the biscuited ware into a light-responsive celadon. He can only surrender his ware to the fire, listen to it, talk to it, so that he and the fire respond to each other's power, and the fired pot is the child.

Some craftsmen seem to be troubled by the question of originality and imitation. My only standard here is that a person be led into a deeper experience of himself and his craft. Human beings learn by imitation; certainly, in the years of childhood, almost exclusively by imitation. One is inspired by someone else's example. One seeks to do likewise. Sometimes the effort to do likewise gradually creates capacities and perceptions that one did not feel before. These periods of imitation are usually temporary. They too may be aspects of the long journey each one of us is on to get where we are bound for, consciously or unconsciously. I have found imitation useful both as a discipline and as a momentary indulgence. People bring each other into activity. If, however, the phase of imitation congeals and one sticks in it out of inertia, then of course the works will begin to look tired too. Ideas do not belong to people. Ideas live in the world as we do. We discover certain ideas at certain times. Someone enjoys a certain revelation and passes it around. A certain person's courage inspires a similar courage in others. People share their culture: there are enjoyable resemblances that make us feel like a community of fellow beings, fellow craftsmen – using a tradition and contributing our own impulses to it.

I have a finger exercise for originality which I sometimes use. Working with a piece of clay, hand-building, I destroy every pleasing result, seeking the unrecognizable. For if it is new, it will not look like something else: not like driftwood nor a Henry Moore perforated torso, not like a coral reef nor a Giacometti sculpture, not like a Haniwa horse nor a madonna nor a "free form," nor the new look in pottery in the sixties. It will look very odd indeed, if it is really new. Insecurity we need perhaps the most when we are inventing: it seems like our philosopher's stone, turning base materials into gold. The image we make in such an exercise will not be our goal, but in creating it we will have performed acts for the first time, and these will bring new structures and coordinations into our hands and into our visions.

In my own work I like to vary my rhythms: from one of a kind to many of a kind. Two sayings from that ancient tract on CENTERING make one passage of my dialogue: "Wherever satisfaction is found, in whatever act, *actualize this*"; and "Just as you have the impulse to do something, stop."

I admire very much the pottery of Karen Karnes, with whom I share a shop in Stony Point, New York. Her work is clean, expert, uncluttered, useful, beautiful, restrained but warm, full of a feeling of original plasticity as well as the advantages of stone. A plastic form with beautifully fitted rims. And the shiny glazes of high heat. Yet my temperament turns equally to ornament, to fooling around, to doing I know not what. And to letting the clay stand naked and untreated. Or any combination of these, at any moment of their intersection. I like a dry scabby surface through which color barely strains as well as depths soaked in lustre. Or just a simple semiglossy easily washable surface, no high jinks. The more a piece confounds me, the more it interests me. At the same time, one of the most thrilling experiences for me is to make tableware: twelve plates of the same size, twelve cups, twelve bowls. One after another. To make a lot of things alike is as exciting as to make one surprise after another. And of course the rewards of sustained working rhythms are marvelous. To throw forty tea bowls and to feel that certain ones have *it*. Have *mu*. Have *shibui*. Then you throw all the others away? No. For the quality of magic is not that clear: where you had been slowest to detect it, there it suddenly stands.

And yet the opposite is also true. There are moments when I could with ease clear all the shelves, clear the board, all the past, plough it under, make it new. Throw everything away. Is this a paradox? To be in love with the material world in all its stages of imperfection and yet to feel that love does not depend upon the permanence of its images? It is not the images per se that we adore but the being who lives within them and will live after the pot is broken. So goes the weather of this love of life and love of death, the feeling that the living and the dead are a permanent family fully alive in an awesome cosmic dialogue.

During the dozen years that I have been working with clay, certain influences from the potter's world have inspired me in special ways. The French potters in Vallauris. The folk potters in North Carolina, living by their craft, producing every day quantities of their unselfconscious simple useful appealing ware. Bernard Leach, as person, as potter, as author of *A Potter's Book, Potter's Portfolio, Potter in Japan*. Raku ware: the Japanese-derived ceremony of making a cup, firing it, and drinking tea out of it, all in a single rhythm: the living relation of the shaping and the drinking and the consecration. Bizen ware. Children who come into my studio to fool around with my clay. Three teachers: Warren McKenzie, fresh from a stint at St. Ives Pottery in England, where he had had to make five hundred mugs before the first one was accepted. Daniel Rhodes, his love for the craft in all the richness of its history and the combination in him of knowledge and feeling. Peter Voulkos, who told me to work with the clay till it collapses, that there's nothing to it, that if pots weren't breakable potters would be sunk, that there's lots more where these come from. Exhibitions of work in clay by sculptors Noguchi and Marisol and Nakian; exhibits at Asia House from Oriental antiquity and the present day; a visit to Mexico, all that carved stone and all that clay; a visit to Picasso's ceramics in Antibes; Henry Takemoto's coiled pots big enough to hide a thief; the paper-thin poetry of Lucy Rie's thrown porcelain.

But perhaps most vivid: a visit to this country by a Japanese potter, Rosanjin. He gave a speech at Greenwich House in New York City. In Japanese. He smiled throughout, and spoke with feeling. At the end, a young lady read an English translation. He began, she said, by saying how glad he was to be here, and how much he had enjoyed looking around the Greenwich House pottery at the potters' work, and how he couldn't help wondering why they all made such hideous things! A great evening ... He spoke about educating one's feeling through a close relationship with nature and through drawing nature and studying the masterpieces of previous ages. Then he gave a demonstration. A potter's wheel was on stage. He did not throw the cylinder, he asked one of the visiting professors to do that. Rosanjin pinched its wall, turned to his translator, and said, "The clay is too wet, but I'll see what I can do with it." He then shaped a bowl. But because he opened it too wide for the wetness of the clay, it collapsed. Then he rolled fat coils between his hands and, lifting the rim of the fallen pot, propped it up. He pinched the rim into ripples and held this extraordinary flop before his horrified audience of American studio potters for admiration. Not only that, but he had it carried through the hall, up one row and down the next, to be examined and enjoyed. His smiling comment was, "It doesn't look like much now, but wait till the fire gets through with it, you never can tell!" I was transported with delight and mirth and admiration. American pieties were being offended right and left. The Orient was with us. Bringing its own joyful reverence, its own pieties to speak with ours.

David Tudor is not a potter but a pianist. He came to Black Mountain College one summer to give concerts. A half-dozen young student composers had arranged a short program of their works and, not being performers, asked him if he would play. I will never forget it. A grand piano. A college dining hall. All of us in blue jeans and T-shirts. The pianist in a sports jacket to lend a formal air. He entered from the "wings" with each small score, played the piece, whatever it was, with absolute sincerity and respect for the composer and the composed; bowed, exited, re-entered. A half-dozen compositions by beginners, handled without reservation nor irony nor sentiment nor anything except the capacity to let the moment *speak,* and us *listen.* Is this not the emptiness for which the sages pray: to be filled as a spring is?

I have been inspired as well by potters who undertake huge tasks and realize them faultlessly. I once saw Mary Scheier throw bowls. Huge beautiful curved thin instruments: like bells. All the clay used and the bowl soaring off the wheel like a bubble.

And Margaret Israel's exhibition of works in clay at the Egan Gallery in New York during the winter of 1961. No pots. All sculpture. Mythic, archetypal, musing, bemused images. Huge impossible forms, all hand built; huge sacks, like grain sacks, made of clay, standing empty in the corner. Caves with rose windows and congregations. A horse's muzzle and a woman's face, emerging out of a clay union, into physiognomy. A book with clay pages. A doorway, eight feet high. A boulder too big to fit in a kiln. A box, with an axis, with an altar, with gears. And I learned that the potter came every day to change something. To smudge a little soot on here and there, to alter the color of the body. To try a little blue paint. To remove a figure, to add a figure, to break something. To put something on a pedestal, to take something off. Chaos still bubbling and seething with possibilities. And the frenzied artist carbonated with creative impulses.

To tear this one down so that we can put this one up. But *we* don't have to do it. Life and time do it. And we discover that what is being created is a single being: its apparent lives and deaths only the appearances of its metamorphosis.

Life in both its outward crafts and inner forms offers us the experience of destruction and creation. We speak in a vocabulary that discriminates between meaningful form and lack of form, between pot and shard. At the same time we cultivate a love for each particular thing, each particular moment, no matter where it stands in the long rhythms of life and death: I have an ancient Egyptian potsherd mounted on my treasure shelf. We discover that now is always alive, and that the generative force within life continuously heals what appear to be separations, by making them fruitful. It is an important thing for us to cherish this living contact, finding through it our poetry, our pots, our love for each other and for life: the centering and the dialogue.

I tried once to put this impression into a poem:

Poem

Pots are for shards,
                    and
shards are
                    for shepherds, to cry with.
SHAPES. taken, and taking
shape:
            avoid it if you can, you can't,
            shape's the void
            we're in; order is
            the chaos we befriend.
                                    SAMSARA: one
thing and not another, one thing
and then another; samsara, is what
it's called, what we're at and what we're
in: forms and naming. Names we bandy and
are scouted by, th'outs and innings, everyday a
requiem-birthday,
                    spilling the shepherd's tears, spoiling the shep-
                    herd's fears —
                            JOB,
the job's
            permanent
at ground level.

Soetsu Yanagi

from
THE UNKNOWN CRAFTSMAN
A Japanese Insight into Beauty

We human beings are accustomed to thinking, "I am now painting a picture" or "I am now weaving cloth." According to Buddhism, however, such phrases express a dualistic relationship from which no true picture or cloth can result. Buddhism says that the root of the dualism is the word "I" and that it must vanish, until the stage where "picture draws picture" or "cloth weaves cloth" is reached. In one of the Buddhist scriptures is the phrase "Buddha with Buddha," which may be taken to mean "from Buddha to Buddha," and that in turn means that all true actions take place between Buddha and Buddha. Instead of man turning to Buddha or Buddha to man, Buddha turns to Buddha, all distinction or opposition between Buddha and man having disappeared. Put in another way, one may say that "the thing turns to the thing itself."

We speak of "offering prayers to God" – but true prayers are not those offered by man to God, they are, so to speak, God's voice whispering to God himself. Plotinus, the most religious minded of the Greek philosophers, concluded the *Enneads* with the words "Flight of the Alone to the Alone," a phrase of remarkable depth. Would it not be possible, then, to say that all beautiful work is work done by the work itself? When an artist creates a work, he and the work are two different things. Only when he becomes the work itself and creates the work (in other words, when the work alone is creating the whole work) does true work become possible. Not the artist but the work should say "I am": when this state is reached, a work of art deserving the name has been produced.

Chuang Tzu

MASTERING LIFE
(The Woodcarver)

Woodworker Chi'ing carved a piece of wood and made a bell stand, and when it was finished, everyone who saw it marveled, for it seemed to be the work of gods or spirits. When the marquis of Lu saw it, he asked, "What art is it you have?"

Ch'ing replied, "I am only a craftsman – how would I have any art? Here is one thing, however. When I am going to make a bell stand, I never let it wear out my energy. I always fast in order to still my mind. When I have fasted for three days, I no longer have any thought of congratulations or rewards, of titles or stipends. When I have fasted for five days, I no longer have any thought of praise or blame, of skill or clumsiness. And when I have fasted for seven days, I am so still that I forget I have four limbs and a form and body. By that time, the ruler and his court no longer exist for me. My skill is concentrated and all outside distractions fade away. After that, I go into the mountain forest and examine the Heavenly nature of the trees. If I find one of superlative form, and I can see a bell stand there, I put my hand to the job of carving; if not I let it go. This way I am simply matching up 'Heaven' with 'Heaven.'9 That's probably the reason that people wonder if the results were not made by spirits."

translated by Burton Watson

Robert Garrison

WOOD GRAIN
AND CARVING

"Do you know why I don't use the power tools?"
  Asked the carver.
"It is because the power motor cannot feel
  The wood grain.
  Things made with power tools may look correct,
  But the eye can only see.
  Something else feels ...

"When the lay of the wood is not followed
  Certain tensions are set up in the work ...

"And so it is with wood grain," he said
  Selecting a piece of curly maple
  Not with effort, not grabbing, either
  But having it just suddenly appear
  Ready in the wood vise.

  Next a sharp carbon-steel tool appeared in his hand
  And its edge reminded me of a canoe in a clear lake,
  Sliding.

"If I were truly a master carver
  I would need no tools except my senses.
  And after a time, I would need nothing
  And there would be nothing more to say."

  Only the stillness after a fish jumps
  On a mirror, cool lake.

Richard B. Derby

from
EARLY HOUSES OF THE CONNECTICUT VALLEY

Man loves any material that he has worked upon in proportion to its resistance to his efforts of bending it to his will, — assuming that he has not attempted the impossible or the absurd with reference to the task at hand. This is why the hand-hewn timber of our old houses is better than the two-by-four sawed stud or the six-by-eight post. I can very well believe that the first settlers in Connecticut took their timbers for their houses with them, as they are said to have done. They had wrought upon them with their own hands, and had a certain affection for them on this account, and what is equally important, the timbers had an affection for the men who had worked them. The frames of our present houses are a pretty good example of efficiency in the economic and modern sense. Its loads have been carefully appraised and distributed proportionately over the members which it supports, so that the strain and stress on each of these is just precisely what each one will bear, and never more or less. This may be all right, as no doubt it is from the scientific or the economic point of view, but it represents for me a very low order of efficiency.

I look at the ten-by-twelve corner posts in the summer kitchen of my great-grandfather's old home, and I wonder whether he knew that four-by-six posts would have done the work of these. Perhaps he did, and perhaps he did not, and perhaps he did not care whether it would have done the work or not; but I feel sure that he would not have had the satisfaction out of our smaller post that he must have experienced from the ten-by-twelve. My great-grandfather had the reputation in his district of being able to square the butt of a log more perfectly than any one else around, and he left a better stump in his wood lot than his neighbors did. I am sure, therefore, that he applied himself with great care to the corner posts, beams, and rafters of his own home, that he had a defensible pride in the result of his hand-iwork, and that he never could have had this pride in any four-by-six. The affection which he had for his timbers was returned by them, and is being returned today. I get back some of it always when I look at the smoky corner posts, or when I lie on the bed in the unfinished attic and let my eyes wander over the hand-hewn rafters.

Connecticut settlers of 1636 forged their way westward from Massachusetts through uncharted forests. They cut their own paths, except, perhaps, for short distances, where they found an Indian trail making in their direction. Besides their axes they must have carried arms; for, though the Indians were politically friendly, they were hardly to be trusted in every case. They must have carried, too, some provisions and their camping outfits, for they did not know that they would always have luck in finding food, and they were quite uncertain in what places or at what times they would pitch their tents. It is hardly to be believed, therefore, that they carried timber along with the other things on their backs, or that they added this to the burdens of their horses. It is not incredible, however, that, the Connecticut Valley once reached, they had their timbers brought in the vessels which made the first long voyage around the cape and up the river to the place of their abode. They were engaged primarily in clearing and planting, and, no doubt, their energies were fully occupied with these exertions.

The first houses, as we know, were merely cellars dug in the side of a hill, the walls lined with stone or logs; the roofs simply lean-tos brushed or thatched. These crude shelters gave place to better habitations in comparatively short time. The very early dwellings were likely built of White Pine, and in certain instances of oak, squared and bored and ready to be raised and pinned together.

Fetching timber from Massachusetts could hardly have continued long. It was too much like bringing coal to Newcastle. The timber was abundant, and the craftsman instinct must have cried aloud to exercise itself.

We are not acquainted with the aspect of the forest which these settlers looked out upon, and we do not know precisely the feelings which the native trees engendered under the conditions which obtained; but some of us are not so young but that we have seen native forests, and the impression these have made upon us (though of a later time and under widely changed conditions) is not perhaps so very different from that made on the earliest inhabitants of western Massachusetts and Connecticut. I myself remember very well the primeval forests of the Allegheny Mountains in Pennsylvania. I remember when I first rode over them on a tote-team, and later tramped my way, with pack on back, beneath the pine and hemlock. The lowest branches of these trees were far above me. I should hardly dare to guess how far, but I can recollect distinctly that the rhododendrons which flourished in the dusk below them interlaced their lowest branches several times my height above my head, and the blossoms of the topmost branches must have been thirty or more feet in height. The butts of the trees themselves were huge, and the whole effect or feeling (one does not observe the forest) for me was the same that I get from looking at a lofty mountain. I do not wish to try to match my strength against a mountain, and I did not (as I now remember) wish to build myself a cabin of these trees.

This was not the feeling, however, of the men who worked among them. These trees, or the making of them into timber, was their life. They were not depressed but rather tempted and exhilarated by the size and number of them; it was their pride, like my great-grandfather's, to square a butt with axes or to notch one so exactly that the tree would fall precisely where they meant it should. They saw only the tree that could be felled and subdivided, barked and piled on skidways and later take its booming way for miles along the frosty slide to water, whence it could be splashed or floated to the saw-mills. These lumbermen had both strength and genius for this work, and no doubt the earlier settlers had it also. In addition, they had an instinct for building their homes.

It would be interesting to do an old house as the old men would have done it, and it is likely that most architects would welcome a chance to do this if it offered. Big White Pine timber grows abundantly today, though no longer in the East and at our very doors, but the facilities of transportation may almost do away with the handicap of this condition. Let some big lumberman offer us his large timbers and see whether this may not result in a reversion in some degree to older architectural types. These types, when added to our present ones, would furnish a broader basis of tradition on which to build our future native work.

Ananda K. Coomaraswamy

SHAKER FURNITURE

Shaker Furniture

Shaker Furniture emphasizes the spiritual significance of perfect craftsmanship and, as the author remarks, "the relationship between a way of life and a way of work invests the present study with special interest."[10] And truly a humane interest, since here the way of life and way of work (*karma yoga* of the *Bhagavad Gita*) are one and the same way; and as the *Bhagavad Gita* likewise tells us in the same connection, "Man attains perfection by the intensity of his devotion to his own proper task," working, that is to say, not for himself or for his own glory, but only "for the good of the work to be done." "It is enough," as Marcus Aurelius says (VI.2), "to get the work done well." The Shaker way of life was one of order; an order or rule that may be compared to that of a monastic community. At the same time, "the idea of worship in work was at once a doctrine and a daily discipline.... The ideal was variously expressed that secular achievements should be as 'free from error' as conduct, that manual labour was a type of religious ritual, that godliness should illuminate life at every point."

In this they were better Christians than many others. All tradition has seen in the Master Craftsman of the Universe the exemplar of the human artist or "maker by art," and we are told to be "perfect, even as your Father in heaven is perfect." That the Shakers were doctrinally Perfectionists is the final explanation of the perfection of Shaker workmanship; or, as we might have said, of its "beauty." We say

"beauty," despite the fact that the Shakers scorned the word in its worldly and luxurious applications, for it is a matter of bare fact that they who ruled that "bead-
ings, mouldings, and cornices, which are merely for fancy, may not be made by
Believers" were consistently better carpenters than are to be found in the world of
unbelievers. In the light of mediaeval theory we cannot wonder at this; for in the
perfection, order, and illumination which were made the proof of the good life we
recognize precisely those qualities (*integritas sive perfectio, consonantia, claritas*) which are
for St. Thomas the "requisites of beauty" in things made by art. "The result was
the elevation of hitherto uninspired, provincial joiners to the position of fine
craftsmen, actuated by worthy traditions and a guildlike pride. ... The peculiar
correspondence between Shaker culture and Shaker artisanship should be seen as
the result of the penetration of the spirit into all secular activity. Current in the
United Society was the proverb: 'Every force evolves a form.'... The eventual result
of this penetration of religion into the workshop as we have noted was the discarding of all values in design which attach to surface decoration in favor of the
values inherent in form in the harmonious relationship of parts and the perfected
unity of form."

Shaker art is, in fact, far more closely related to the perfection and severity of
primitive and "savage" art (of which the Shakers probably knew nothing and which
they would not have "understood") than are the "many shrewdly reticent modern
creations" in which the outward aspects of primitive and functional art are consciously imitated. Shaker art was not in any sense a "crafty" or "mission style," deliberately "rustic," but one of the greatest refinement, that achieved "an effect of
subdued elegance, even of delicacy ... at once precise and differentiated." One thing
that made this possible was the fact that given the context in which the furniture was
to be used "the joiners were not forced to anticipate carelessness and abuse."

The style of Shaker furniture, like that of their costume, was impersonal; it was,
indeed, one of the "millennial laws" that "No one should write or print his name
on any article of manufacture, that others may hereafter know the work of his
hands." And this Shaker style was almost uniform from beginning to end; it is a
collective and not an individualistic expression. Originality and invention appear
not as a sequence of fashions or as an "aesthetic" phenomenon, but whenever there
were new *uses* to be served; the Shaker system coincided with and did not resist "the
historic transference of occupations from the home to the shop or small factory;
and new industries were conducted on a scale requiring laborsaving devices and
progressive methods. The versatility of the Shaker workmen is well illustrated by
the countless tools invented for unprecedented techniques."

We cannot refrain from observing how closely the Shaker position corresponds
to the mediaeval Christian in this matter of art. The founders of the Shaker order
can hardly have read St. Thomas, yet it might have been one of themselves that had
said that if ornament (*decor*) is made the chief end of a work it is mortal sin, but
if a secondary cause may be either quite in order or merely a venial fault; and that
the artist is responsible as a man for whatever he undertakes to make, as well as re-

sponsible as an artist for making to the best of his ability (*Sum. Theol.* ii–ii.167.2c and ii–ii.169.2 *ad* 4): or that "Everything is said to be *good* insofar as it is perfect, for in that way only is it desirable.... The perfections of all things are so many similitudes of the divine being" (*ibid.* 1.5.5c, 1.6.1 *ad* 2) — "all things," of course, including even brooms and hoes and other "useful articles" made *secundum rectam rationem artis.* The Shaker would have understood immediately what to the modern aesthetician seems obscure, Bonaventura's "light of a mechanical art."

It would, indeed, be perfectly possible to outline a Shaker theory of beauty in complete agreement with what we have often called the "normal view of art." We find, for example in Shaker writings that "God is the great artist or master-builder"; that only when all the parts of a house or a machine have been perfectly *ordered,* "then the beauty of the machinery and the wisdom of the artist are apparent"; that "order is the creation of beauty. It is heaven's first law [cf, Gk. κόσμος, Skr. *rta*] and the protection of souls.... Beauty rests on utility"; and conversely, that "the falling away from any spiritual epoch has been marked by the ascendancy of the aesthetics [*sic*]." Most remarkable is the statement that that beauty is best which is "peculiar to the flower or generative period" and not that "which belongs to the ripened fruit and grain." Nor is the matter without an economic bearing. We treat "art" as a luxury, which the common man can hardly afford, and as something to be found in a museum rather than a home or business office: yet although Shaker furniture is of museum quality, "the new Lebanon trustees reported that the actual cost of furnishing one of our dwellings for the comfortable accommodations of sixty or seventy inmates would fall far short of the sum often expended in furnishing some single parlors in the cities of New York and Albany." One is moved to ask whether our own "high standard of living" is really more than a high standard of paying, and whether any of us is really getting our money's worth. In the case of furniture, for example, we are certainly paying much more for things of inferior quality.

In all this there would appear to be something that has been overlooked by our modern culturalists who are engaged in the teaching of art and of art appreciation, and by our exponents of the doctrine of art as self-expression, in any case as an expression of emotions, or "feelings." The primary challenge put by this splendid book, a perfect example of expertise in the field of art history, may be stated in the form of a question: Is not the "mystic," after all, the only really "practical" man?

Our authors remark that "as compromises were made with principle, the crafts inevitably deteriorated." In spite of their awareness of this, the authors envisage the possibility of a "revival" of Shaker style. The furniture "can be produced again, never as the inevitable expression of time and circumstance, yet still as something to satisfy the mind which is surfeited with over-ornamentation and mere display," produced — shall we say at Grand Rapids? — for "people with limited means but educated taste ... who will seek a union of practical convenience and quiet charm." In other words, a new outlet is to be provided for the bourgeois fantasy of "cult"-ure when other period furnitures have lost their "charm." The museums will undoubtedly be eager to assist the interior decorator. It does not seem to occur to anyone that things are only beautiful in the environment for which they were designed, or as the Shaker expressed it, when "adapted to condition" (62). Shaker style was not a "fashion" determined by "taste," but a creative activity "adapted to condition."

Innumerable cultures, some of which we have destroyed, have been higher than our own: still, we do not rise to the level of Greek humanity by building imitation Parthenons, nor to that of the Middle Ages by living in pseudo-Gothic chateaux. To imitate Shaker furniture would be no proof of a creative virtue in ourselves: their austerity, imitated for our convenience, economic or aesthetic, becomes a luxury in us: their avoidance of ornament an interior "decoration" for us. We should rather say of the Shaker style *requiescat in pace* than attempt to copy it. It is a frank confession of insignificance to resign oneself to the merely servile activity of reproduction; all archaism is the proof of a deficiency. In "reproduction" nothing but the accidental appearance of a living culture can be evoked. If we were now such as the Shaker was, an art of our own, "adapted to condition," would be indeed essentially like, but assuredly accidentally unlike, Shaker art. Unfortunately we do not desire to be such as the Shaker was; we do not propose to "work as though we had a thousand years to live, and as though we were to die tomorrow" (12). Just as we desire peace but not the things that make for peace, so we desire art but not the things that make for art. We put the cart before the horse. *Il pittore pinge se stesso;* we have the art that we deserve. If the sight of it puts us to shame, it is with ourselves that the re-formation must begin. A drastic transvaluation of accepted values is required. With the re-formation of man, the arts of peace will take care of themselves.

Studs Terkel

---✦---

THE MASON:
CARL MURRAY BATES

(An Interview)

We're in a tavern no more than thirty yards from the banks of the Ohio. Toward the far side of the river, Alcoa smokestacks belch forth: an uneasy coupling of a bucolic past and an industrial present. The waters are polluted, yet the jobs out there offer the townspeople their daily bread.

He is fifty-seven years old. He's a stonemason who has pursued his craft since he was seventeen. None of his three sons is in his trade.

As far as I know, masonry is older than carpentry, which goes clear back to Bible times. Stone mason goes back way *before* Bible time: the pyramids of Egypt, things of that sort. Anybody that starts to build anything, stone, rock, or brick, start on the northeast corner. Because when they built King Solomon's Temple, they started on the northeast corner. To this day, you look at your courthouses, your big public buildings, you look at the cornerstone, when it was created, what year, it will be on the northeast corner. If I was gonna build a septic tank, I would start on the northeast corner. (Laughs.) Superstition, I suppose.

With stone we build just about anything. Stone is the oldest and best building material that ever was. Stone was being used even by the cavemen that put it together with mud. They built out of stone before they even used logs. He got him a cave, he built stone across the front. And he learned to use dirt, mud, to make the stones lay there without sliding around – which was the beginnings of mortar, which we still call mud. The Romans used mortar that's almost as good as we have today.

Everyone hears these things, they just don't remember 'em. But me being in the profession, when I hear something in that line, I remember it. Stone's my business. I, oh, sometimes talk to architects and engineers that have made a study and I pick up the stuff here and there.

Every piece of stone you pick up is different, the grain's a little different and this and that. It'll split one way and break the other. You pick up your stone and look at it and make an educated guess. It's a pretty good day layin' stone or brick. Not tiring. Anything you like to do isn't tiresome. It's hard work; stone is heavy. At the same time, you get interested in what you're doing and you usually fight the clock the other way. You're not lookin' for quittin'. You're wondering you haven't got enough done and it's almost quittin' time. (Laughs.) I ask the hod carrier what time it is and he says two-thirty. I say, "Oh, my Lord, I was gonna get a whole lot more than this."

I pretty well work by myself. On houses, usually just one works. I've got the hod carrier there, but most of the time I talk to myself, "I'll get my hammer and I'll knock the chip off there." (Laughs.) A good hod carrier is half your day. He won't work as hard as a poor one. He knows what to do and make every move count makin' the mortar. It has to be so much water, so much sand. His skill is to see that you don't run out of anything. The hod carrier, he's above the laborer. He has a certain amount of prestige.

I think a laborer feels that he's the low man. Not so much that he works with his hands, it's that he's at the bottom of the scale. He always wants to get up to a skilled trade. Of course he'd make more money. The main thing is the common laborer – even the word common laborer – just sounds so common, he's at the bottom. Many that works with his hands takes pride in his work.

I get a lot of phone calls when I get home: how about showin' me how and I'll do it myself? I always wind up doin' it for 'em. (Laughs.) So I take a lot of pride in it and I do get, oh, I'd say, a lot of praise or whatever you want to call it. I don't suppose anybody, however much he's recognized, wouldn't like to be recognized a little more. I think I'm pretty well recognized.

One of my sons is an accountant and the other two are bankers. They're mathematicians, I suppose you'd call 'em that. Air-conditioned offices and all that. They always look at the house I build. They stop by and see me when I'm aworkin'. Always want me to come down and fix somethin' on their house, too. (Laughs.) They don't buy a house that I don't have to look at it first. Oh sure, I've got to crawl under it and look on the roof, you know ...

I can't seem to think of any young masons. So many of 'em before, the man lays stone and his son follows his footsteps. Right now the only one of these sons I can think of is about forty, fifty years old.

I started back in the Depression times when there wasn't any apprenticeships. You just go out and if you could hold your job, that's it. I was just a kid then. Now I worked real hard and carried all the blocks I could. Then I'd get my trowel and I'd lay one or two. The second day the boss told me: I think you could lay enough blocks to earn your wages. So I guess I had only one day of apprenticeship. Usually it takes about three years of being a hod carrier to start. And it takes another ten or fifteen years to learn the skill.

I admired the men that we had at that time that were stonemasons. They knew their trade. So naturally I tried to pattern after them. There's been very little change in the work. Stone is still stone, mortar is still the same as it was fifty years ago. The style of stone has changed a little. We use a lot more, we call it golf. A stone as big as a baseball up to as big as a basketball. Just round balls and whatnot. We just fit 'em in the wall that way.

Automation has tried to get in the bricklayer. Set 'em with a crane. I've seen several put up that way. But you've always got in-between the windows and this and that. It just doesn't seem to pan out. We do have a power saw. We do have an electric power mix to mix the mortar, but the rest of it's done by hand as it always was.

In the old days they all seemed to want it cut out and smoothed. It's harder now because you have no way to use your tools. You have no way to use a string, you have no way to use a level or a plumb. You just have to look at it because it's so rough and many irregularities. You have to just back up and look at it.

All construction, there's always a certain amount of injuries. A scaffold will break and so on. But practically no real danger. All I ever did do was work on houses, so we don't get up very high — maybe two stories. Very seldom that any more. Most of 'em are one story. And so many of 'em use stone for a trim. They may go up four, five feet and then paneling or something. There's a lot of skinned fingers or you hit your finger with a hammer. Practically all stone is worked with hammers and chisels. I wouldn't call it dangerous at all.

Stone's my life. I daydream all the time, most times it's on stone. Oh, I'm gonna build me a stone cabin down on the Green River. I'm gonna build stone cabinets in the kitchen. That stone door's gonna be awful heavy and I don't know how to attach the hinges. I've got to figure out how to make a stone roof. That's the kind of thing. All my dreams, it seems like it's got to have a piece of rock mixed in it.

If I got some problem that's bothering me, I'll actually wake up in the night and think of it. I'll sit at the table and get a pencil and paper and go over it, makin' marks on paper or drawin' or however ... this way or that way. Now I've got to work this and I've only got so much. Or they decided they want it that way when you already got it fixed this way. Anyone hates tearing his work down. It's all the same price but you still don't like to do it.

These fireplaces, you've got to figure how they'll throw out heat, the way you curve the fireboxes inside. You have to draw a line so they reflect heat. But if you throw too much of a curve, you'll have them smoke. People in these fine houses don't want a puff of smoke coming out of the house.

The architect draws the picture and the plans, and the draftsman and the engineer, they help him. They figure the strength and so on. But when it comes to actually makin' the curves and doin' the work, you've got to do it with your hands. It comes right back to your hands.

When you get into stone, you're gettin' away from the prefabs, you're gettin' into the better homes. Usually at this day and age they'll start into sixty to seventy thousand and run up to about half a million. We've got one goin' now that's mighty close, three or four hundred thousand. That type of house is what we build.

The lumber is not near as good as it used to be. We have better fabricating material, such as plywood and sheet rock and things of that sort, but the lumber itself is definitely inferior. Thirty, forty years ago a house was almost entirely made of lumber, wood floors ... Now they have vinyl, they have carpet, everything, and so on. The framework wood is getting to be of very poor quality.

But stone is still stone and the bricks are actually more uniform than they used to be.

Originally they took a clay bank ... I know a church been built that way. Went right on location, dug a hole in the ground, and formed bricks with their hands. They made the bricks that built the building on the spot.

Now we've got modern kilns, modern heat, the temperature don't vary. They got better bricks now than they used to have. We've got machines that make brick, so they're made true. Where they used to, they were pretty rough. I'm buildin' a big fireplace now out of old brick. They run wide, long, and it's a headache. I've been two weeks on that one fireplace.

The toughest job I ever done was this house, a hundred years old plus. The lady wanted one room left just that way. And this doorway had to be closed. It had deteriorated and weathered for over a hundred years. The bricks was made out of broken pieces, none of 'em were straight. If you lay 'em crooked, it gets awful hard right there. You spend a lifetime trying to learn to lay bricks straight. And it took a half-day to measure with a spoon, to try to get the mortar to match. I'd have so much dirt, so much soot, so much lime, so when I got the recipe right I could make it in bigger quantity. Then I made it with a coffee cup.

Half a cup of this, half a cup of that ... I even used soot out of a chimney and sweepin's off the floor. I was two days layin' up a little doorway, mixin' the mortar and all. The boss told the lady it couldn't be done. I said, "Give me the time, I believe I can do it." I defy you to find where that door is right now. That's the best job I ever done.

There's not a house in this country that I haven't built that I don't look at every time I go by. (Laughs.) I can set here now and actually in my mind see so many that you wouldn't believe. If there's one stone in there crooked, I know where it's at and I'll never forget it. Maybe thirty years, I'll know a place where I should have took that stone out and redone it but I didn't. I still notice it. The people who live there might not notice it, but I notice it. I never pass that house that I don't think of it. I've got one house in mind right now. (Laughs.) That's the work of my hands. 'Cause you see, stone, you don't prepaint it, you don't camouflage it. It's there, just like I left it forty years ago.

I can't imagine a job where you go home and maybe go by a year later and you don't know what you've done. My work, I can see what I did the first day I started. All my work is set right out there in the open and I can look at it as I go by. It's something I can see the rest of my life. Forty years ago, the first blocks I ever laid in my life, when I was seventeen years old. I never go through Eureka — a little town down there on the river — that I don't look thataway. It's always there.

Immortality as far as we're concerned. Nothin' in this world lasts forever, but did you know that stone — Bedford limestone, they claim — deteriorates one-sixteenth of an inch every hundred years? And it's around four or five inches for a house. So that's gettin' awful close. (Laughs.)

Donald Hall

⟶⟩⟩⊙⟨⟨⟵

from
LIFE WORK

When I hear talk about "the work ethic" I puke. CEOs talk about it, whose annual salaries average one hundred and thirty times their workers' wages. Whatever the phrase purports to describe, it is not an ethic; it is not an idea of work's value or a moral dictate but a feeling or tone connected to work, and it is temperamental and cultural. Studs Terkel's stonemason has it, and his line-worker does not; instead, the line-worker has a work anger, or a work malevolence, which is entirely appropriate. Mind you, the stonemason works alone with his hands solving problems that change with every stone. He does something that he can look at and put his name to. He can measure what he has done in walls and buildings, not in units of the same thing, like so many Chevrolet Impalas or so many distributor cap linings. Shades of John Ruskin. I no more have a work ethic than I have self-discipline. I have so many pages a day, so many books and essays.

Elizabeth Wayland Barber

from
BEHIND THE MYTHS:
ATHENA & WEAVING

Weaving, as opposed to thread making, was the special province of Athena. Wherever divine weaving was to be done, ancient Greek storytellers looked to Athena. In Hesiod's tale of Pandora ("All-gifts") and her infamous box – a box filled with all the evils of the world, including hope (no better than delusion, to the Greek mind) – Zeus orders Hephaistos to make the image of a beautiful girl out of clay. Aphrodite is to "shed grace on her head" and "Athena to teach her skills – to weave a complex warp." As the various gods busy themselves in tricking Pandora out,

> The owl-eyed goddess Athena girdled her, and bedecked her
> with a shining garment, and on her head a fancy veil
> she spread with her hands, a wonder to behold.

Thus Athena provides for the young bride both her clothing and her instruction in weaving, the basic household craft.

Perhaps the most famous story of Athena's weaving is that of Arachne. This uppity girl boasted that she could weave better than Athena, the patron goddess of weaving. Not a wise thing to do: Athena heard and challenged her to a weaving contest. According to Ovid, again embroidering his tale to the utmost, Arachne boldly wove into her web the stories of the most scandalous love affairs of the gods: how Zeus, the king of the gods, repeatedly was unfaithful to his wife as he disguised himself to rape or seduce a dozen women – appearing to Leda as a swan, to Europa as a bull, to Danaë as a shower of gold, and, most treacherously of all, to Alkmene as her own absent husband, Amphitryon. Not content with that, Arachne depicted Poseidon, Apollo, Bacchus, and Hades as they also assumed false forms to take advantage of various hapless maidens. Athena, for her part, grimly wove mortals who had lost contests with the gods and been soundly punished. (We have a representation of this weaving contest on a little oil flask from Corinth, from about 600 BC. Athena, a divine being, is so much taller than the human that her head scrapes the top of the picture.) Gods always win, of course. When the cloths were finished, in wrath Athena turned Arachne into the Spider, doomed to weave in dark corners for the rest of time.

But Athena's purview is much wider than just the making of cloth and clothing. Athenians worshipped her also as the one who brings fertility to the crops and protection to the city, as the inventor of the cultivated olive (one of the central crops in the Aegean), as the patroness of shipbuilders and other handcrafters, as a goddess of war, and so on. In fact, she is the goddess of so many things that modern commentators lose sight of her central nature.

That nature is most clearly seen by looking at what she is not, what opposes her. Her traditional opponent is Poseidon, with whom she strove first for possession of Athens. As a sign of supremacy, Poseidon hit the rock with his trident and a salt spring gushed forth, but Athena produced the first olive tree. (Both the trident mark and the "original" olive tree were proudly shown to visitors at the Erechtheum, on the Athenian Acropolis, in Classical times.) The citizens of the new state judged that Athena's gift was going to be much more useful to them than a salt spring and awarded her the prize. But Poseidon was a poor loser and in revenge sent a tidal flood, which Athena barely halted at the foot of the Acropolis, protecting her people. (Bad tidal waves did occur in the Aegean.)

This whole tale, despite its anchors in reality, is obviously another packet of "just so" stories to explain origins, but the nature of the opposition shows us that Athena is the beneficent deity that protects humans and makes them prosper, pushing back the untamed forces of nature represented by Poseidon. More exactly, she represents everything that human skill and know-how (*tekhnē*, whence our word *technology*) can accomplish; she is goddess of "civilization" itself. Exactly this same opposition motivates *The Odyssey*, where Athena helps Odysseus by means of clever stratagems and skills (including building a seagoing raft) to escape the wrath of Poseidon, who for his part throws an endless barrage of storms, gales, and wild seas at the poor mortal. Homer treats Athena in both epics as the goddess of good advice and clever plans. Hence she functions as the embodiment of one's "conscience" and bright ideas.

If human skill and cunning are personified by Athena, and the central womanly skill is weaving, then weaving can itself become a metaphor for human resourcefulness. One's life-span was conceived by the Greeks as a thread, formed by the Fates at birth, but the act of weaving the thread symbolized what one did with that life, the choices of the individual. Thus throughout *The Odyssey* Athena and "the wily Odysseus" (her favorite devotee) are constantly hatching ingenious plots to escape one tight situation or another, rallying with the words "Come, let us weave a plan!"

Odysseus's clever wife, Penelope, is from the same mold. Not only does she, too, use this phrase, but she actually attempts to weave her way out of trouble, telling the suitors who pester her in Odysseus's prolonged absence that she cannot marry until she finishes an important funeral cloth for her aged father-in-law. For three years she tricks these men by unraveling at night what she has woven during the day-time. Truly she was a worthy wife for the trickiest of all the Greeks.

Good evidence exists that the basis of Athena's mythology lies far back in Aegean prehistory, long before the Greeks themselves arrived. The names of Athena and Athens are not Greek or Indo-European names but come from an ear-lier linguistic layer. Furthermore, most of the Greek weaving vocabulary is not Indo-European. The proto-Indo-Europeans seem to have had scant knowledge of weaving, their women knowing only how to weave narrow belts and bands. Probably they were ignorant even of heddles, which mechanize the weaving process and make it efficient. The Greeks clearly learned how to use the large European warp-weighted loom *after* they broke off and moved away from the proto-Indo-European community since all their terms for using a large loom (as opposed to a small band loom) have been borrowed. The people who taught the Greeks this technology, vocabulary, and associated mythical lore must have been the "indige-nous" inhabitants of the Balkans (skilled in weaving since the middle of the Neolithic, perhaps even 5000 BC). The Athenians referred to these natives as "au-tochthonous" – born of the land itself – and Athena must belong originally to them. After all, no one develops a major deity around a technology one doesn't even know yet.

The antiquity of Athena as a local, non-Indo-European deity is hinted at fur-ther by her frequent representation as an owl, that wise-looking bird so common in parts of Greece. In Classical times, after money had been invented, the Athenians chose Athena's owl to stamp on their silver coins. But we also have, from the same period, loom weights stamped with the owl of their favorite goddess. A particularly charming weight shows the owl with human hands, spinning wool from a wool bas-ket at its feet as it looks cockily out at the spectator. It gives a new image to Homer's stock epithet, "owl-eyed Athena," and it underscores once again the importance of this deity to the women on whose textiles so much of Aegean commerce and social interaction was built.

Saint Benedict

THE RULE OF
SAINT BENEDICT

1 If there are artisans in the monastery, they are to practice their craft with all humility, but only with the abbot's permission. 2 If one of them becomes puffed up by his skillfulness in his craft and feels that he is conferring something on the monastery, 3 he is to be removed from practicing his craft and not allowed to resume it unless, after manifesting his humility, he is so ordered by the abbot.

4 Whenever products of these artisans are sold, those responsible for the sale must not dare to practice any fraud. 5 Let them always remember Ananias and Sapphira, who incurred bodily death (Acts 5:1–11), 6 lest they and all who perpetrate fraud in monastery affairs suffer spiritual death.

Hayden Carruth

REGARDING CHAINSAWS

The first chainsaw I owned was years ago,
an old yellow McCulloch that wouldn't start.
Bo Bremmer give it to me that was my friend,
though I've had enemies couldn't of done
no worse. I took it to Ward's over to Morrisville,
and no doubt they tinkered it as best they could,
but it still wouldn't start. One time later
I took it down to the last bolt and gasket
and put it together again, hoping somehow
I'd do something accidental-like that would
make it go, and then I yanked on it
450 times, as I figured afterwards,
and give myself a bursitis in the elbow
that went five years even after
Doc Arrowsmith shot it full of cortisone
and near killed me when he hit a nerve
dead on. Old Stan wanted that saw, wanted it bad.
Figured I was a greenhorn that didn't know
nothing and he could fix it. Well, I was,
you could say, being only forty at the time,
but a fair hand at tinkering. "Stan," I said,
"you're a neighbor. I like you. I wouldn't
sell that thing to nobody, except maybe
Vice-President Nixon." But Stan persisted.
He always did. One time we was loafing and
gabbing in his front dooryard, and he spied
that saw in the back of my pickup. He run
quick inside, then come out and stuck a double
sawbuck in my shirt pocket, and he grabbed
that saw and lugged it off. Next day, when I
drove past, I seen he had it snugged down tight
with a tow-chain on the bed of his old Dodge
Powerwagon, and he was yanking on it

with both hands. Two or three days after,
I asked him, "How you getting along with that
McCulloch, Stan?" "Well," he says, "I tooken
it down to scrap, and I buried it in three
separate places yonder on the upper side
of the potato piece. You can't be too careful,"
he says, "when you're disposing of a hex."
The next saw I had was a godawful ancient
Homelite that I give Dry Dryden thirty bucks for,
temperamental as a ram too, but I liked it.
It used to remind me of Dry and how he'd
clap that saw a couple times with the flat
of his double-blade axe to make it go
and how he honed the chain with a worn-down
file stuck in an old baseball. I worked
that saw for years. I put up forty-five
run them days each summer and fall to keep
my stoves het through the winter. I couldn't now.
It'd kill me. Of course they got these here
modern Swedish saws now that can take
all the worry out of it. What's the good
of that? Takes all the fun out too, don't it?
Why, I reckon. I mind when Gilles Boivin snagged
an old sap spout buried in a chunk of maple
and it tore up his mouth so bad he couldn't play
"Tea for Two" on his cornet in the town band
no more, and then when Toby Fox was holding
a beech limb that Rob Bowen was bucking up
and the saw skidded crossways and nipped off
one of Toby's fingers. Ain't that more like it?
Makes you know you're living. But mostly they wan't
dangerous, and the only thing they broke was your
back. Old Stan, he was a buller and a jammer
in his time, no two ways about that, but he
never sawed himself. Stan had the sugar
all his life, and he wan't always too careful
about his diet and the injections. He lost
all the feeling in his legs from the knees down.
One time he started up his Powerwagon
out in the barn, and his foot slipped off the clutch,
and she jumped forwards right through the wall
and into the manure pit. He just set there,
swearing like you could of heard it in St.

Johnsbury, till his wife come out and said,
"Stan, what's got into you?" "Missus," he says,
"ain't nothing got into me. Can't you see?
It's me that's got into this here pile of shit."
Not much later they took away one of his
legs, and six months after that they took
the other and left him setting in his old chair
with a tank of oxygen to sip at whenever
he felt himself sinking. I remember that chair.
Stan reupholstered it with an old bearskin
that must of come down from his great-great-
grandfather and had grit in it left over
from the Civil War and a bullet-hole as big
as a yawning cat. Stan latched the pieces together
with rawhide, cross fashion, but the stitches was
always breaking and coming undone. About then
I quit stopping by to see old Stan, and I
don't feel so good about that neither. But my mother
was having her strokes then. I figured
one person coming apart was as much
as a man can stand. Then Stan was taken away
to the nursing home, and then he died. I always
remember how he planted them pieces of spooked
McCulloch up above the potatoes. One time
I went up and dug, and I took the old
sprocket, all pitted and et away, and set it
on the windowsill right there next to the
butter mold. But I'm damned if I know why.

Denise Levertov

—————◦————

THE ARTIST

The artist: disciple, abundant, multiple, restless.
The true artist: capable, practicing, skillful;
maintains dialogue with his heart, meets things with his mind.

The true artist: draws out all from his heart,
works with delight, makes things with calm, with sagacity,
 works like a true Toltec, composes his objects, works dexterously, invents;
arranges materials, adorns them, makes them adjust.

The carrion artist: works at random, sneers at the people,
makes things opaque, brushes across the surface of the face of things,
works without care, defrauds people, is a thief.

From the Spanish translation of Toltec Codice de la Real Academia,
fol. 315, v. With the help of Elvira Abascal, who understood the original Toltec.

Lu Chi

PREFACE
from *Wen Fu: The Art of Writing*

When studying the work of the Masters, I watch the working of their minds.

Surely, facility with language & the charging of the word with energy are effects which can be achieved by various means.

Still, the beautiful can be distinguished from the common, the good from the mediocre.

Only through writing and then revising and revising may one gain the necessary insight.

We worry whether our ideas fall short of their subjects, whether the form rhymes with the content.

This may be easy to know, but it is difficult to put into practice.

I have composed this rhymed prose on the Ars Poetica to introduce past masterpieces as models for an examination of the good and the bad in writing.

Perhaps it will be said one day that I have written something of substance and use, that I have entered the Mystery.

When cutting an axe handle with an axe, surely the model is at hand.

Each writer finds a new entrance into the Mystery, and it is difficult to explain.

Nonetheless, I have set down my thinking as clearly as I am able.

translated by Sam Hamill

Gary Snyder

AXE HANDLES

One afternoon the last week in April
Showing Kai how to throw a hatchet
One-half turn and it sticks in a stump.
He recalls the hatchet-head
Without a handle, in the shop
and go gets it, and wants it for his own.
A broken-off axe handle behind the door
Is long enough for a hatchet,
We cut it to length and take it
With the hatchet head
And working hatchet, to the wood block.
There I begin to shape the old handle
With the hatchet, and the phrase
First learned from Ezra Pound
Rings in my ears!
"When making an axe handle
          the pattern is not far off."
And I say this to Kai
"Look: We'll shape the handle
By checking the handle
Of the axe we cut with – "
And he sees. And I hear it again:
It's in Lu Ji's *Wên Fu*, fourth-century
A.D. "Essay on Literature" – in the
Preface: "In making the handle
Of an axe
By cutting wood with an axe
The model is indeed near at hand."
My teacher Shih-hsiang Chen
Translated that and taught it years ago
And I see: Pound was an axe,
Chen was an axe, I am an axe
and my son a handle, soon
To be shaping again, model
And tool, craft of culture,
How we go on.

Mirabai

MIRA IS DANCING

Bending my ankles with silver
I danced —
people in town called me crazy.
She'll ruin the clan,
said my mother-in-law,
and the prince
had a cup of venom delivered.
I laughed as I drank it.
Can't they see? —
body and mind aren't something to lose,
the Dark One's already seized them.
Mira's lord can lift mountains,
he is her refuge.

                    translated by Andrew Schelling

John Haines

from
LIVING OFF THE COUNTRY

The extreme and growing transience of persons, places, and things makes even more difficult the task of discovering who and what we are. Yet this discovery remains the most important thing we have to accomplish. For it is mainly by the intensity of his association with things, persons, and events of this world that the inner person is awakened. All else comes from this. And there are no easy terms for it. We must take thought now, in the truest and deepest sense; and to take thought means that we must, for a while, stop doing. A deliberate slowness is needed, a staying or a standing aside, a waiting, to arrive at where we really ought to be. From that known place, that *felt* place, it may be possible to go on, to do and become many things. Separated from it, we will be lost to the present and future, and our poems, if they come at all, will be brief reports of disaster.

Rainer Maria Rilke

from
LETTERS ON CEZANNE

I can tell how I've changed by the way Cezanne is challenging me now. I am on the way to becoming a worker, on a long way perhaps, and probably I've only reached the first milestone; but still, I can already understand the old man who walked somewhere far ahead, alone.... Today I went to see his pictures again; it's remarkable what an environment they create. Without looking at a particular one, standing in the middle between the two rooms, one feels their presence drawing together into a colossal reality. As if these colors could heal one of indecision once and for all. The good conscience of these reds, these blues, their simple truthfulness, it educates you; and if you stand beneath them as acceptingly as possible, it's as if they were doing something for you. You also notice, a little more clearly each time, how necessary it was to go beyond love, too; it's natural, after all, to love each of these as one makes it: but if one shows this, one makes it less well; one *judges* it instead of *saying* it. One ceases to be impartial; and the very best — love, stays outside the work, does not enter it, is left aside, untranslated: that's how the painting of sentiments came about (which is in no way better than the painting of things). They'd paint: I love this here; instead of painting: here it is. In which case everyone must see for himself whether or not I have loved it. This is not shown at all, and some would even insist that love has nothing to do with it. It's that thoroughly exhausted in the making; there is no residue. It may be that this emptying out of love in anonymous work, which produces such pure things, was never achieved as completely as in the work of this old man.

to Clara Rilke, October 13, 1907
translated by Joel Agee

Donald Hall

from
LIFE WORK

Henry Moore is a model for work. I met him first in 1959 when I lived with my family for a year in an English village about fifteen miles from Moore's house. I had first known Moore for his shelter drawings; and as an undergraduate I thumb-tacked to my Eliot House wall a Penguin Print of a study for sculpture. In 1951, coming to Europe for the first time, I saw many of his sculptures outdoors (where they stand in happy competition with the natural world) at the Festival of Britain. In 1959 the American magazine *Horizon* commissioned me to conduct an interview with him, *Paris Review* style. That year, on leave without pay from the university, I lived by my wits for the first time – BBC work, reviews for the *New Statesman* and *Encounter*, an encyclopedia of poetics co-edited with Stephen Spender – and the interview would contribute to the family budget. I wrote him a letter with the suggestion; he asked me for tea to talk about it, and I took a bus from Thaxted to Bishop's Stortford seven miles from his house and studios that occupied Hertfordshire farmland. He met the bus in his Rover, generous to take time away from work, and after tea agreed to be interviewed. We met two or three times again, sitting in his living room with a tape recorder between us. He and I played Ping-Pong. He and his wife Irina drove to our house for dinner.

Irina was a beautiful and intelligent woman whom Henry had met when she was an art student and Henry a teacher, who had given up her drawing to concentrate on gardening, who loved silence and solitude. Moore was gregarious by nature, but in their household she led the way: Solitude won out over company, which satisfied another powerful portion of Henry Moore, because he loved dearly to work. If he had married a woman who enjoyed society and conversation, Moore would have wasted his time at parties. He wanted most to get up in the morning, pick up a piece of clay, and work all day into the night. His work was various: modeling new ideas in a little old studio filled with oddly shaped pebbles, old maquettes, and bone; working over waxes that came from the foundry before they returned to become bronzes; carving in stone or wood; sketching; or overseeing assistants, young sculptors who translated models into larger versions – six inches to three feet, three feet to fourteen, fourteen to twenty-seven. Maybe I felt free to hire typists and researchers because Henry hired assistants.

Moore interrupted himself for lunch, tea, drinks, and supper; for mail, although mail was a burden; for the telephone; for the founder's truck that came to haul away a great plaster for casting. All day he rode a bicycle over his acreage in the rolling farmland, patrolling his studios to work on different projects. At night after supper he and Irina might watch a BBC detective mystery, but as he watched he kept a pad open on his lap and made automatic or random marks in pencil – and sometimes ideas derived from his idle doodles. When I last saw him at eighty he had built a new graphic studio next to the house, where he retreated for an hour after television, working again between nine and ten at night.

Moore did not arrive among the rich and the famous until he was in his forties. Earlier, he had taught for a living, sculpting as much as he could the rest of the day in a Hampstead studio, or at a cottage in the country during holidays. He grew up in Castleford near Leeds, where his father was a coal miner who swore that none of his children would ever go down to the pits. They didn't – except when Henry sketched coal mining during the second world war; most of the children taught school, as Henry might have done if he had not served in the Great War and attended art school, first in Leeds and then at the Royal Academy, on something like the GI Bill. His whole life felt lucky to him, to have escaped the pits for the studio, to have traded work at the surface of a coal seam for work at the surface of marble and alabaster, of wood and clay.

Although he refused to attend some openings, others took him away from his work; so did lectures, which he mostly refused, and ceremonial occasions and honorary degrees or investitures. Celebrity dogged him and he fought it. Yet he gave up work one afternoon for a photo session, or a morning for a meeting of the directors of the Tate Gallery. During the years when I knew him he was celebrated all over the world, and he enjoyed his fame no end, but remained vigilant to combat its cost in work. I returned three years after the interview to do his *New Yorker* profile, and again when he was eighty for another magazine piece. He wrote me postcards and letters from time to time (I bought etchings; I lectured about him and required slides, which he provided; or he just said hello.) Always he asked me to drop by when I visited England, but we dropped by only twice, because I understood that although his invitations were genuine we would interrupt his day. Only once did I feel impatience from him – he wanted to be working – when Jane and I came calling in the autumn after his summer had been wasted by the huge show in Florence in the 1970s.

The last time I saw him I cherish. He talked about his new grandson and showed us drawings in a studio he had just built to extend his workday. We sat with a drink in the sunny living room he had added to the house which, when he moved to it during the war, had been a broken-down farm-worker's cottage. I knew my man, and I asked him, "Now that you're eighty, you must know the secret of life. What is the secret of life?" With anyone else the answer would have begun with an ironic laugh, but Henry Moore answered me straight: "The secret of life is to have a task, something you devote your entire life to, something you bring everything to, every minute of the day for your whole life. And the most important thing is – it must be something you cannot possibly do!"

Kathleen Norris

DEGENERATES

Not long ago I accompanied a Trappist abbot as he unlocked a door to the cloister and led me down a long corridor into a stone-walled room, the chapter house
of the monastery, where some twenty monks were waiting for me to give a reading.
Poetry does lead a person into some strange places. His wonderfully silent, hidden-
away place was not alien to me as it might have been, however, as I'd been living on
the grounds of a Benedictione monastery for most of the last three years. Trappists
are more silent than the Benedictines, far less likely to have work that draws them
into the world outside the monastery. But the cumulative effect of the Liturgy of
the Hours — at a bare minimum, morning, noon, and evening prayer, as well as the
Eucharist — on one's psyche, the sense it gives a person of being immersed in the
language of scripture, is much the same in any monastery. What has surprised me,
in my time among monastic people, is how much their liturgy feeds my poetry; and
also how much correspondence I've found between monastic practice and the discipline of writing.

Before I read a few poems of mine that had been inspired by the psalms (the
mainstay of all monastic liturgy), I discussed some of those connections. I told the
monks that I had come to see both writing and monasticism as vocations that require periods of apprenticeship and formation. Prodigies are common in mathematics, but extremely rare in literature, and, I added, "As far as I know, there are no
prodigies in monastic life." The monks nodded, obviously amused. (The formal
process of entering a monastery takes at least five years, and usually longer, and
even after monks have made final vows, they often defer to the older members of
the community as more "fully formed" in monastic life.)

Related to this, I said, was recognizing the dynamic nature of both disciplines;
they are not so much subjects to be mastered as ways of life that require continual
conversion. For example, no matter how much I've written or published, I always
return to the blank page; and even more important, from a monastic point of view,
I return to the blankness within, the fears, laziness, and cowardice that, without
fail, will mess up whatever I'm currently writing and, in turn, require me to revise
it. The spiritual dimension of this process is humility, not a quality often associated with writers, but lurking there, in our nagging sense of the need to revise, to
weed out the lies you've told yourself and get real. As I put it to the monks, when

you realize that anything good you write comes *despite* your weaknesses, writing be-comes a profoundly humbling activity. At this point, one of the monks spoke up. "I find that there's a redemptive quality," he said, "just in sitting in front of that blank piece of paper."

His comment reflects an important aspect of monastic life, which has been de-scribed as "attentive waiting." I think it's also a fair description of the writing process. Once, when I was asked, "What is the main thing a poet does?" I was in-spired to answer, "We wait." A spark is struck; an event inscribed with a message – *this is important, pay attention* – and a poet scatters a few words like seeds in a notebook. Months or even years later, those words bear fruit. The process requires both dis-cipline and commitment, and its gifts come from both preparedness and grace, or what writers have traditionally called inspiration. As William Stafford wrote, with his usual simplicity, in a poem entitled "For People with Problems About How to Believe": "a quality of attention has been given to you: / when you turn your head the whole world / leans forward. It waits there thirsting / after its names, and you speak it all out / as it comes to you …"

Anyone who listens to the world, anyone who seeks the sacred in the ordinary events of life, has "problems about how to believe." Paradoxically, it helps that both prayer and poetry begin deep within a person, beyond the reach of language. The fourth-century desert monk St. Anthony said that perfect prayer is one you don't understand. Poets are used to discovering, years after a poem is written, what it's re-ally about. And it's in the respect for the mystery and power of words that I find the most profound connections between the practice of writing and monastic life.

"Listen" is the first word of St. Benedict's Rule for monasteries, and listening for the eruptions of grace into one's life – often from unlikely sources – is a "qual-ity of attention" that both monastic living and the practice of writing tend to cul-tivate. I'm trained to listen when words and images begin to converge. When I wake up at three AM, suddenly convinced that I had better look into an old notebook, or get to work on a poem I'd abandoned years before, I do not turn over and go back to sleep. I obey, which is an active form of listening (the two words are etymolog-ically related).

In fact, I tell the monks, when I first encountered the ancient desert story about obedience – a monastic disciple is ordered by his *abba* to water a dead stick – I laughed out loud. I know that abba's voice from those three-AM encounters; I know the sinking, hopeless feeling that nothing could possibly come out of this writing I feel compelled to do. I also know that good things often come when I persevere. But it took me a long time to recognize that my discipline as a writer, some of it at least, could translate into the monastic realm.

The monastic practice of *lectio divina* – which literally means holy reading – seemed hopelessly esoteric to me for a long time. When I'd read descriptions of it, I'd figure that my mind was too restless, too impatient, too flighty to do it well. But then the monk who was my oblate director said, "What do you mean? You're *doing*

it!" He explained that the poems I was writing in response to the scripture I'd encounter at the Divine Office with the monks, or in my private reading, were a form
of *lectio*. He termed this writing active *lectio*, at least more active than the usual form
of meditating on scripture. I had thought that because I was writing, because I was
doing something, it couldn't be *lectio*. But writing was not what I'd set out to do;
words came as if organically, often simply from hearing scripture read aloud. I was
learning the truth of what the Orthodox monk Kallistos Ware has said about the
monastic environment; that in itself it can be a guide, offering a kind of spiritual
formation. Not all my poems are *lectio* — to believe that would be too easy, a form
of self-indulgence — but the practice of *lectio* does strike me as similar to the practice of writing poetry, in that it is not an intellectual procedure so much as an existential one. Grounded in a meditative reading of scriptures, it soon becomes
much more; a way of reading the world and one's place in it. To quote the fourth-
century monk, it is a way of reading that "works the earth of the heart."

I should try telling my friends who have a hard time comprehending why I like
to spend so much time going to church with Benedictines that I do so for the same
reasons that I write: to let words work the earth of my heart. To sing, to read poetry aloud, and to have the poetry and the wild stories of scripture read to me. To
respond with others, in blessed silence. That is a far more accurate description of
morning or evening prayer in a monastery than what most people conjure up when
they hear the word "church." Monks have always recognized reading as a bodily experience, primarily oral. The ancients spoke of masticating the words of scripture
in order to fully digest them. Monastic "church" reflects a whole-body religion,
still in touch with its orality, its music. In the midst of today's revolution in "instant communication" I find it a blessing that monks still respect the slow way that
words work on the human psyche. They take the time to sing, chant, and read the
psalms aloud, leaving plenty of room for silence, showing a respect for words that
is remarkable in this culture, which goes for the fast talk of the hard sell, the de-
ceptive masks of jargon, the chatter of television "personalities." Being with monks
is more like imbibing language — often powerfully poetic langauge — at full strength.
One night, when we ended a vespers reading with a passage from Job; "My lyre is
turned to mourning, and my pipe to the voice of those who weep," I was awestruck,
not only by the beauty of the words but also by the way those words gave a new dimension to watching the nightly news later that night, leading me to reflect on the
communal role of the poet.

Poets and monks do have a communal role in American culture, which alternately ignores, romanticizes, and despises them. In our relentlessly utilitarian society, structuring a life around writing is as crazy as structuring a life around prayer,
yet that is what writers and monks *do*. Deep down, people seem glad to know that
monks are praying, that poets are writing poems. That is what others want and expect of us, because if we do our job right, we will express things that others may
feel, or know, but can't or won't say. At least this is what writers are told over and
over again by their readers, and I suspect it's behind the boom in visits to monastic

retreat houses. Maybe it is the useless silence of contemplation, that certain "quality of attention" that distinguishes both the poem and the prayer.

I regard monks and poets as the best degenerates in America. Both have a finely developed sense of the sacred potential in all things; both value image and symbol over utilitarian purpose or the bottom line; they recognize the transformative power hiding in the simplest things, and it leads them to commit absurd acts: The poem! The prayer! What nonsense! In a culture that excels at creating artificial, tightly controlled environments (shopping malls, amusement parks, chain motels), the art of monks and poets is useless, if not irresponsible, remaining out of reach of commercial manipulation and ideological justification.

Not long ago I viewed an exhibition at the New York Public Library entitled "Degenerate Art," which consisted of artworks approved by Hitler's regime, along with art the Nazis had denounced. As I walked the galleries it struck me that the real issue was one of control. The meaning of the approved art was superficial, in that its images (usually rigidly representational) served a clear commercial and/or political purpose. The "degenerate" artworks, many crucifixes among them, were more often abstract, with multiple meanings, or even no meaning at all, in the conventional sense. This art – like the best poetry, and also good liturgy – allowed for a wide freedom of response on the part of others; the viewer, the reader, the participant.

Pat Robertson once declared that modern art was a plot to strip America of its vital resources. Using an abstract sculpture by Henry Moore as an example, he said that the material used could more properly have been used for a statue of George Washington. What do poets mean? Who needs them? Of what possible use are monastic people in the modern world? Are their lives degenerate in the same sense that modern art is: having no easily perceptible meaning yet of ultimate value, concerned with ultimate meanings? Maybe monks and poets know, as Jesus did when a friend, in an extravagant, loving gesture, bathed his feet in nard, an expensive, fragrant oil, and wiped them with her hair, that the symbolic act *matters*; that those who know the exact price of things, as Judas did, often don't know the true cost or value of anything.

Sam Hamill

—————

SHADOW WORK

Plato, who despised and distrusted poets, believed that love (in its largest sense) was *gnosis*, the binding (*re-ligio*) which transforms opposites into a unity. For Plotinus, love was the result of "strenuous contemplation in the soul." Kenneth Rexroth, in his beautiful "Letter to William Carlos Williams," defines a poet as one "who creates sacramental relationships that last always." And in the *Timaeus*, Plato says, "It is impossible for the determination or arrangement of two of anything, so long as there are only two, to be beautiful without a third. There must come between them, in the middle, a bond which brings them into union."

Horace wrote, "By right means, if possible, but by any means, make money." Dr. Johnson wrote, on April 5, 1776, working on his "own time" and without remuneration for his thinking, "No man but a blockhead ever wrote, except for money." And Nigel Dennis exclaimed, "One is always excited by descriptions of money changing hands — it's much more fundamental than sex!"

A poet's work was defined by Dr. Williams in *Spring and All:* "To refine, to clarify, to intensify that eternal moment in which we alone live." Williams sought a poetry which would not control energy, but would release it. A re-invigoration of the spirit.

A poet's work is shadow work. I borrow the term, altering it slightly, from Ivan Illich's 1981 *Shadow Work* (Marion Boyars), and it would be improper not to permit him the initial definition:

> I do not mean badly paid work, nor unemployment; I mean unpaid work. The unpaid work which is unique to the industrial economy is my theme. In most societies men and women together have maintained and regenerated the subsistence of their households by unpaid activities. The household itself created most of what it needed to exist. These so-called subsistence activities are not my subject. My interest is in that entirely different form of unpaid work which an industrial society demands as a necessary complement to the production of goods and services. This kind of unpaid servitude does not contribute to subsistence. I call this complement to wage labor "shadow work." It comprises most housework ... shopping ... the homework of students, the toil expended commuting to and from the job ... compliance with bureaucrats ... and the activities usually labeled "family life."

A poet's work is shadow work, it is work performed without regard for remuneration of any kind, most often without consideration for even the possibility of remuneration. The major difference between the shadow work of the poet and that of all of us lies in the fact that a poet's work contributes virtually nothing to the formal economy. Nor is the poet's work (except in certain "chairs" of certain universities) an unpaid condition of employment. Poetry has nothing to do with "employment" except in its most Latinate sense *implicare* – to enfold or involve. The poet's involvement is most likely to be through the employment of contemplation, a sublime activity which is not an action.

The poet, contemplating the experience of love, creates an expression of the irrefutable unity of opposites; that is, the poet seeks to discover the third thing, the bond that binds, the "sacramental relationship" that can, through the poem, be rediscovered again and again. When Buson writes his poem,

> By white chrysanthemums
> scissors hesitate
> only an instant

his poem is not "about" scissors and chrysanthemums. It is an essay on birth and life and death and the rhythm of days and seasons, and it suggests profound unity. He balances action against perfect stillness, life against death, beauty against emptiness. But he excludes none of them. Against the death of chrysanthemums, he places the human hand with all its implications of beauty and life in flowers which the human mind holds dear. Against the cutting, he places the moment's hesitation, a perfect stillness. And in that perfect stillness, we glimpse the great void of which we are a part. Through the poem we are invited into the reality of the "other" life.

Poetry is not commerce. It is not something to be exchanged or traded. It is a gift to the poet, a gift for which the poet, eternally grateful, spends a lifetime in preparation, and which the poet, in turn, gives away and gives away again. The actual work of preparation is shadow work: it must be performed without thought of money and it is "essential" work in that it enables the poet to recognize and accept the gift and, in giving the gift away, do so with a great accompanying energy. But that energy, that experience we name poem, cannot be traded in the marketplace because it cannot be subverted. It won't light a lightbulb, run a heater or an air conditioner or a microwave oven. It is only a poem – necessary, and inviolable, an articulation of a world beyond the possibilities of money.

As the audience for poetry shrank, as social awareness even of the existence of poetry evaporated, poetry turned more and more toward the inner, other world. Poetic language has always been confused with religious language. Since World War II, poetry has spoken almost as a religion, but as a religion without a bureaucracy and with an almost complete absence of dogma. As Heidegger said, "We were too late for the gods, and too early for being, whose poem, already begun, is being."

"All the new thinking," Robert Hass writes, "is about loss. / In this it resembles all the old thinking."

Illich has some illuminating observations on the nature of what we call work: "Both 'work' and 'job' are key words today. Neither had its present prominence three hundred years ago. Both are still untranslatable from European languages into many others. Most languages never had one single word to designate all activities that are considered useful. Some languages happen to have a word for activities demanding pay. This word usually connotes graft, bribery, tax or extortion of interest payments. None of these words would comprehend what we call 'work.'"

To the Greek mind, handwork was anti-aristocratic and best left for servants. St. Paul's declaration that "who does not work does not eat" was generally ignored by the Christian hierarchy. The Rinzai Buddhists had their own version, "No work, no food," which they generally honored. Yet throughout these cultures, as throughout most others, there has been a consistent shadow work that provided, necessarily, for the health of the spirit or soul. It is *gnosis*, the work of knowing. It is not the same as "scientific" work, which is often more the exercise of technology than the labor after knowledge and which is subsidized. The poet's work cannot be subsidized except that subsidies can "purchase time" for a poet. And that "purchased time" is used almost in its entirety for shadow work.

But before examining the poet's shadow work, it might be helpful to understand just when and how the economic division of labor into "productive" and "non-productive" types came about. Illich claims that it was "pioneered and first enforced through the domestic enclosure of women." And while its roots pre-date the Industrial Revolution, it was indeed our faith in technology combined with our insatiable lust for "goods" that divided the home and that removed the hearth from the center of production, transforming it into a center of consumption only. "An unprecedented economic division of the sexes," Illich says, "an unprecedented economic conception of the family, an unprecedented antagonism between domestic and public spheres made wage work into a necessary adjunct of life. All this was accomplished by making working men into the wardens of their domestic women, one by one, and making this guardianship into a burdensome duty."

While men were encouraged to pursue new vocations beyond the home (and beyond "mere" subsistence), women were being redefined through the lenses of biology and philosophy. This newly defined "nature of woman" has been amply explored in Susan Griffin's magnificent *Woman and Nature* (Harper and Row, 1978). Woman was thought to be the matrix of society, one for whom common economics should have no meaning, one for whom the keeping of the household and the overseeing of children would be reward enough. "This new conception of her 'nature' destined her," Illich says, "for activities in a kind of home which discriminated against her wage labor as effectively as it precluded any real contribution to the household's subsistence. In practice, the labor theory of value made man's work into the catalyst of gold, and degraded the homebody into a housewife economically dependent and, as never before, unproductive. She was now man's beautiful property and faithful support needing the shelter of home for her labor of love."

But in materialist culture, what is the "value" of "labors of love"? Man began to perceive himself as utterly dependent upon wage work, he began to perceive himself as sole arbiter of society's problems, and he began to see the "requirements" of woman and wife and family as a kind of extortion. Suddenly, man and woman were completely estranged from subsistence work. The family cow disappeared. The family garden went fallow or turned into a small flower garden.

"Capital gains" replaced the family's customary re-investment in the *means* of family production, and the family-as-means-of-production disappeared.

Womankind became mystified. "Woman's work" was born simultaneously with the devaluation of shadow work and subsistence labor. The sexes became increasingly divided, with man perceived as the "provider" and woman as the "consumer." We consoled woman, whose work was perceived as "non-productive," by further mystifying her "re-productive" capacities. In practical terms, sex became the paradigm for the economics of "women's work" at the direct expense of all notions of partnership and communion and true cohabitation.

The soap-making, weaving, sewing, broom-making, quilting, canning, planting and harvesting, rug-making, animal husbandry, and household repairs at which woman excelled were taken over by technology. When women did begin to re-emerge from the domicile and as they entered the marketplace, they found that, because their work was mystified and devalued, they would find employment only as menial assistants to production – at sewing machines, then at typewriters and telephones – for which they were paid second-class wages, and at which they labored without benefit of union or insurance or retirement benefits – a position which was not in fact greatly different from that position now occupied by the poet or by the free-lance "literary" writer except that woman had little or no hope for advancement.

Shadow work was born with the invention of wage labor, and, as Illich says, both alienate equally. Both become forms of bondage – wage labor through the issuing of long-term credit, shadow work through its devalued "non-productive" and non-capitalist characteristics. Industrial society produces victims as surely, and proportionately, as it produces "wealth" in the form of consumable goods. Just as South African apartheid supplies the white economy with "prosperity," Hitler expected his victims to "produce" while waiting for their inevitable extinction. It is the ultimate exclamation of the Work Ethic: *Arbeit macht frei.*

For the poet, whose work is a "labor of love," whose labor is to "refine, to clarify, to intensify that eternal moment," the real work becomes "feminized" and mystified in the eyes of the public. Poetry is perceived as something rarefied, semi-precious, and nonproductive (to say nothing of counterproductive). Alienated from all forms of subsistence, from virtually all personal productivity, isolated on the assembly line of manufacturing or in the sterile executive suite in which no real product is actually produced, the contemporary male has relegated care of the culture, social work, family lay ministry, education, and all form of housework to the shadow economy. Divorced from the foundation of immaterial good, he struggles to make sense of his life, a life dictated to by forces entirely outside the self, outside part-nership with spouse, and outside the domicile. He neither understands nor values gift labor.

To clarify the difference between "gift labor" (the work the poet invests in mak-ing the poem which will then be given away) and what I have termed "shadow work" (that work performed by the poet in preparation for the gift of inspiration) let me quote Lewis Hyde's remarkable study, *The Gift: Imagination and the Erotic Life of Property* (Random House, 1983): "The costs and benefits of tasks whose procedures are adversarial and whose ends are easily quantified can be expressed through a mar-ket system. The costs and rewards of gift labors cannot. The cleric's larder will al-ways be filled with gifts; artists will never 'make' money."

The poet's necessity to speak is bound to society's need for cultural, social, and spiritual livelihood. There is no "price" for a great painting or poem or musical composition. A true "bardic" tradition in which a poet is paid to sing the praises of the king produces less real poetry than does the shotgun granting we now see under the auspices of the National Endowment for the Arts. The poet can neither buy nor sell the poem just completed. There is no marketplace for poetry. But to quote from Hyde again,

> There is a place for volunteer labor, for mutual aid, for in-house work,
> for healings that require sympathetic contact or a cohesive support
> group, for strengthening the bonds of kinship, for intellectual com-
> munity, for creative idleness, for the slow maturation of talent, for the
> creation and preservation and dissemination of culture, and so on. To
> quit the confines of our current system of gender means not to in-
> troduce market value into these labors but to recognize that they are
> not "female" but human tasks. And to break the system that oppresses
> women, we need not convert all gift labor [and all shadow work] to
> cash work; we need rather to admit women to the "male" money-
> making jobs while at the same time including supposedly "female"
> tasks and forms of exchange in our sense of possible masculinity.

May Sarton has written that the greatest deprivation is that of being unable to give one's gift to those one loves. Then, she says, "the gift turned inward, unable to be given, becomes a heavy burden, even sometimes a kind of poison."

Without the shadow work, without the years of study and contemplation and self-searching, without the mastering of discipline from within, and without the years of trial and error, the years of work to know language and to gain a sense of craft in language, how can the abstract inspiration be transformed (through the ap-propriate infusion and release of human energy) into something worthy of being given? The "product" of love's labor. The quality of the economy in gift-economics is determined in part by the quality of the shadow work which attends it.

A man I shall call Joe has a family. He is in his thirties. He has a dull office job in the city. Having been born and raised in the heart of the USA, he rarely attends a church or a civic function, but has a deep abiding faith in God and Country. He loves his wife. He loves his three children. But his life is hard. He has very little vocabulary for his emotions. He often drinks too much in order to avoid his emotions, in order to obliterate them. He produces nothing with his own hands and knows of no one in whom he can comfortably and intimately confide. His closest friend is a man almost identical to himself. They work together, they play together, they drink to obliterate their feelings together, and sometimes in order to gain courage to discuss what they cannot, when they are sober, comfortably discuss.

But Joe is afraid. He fears the blank gray future with its office dust and telephone and file drawers. He fears the twenty-three years left on his mortgage. He fears the two years left on his automobile loan and the loan he took last year to pay for the birth of his youngest.

He cannot give the quality of love to his family which he would like to give. He is overcome, almost daily, by a dreadful ennui. His nightly entertainment consists almost entirely of televised violence, and he often fantasizes himself as one who is physically inviolable, able to overcome all problems by sheer physical will.

It is one of the most common portraits in twentieth-century literature. From "The Hollow Men" to Willie Loman, from Tennessee Williams to Ernest Hemingway, modern man is filled with existential dread which can be relieved only in shadow work and gift economics, those two "other" kinds of economics for which our families and schools leave us totally unprepared.

Joe needs and wants to give his family an enormous gift, but in order for that gift to be understood it must be articulated in such a manner as to preclude any possibility of misunderstanding. He would also like to share his sense of frustration and, indeed, grief. The greatest gift he might receive from his family is the gift of understanding. His habitual drinking to escape reality may well turn to drunken expressions of rage that take the form of physical violence because he remains unable to articulate either his deepest love or his enormous frustration and his personal agony. Neither his home life nor his education has prepared him to meet the responsibilities that are concomitant with emotional health.

The poet's gift to Joe is the gift of articulation, the gift of good words. But the poet is also left to his or her own resources, for the shadow work of language has no place in public education, and even the language itself resists a poet's use. The actual working material of language, of poetics especially, was articulated by Paul Valery in his essay "Pure Poetry" (*The Art of Poetry*, Bollingen, 1958):

> Language falls successively under the jurisdiction of *phonetics*, *metrics* and *rhythmics*; it has a *logical* and a *semantic* aspect; it includes rhetoric and *syntax*. One knows that all these different disciplines study the same text in many different ways. Here, then, is the poet at grips with this diverse and too rich collection of primal qualities – too rich, in fact, not to be confused; it is from this that he must draw his *objet d'art*,

his machine for producing the poetic emotion, which means that he must compel the practical instrument, the clumsy instrument created by everyone, the everyday instrument used for immediate needs and constantly modified by the living, to become – for the duration that his attention assigns to the poem – the substance of a chosen emotive state quite distinct from all the accidental states of unforeseen duration which make up the ordinary sensitive or psychic life. One may say without exaggeration that common language is the fruit of the disorder of life in common, since beings of every nature, subjected to an innumerable quantity of conditions and needs, receive it and use it to further their desires and their interests, to set up communications among themselves; whereas the poet's language, although he necessarily uses the elements provided by this statistical disorder, constitutes, on the contrary, *an effort by one man* to create an artificial and ideal order by means of a material of vulgar origin.

In order for the poet to be in a position to give a gift that is useful, the poet must master the use of a material which is itself created and used every day by people who have no conscious use for nor faith in poetry. The poem exists in a condition of gift economics. But the work that precedes the poem, the years and years of preparation, come under the category of shadow work, just as the true poet continues to be dependent on shadow work in the form of reading, note-taking, researching, as well as furthering one's self-discipline, one's shamanistic practices, and one's spiritual life.

Poetry subverts materialistic economics because there is no "product" in the marketplace sense of the term, and because poetry teaches us to participate in the economy of the gift and in the economy of shadow work. For Joe, who suffers as a result of his inability to articulate both his needs and his gifts of true emotion, life in the material economy alone is supremely dangerous – it leaves him "emotionally bankrupt" – and he is left with a television serving as a substitute for friendship, as a substitute for partnership, and, ultimately, with himself alone with his loneliness. The loves and hopes and fears that threaten to overcome Joe may well also overcome his family, taking domestic violence (which is after all an inarticulate expression of self-hatred) as their form. Not only does Joe require emergency help, but his family is similarly endangered. Unless the necessary shadow work is done the exchange of true gifts (the gift of one's self, the gift of giving) cannot take place in any comprehensible way.

The quality of time and attention invested in the shadow work contributes directly to the *quality* of transformation of the gift (inspiration) in the hands of the maker (poet). The hunter says, "If you want to catch fish, think like a fish; if you want to catch bear, think like a bear." Wanting to speak for the voiceless, the poet must spend time with those for whom the articulation of complex ideas and emotions is an enormous (and, often, losing) struggle. Wanting to participate fully in the economy of gift-giving, in the economy of love and hope, the shadow work must be attended to, and attended to with all due care and commitment.

The blockhead who writes nothing except for remuneration remains isolated in the material economy alone. The holistic life, the life of health, requires finding a balance within the boundaries of all three separate but interlocking economies; all three are bound together in a sacramental relationship that lasts always.

Lewis Hyde

—⟫●⟪—

from
THE GIFT
Imagination and the Erotic Life of Property

There are many other examples of teachings as transformative gifts. Spiritual conversions have the same structure as the AA experience: the Word is received, the soul suffers a change (or is released, or born again), and the convert feels moved to testify, to give the Word away again. Those whose lives have been touched by a true mentor will have known a similar history. I once met a man who ran a research lab for a large petrochemical firm. He had started to work for the company just out of high school, literally pushing a broom. An older man, a Ph.D., had then asked him to be the handyman in his research lab. The two of them worked together for years, the older man training the younger. When I met him in his late forties, the former handyman had earned a master's degree in chemistry and was working in the same situation his mentor had filled when they first met. When I asked this man what he planned to do in the coming years, he said that he wanted to teach, "to pass it on to the younger men."

We could speak of artists' lives and artists' creations in a similar fashion. Most artists are brought to their vocation when their own nascent gifts are awakened by the work of a master. That is to say, most artists are converted to art by art itself. The future artist finds himself or herself moved by a work of art, and, through that experience, comes to labor in the service of art until he can profess his own gifts. Those of us who do not become artists nonetheless attend to art in a similar spirit. We come to painting, to poetry, to the stage, hoping to revive the soul. And any artist whose work touches us earns our gratitude. The connection between art and gift ... deserves mention here, for it is when art acts as an agent of transformation that we may correctly speak of it as a gift. A lively culture will have transformative gifts as a general feature — it will have groups like AA which address specific problems, it will have methods of passing knowledge from old to young, it will have spiritual teachings available at all levels of maturation and for the birth of the spiritual self. And it will have artists whose creations are gifts for the transformation of the race.

In each example I have offered of a transformative gift, if the teaching begins to "take," the recipient feels gratitude. I would like to speak of gratitude as a labor undertaken by the soul to effect the transformation after a gift has been received.

Between the time a gift comes to us and the time we pass it along, we suffer gratitude. Moreover, with gifts that are agents of change, it is only when the gift has
worked in us, only when we have come up to its level, as it were, that we can give it
away again. Passing the gift along is the act of gratitude that finishes the labor. The
transformation is not accomplished until we have the power to give the gift on our
own terms....

I want to offer a final example of transformation and gratitude, this one at quite a
different level. Meister Eckhart, the fourteenth-century Christian mystic, presents
a high spiritual statement of the commerce I have tried to outline between man and
spirit.... For Eckhart, all things owe their being to God. God's initial gift to man
is life itself, and those who feel gratitude for this gift reciprocate by abandoning attachment to worldly things, that is, by directing their lives back toward God. A second gift comes to any soul that has thus emptied itself of the world – a Child is
born (or the Word is spoken) in the soul emptied of "foreign images." This gift,
too, can be reciprocated, the final stage of the transformation being the soul's entrance into the Godhead.

Eckhart says: "That man should receive God in himself is good, and by this re-
ception he is a virgin. But that God should become fruitful in him is better; for the
fruitfulness of a gift is the only gratitude for the gift." Eckhart is speaking his own
particular language here. To understand what he means we need to know, first, that
according to his theology, "God's endeavor is to give himself to us entirely." The
Lord pours himself into the world, not on a whim or even by choice, but by nature:
"I will praise him," says this mystic, "for being of such a nature and of such an
essence that he must give."

When Eckhart says that it is best if God becomes fruitful in man, he is com-
menting on a verse from the Bible which he translates as: "Our Lord Jesus Christ
went up into a little castle and was received by a virgin who was a wife." He inter-
prets the verse symbolically: to be a "virgin" has nothing to do with carnal life but
refers to "a human being who is devoid of all foreign image and who is as void as
he was when he was not yet." A virgin is detached, someone who no longer regards
the things of this life for themselves or for their usefulness. Detachment is the first
station in Eckhart's spiritual itinerary. When God finds the soul detached he enters
it: "Know then, that God is bound to act, to pour himself out into thee as soon as
ever he shall find thee ready.... It were a very grave defect in God if, finding thee
so empty and so bare, he wrought no excellent work in thee nor primed thee with
glorious gifts." When God pours himself into the soul, the Child is born and this
birth is the fruit of the gratitude for the gift.

> If a human were to remain a virgin forever, he would never bear
> fruit. If he is to become fruitful, he must necessarily be a wife.
> "Wife," here, is the noblest name that can be given to the soul, and
> it is indeed more noble than "virgin." That man should receive God
> in himself is good, and by this reception he is a virgin. But that God

should become fruitful in him is better; for the fruitfulness of a gift
is the only gratitude for the gift. The spirit is wife when in gratitude
it gives birth in return and bears Jesus back into God's fatherly heart.

For Eckhart we are not really alive until we have borne the gift back into the
Godhead. Whatever has proceeded from God comes to life, or receives its being,
only at that moment when it "gazes back" toward Him. The circuit must be completed. "Man ought to be flowing out into whatever can receive him." As in the
other stories we have read, we come alive when we give away what has been received.
In Eckhart the passage is purely spiritual. He tells us not to pray to God for things,
because things are nothing – we should simply pray to be closer to the Godhead.
The final fruit of gratitude toward God is to be drowned in Him.

In the abstract Godhead there is no activity: the soul is not perfectly
beatified until she casts herself into the desolate Deity where neither
act nor form exists and there, merged in the void, loses herself: as self
she perishes, and has no more to do with things than she had when
she was not. Now, dead to self, she is alive in God.

The labor of gratitude accomplishes the transformation that a gift promises.
And the end of gratitude is similarity with the gift or with its donor. The gifted
become one with their gifts. For Eckhart, the child born in the soul is itself a god:
whoever gratefully returns all that God has bestowed will, by that act of donation,
enter the Godhead.

William Everson

from
BIRTH OF A POET

I have stopped at many oases in my life. Vocation is the force that carries you beyond them, that won't let you rest, that seizes you and possesses you and carries you along. When you have your vocation, you have your archetype. Like calls to like, and dislike spits at dislike. No matter how much you try to rest in an oasis, sooner or later it evacuates you. You might be willing to settle for everything it offers because you're tired of the journey, but at that time something else comes to your rescue, the innate disposition of what you are. It is your vocation, and that is what sets you apart and says go. You feel that spiritual craving which is a different thing from either sensual or intellectual thirst; that spiritual thirst to be with your own kind, to associate with them and participate with them, sends you once again on your way across the desert.

Thomas Merton

KARL BARTH'S DREAM

Karl Barth had a dream about Mozart.

Barth had always been piqued by the Catholicism of Mozart, and by Mozart's rejection of Protestantism. For Mozart said that "Protestantism was all in the head" and that "Protestants did not know the meaning of the *Agnus Dei qui tollis peccata mundi."*

Barth, in his dream, was appointed to examine Mozart in theology. He wanted to make the examination as favorable as possible, and in his questions he alluded pointedly to Mozart's masses.

But Mozart did not answer a word.

I was deeply moved by Barth's account of this dream and almost wanted to write him a letter about it. The dream concerns his salvation, and Barth perhaps is striving to admit that he will be saved more by the Mozart in himself than by his theology.

Each day, for years, Barth played Mozart every morning before going to work on his dogma: unconsciously seeking to awaken, perhaps, the hidden sophianic Mozart in himself, the central wisdom that comes in tune with the divine and cosmic music and is saved by love, yes, even by *eros.* While the other, theological self, seemingly more concerned with love, grasps at a more stern, more cerebral *agape:* a love that, after all, is not in our own heart but *only in God* and revealed only to our head.

Barth says, also significantly, that "it is a child, even a 'divine' child, who speaks in Mozart's music to us." Some, he says, considered Mozart always a child in practical affairs (but Burckhardt "earnestly took exception" to this view). At the same time, Mozart, the child prodigy, "was never allowed to be a child in the literal meaning of that word." He gave his first concert at the age of six.

Yet he was always a child "in the higher meaning of that word."

Fear not, Karl Barth! Trust in the divine mercy. Though you have grown up to become a theologian, Christ remains a child in you. Your books (and mine) matter less than we might think! There is in us a Mozart who will be our salvation.

FROM THE CITY
TO SABBATH

From one point of view the townsman is right. It is a lot of nonsense all this cackle about the beauty of the country. And the cackle would never have been heard if the towns had not become such monsters of indecency and indignity. The right and proper and natural development of human life unsullied by an insubordinate commercialism no more leads to ugly towns than to an ugly country side. On the contrary, the town properly thought of is the very crown and summit of man's creativeness and should be the vehicle for the highest manifestation of his sensibility, his love of order and seemliness of dignity and loveliness. Man collaborates with God in creating — that, physically speaking is what he is for. The natural world, following, without the slightest deviation, the line of least resistance, blooms in a million million marvels of natural beauty. The beauty of flowers and trees and beasts and insects, the beauty of bones and muscles and crystals and clouds, is product of this unswerving but unconscious obedience. Man alone among created things can resist: man alone can willingly obey. Man alone can give thanks: man alone can respond and take a conscious and willing part in the universal creativity. Thus, properly thought of, man's works, alone of all material things, can have the spiritual qualities of tenderness and love, of humour and gaiety: and they alone can, on the other hand, have the qualities of wickedness and pride and silliness.

— *Eric Gill, from* A Holy Tradition of Working

⟶⟩●⟨⟵

Answer this to yourselves, & expel from among you those who pretend to despise the labours of Art & Science, which alone are the labours of the Gospel: Is not this plain & manifest to the thought? Can you think at all & not pronounce heartily! That to Labour in Knowledge is to Build up Jerusalem: and to Despise Knowledge, is to Despise Jerusalem & her Builders. . . .

Let every Christian as much as in him lies engage himself openly & publicly before all the World in some Mental pursuit for the Building up of Jerusalem.

— *William Blake, from* Jerusalem

A recent novel by Mary Stolz tells the story of a manuscript now in the monastery of St. Paul in Carinthia. Dating from the ninth century, this illuminated missal includes an unusual marginal notation set down by the nameless monk who was then, 1200 years ago, hard at work upon it. Written alongside the holy words we may still find, should we look, the monk's own verse:

> Hunting mice is his delight,
> Hunting words I sit all night.
> So in peace our task we ply,
> Pangur Ban, my cat, and I:
> In our arts we find our bliss,
> I have mine and he has his.

One reviewer of the novel commented upon the monk's apparent arrogance, asserting his own identity into a divine text. I, however, don't hear arrogance. Rather I hear a kind of joy that spills over onto the margins. The monk is at play in the fields of the Lord. He's cultivating, plowing with pen and ink the edges of God's good earth.

The cat hunts. The man works. I imagine his hands are cold; he blows on them and then places them back upon the manuscript, the words still wet with ink. Candlelight flickers over the page.

The poem results from a particular moment in a particular place, a moment long since, like the monk himself, turned to ash. He is there simply to copy the prayers into the new missal. He couldn't anticipate the poem, but there it is, this brief lingering which now finds its own spot within the boundaries of the divine book. Anarchic, frivolous, and true, the poem sneaks into heaven unannounced.

How do we ever explain this joy in creation, or the depths out of which true labor arises? I think of William Carlos Williams's "January Morning," with its brief, imagist descriptions of the working life of New Jersey, of "the domes of /

the Paulist Fathers in Weehawken / against a smoky dawn." The young doctor – Williams surely – finds himself "dancing with happiness / in the sparkling wind, alone / at the prow of the ferry," delighting in "the tall probationers / in their tan uniforms / hurrying to breakfast," and even in the "semicircle of dirt-colored men / about a fire bursting from an old ash can." How to explain this? It's the way things are when seen in a certain light. "But you got to try hard" he says; and then, again, "But –" as if struggling against the boundaries of what *can* be said:

> But –
>
>   Well, you know how
> the young girls run giggling
> on Park Avenue after dark
> when they ought to be home in bed?
> Well,
>   that's the way it is with me somehow.[1]

We know so little of the final meaning of what we do, where our tiny piece of the puzzle fits into the whole. We work, blindly set upon our "real" tasks, when something winged interrupts. The arrow flies.

However marginal that moment may appear, it too takes its place on the pages of our work. And – who knows? – perhaps that moment is the real work, the small piece of us destined to endure.

How often have we heard the irony: to focus your labor on the center is to miss the point, because the center at which you aim is nowhere to be found. By not aiming, the student *becomes* the center that she seeks. Aim is abandoned, yet abandoned through the most rigorous of disciplines. "All is emptiness," the Master says. "Your own self, the flashing sword, and the arms that wield it. Even the thought of emptiness is no longer there." So too in a work of art. Painting, for example, "becomes spontaneous calligraphy. Here again the painter's instructions might be: spend ten years observing bamboo, become a bamboo yourself, then forget everything and – paint."[2]

Which suggests: only through the marginal is it possible to hit the mark. Recall the shared etymology of these words, *mark, marginal,* and recall too the metaphor within St. Paul's word for sin, *hamartia.* To sin, to miss the mark, means, paradoxically, to miss the margin. I fail to see the margin because I'm so intent upon the center, forgetting what the fairy tales always say: that it's the no-account who will find the way to the riddle's answer, who wins the kingdom because he took the time to befriend the lowly duck, the fox, the ant. These foolish ones gain all by attending to the simple things of the world.

Always these contradictions come together in the city, as both Blake and Eric Gill remind us, which we think of as the center of human civilization, the focus of all that Athena has given us: all of that software, all that technology. Here unimaginable destitution rubs up against ungraspable wealth. These two are sisters, light and dark twins. They are who we are: splintered selves. Which helps explain why one Catholic Worker in Manhattan can write,

> I think of God more passionately and with a kind of insight I cannot imagine possessing in a place of more natural beauty, in a landscape more conducive to tranquility of soul. It is here that I grasp, if ever so slightly, the Passion and Death, and, lastly, the Resurrection of Jesus. For it was Jesus who went where all roads crossed and all iniquity was revealed. It was there that he met his destiny, and where Mary found the empty tomb.[3]

The marginal way leads, curiously enough, to the center – for Jesus as for Oedipus. One chooses consciously, one blindly, but the result is much the same. Both find the narrow path, the needle's eye into the City.

The marginal is Flannery O'Connor's Misfit, the criminal through whom the Grandmother discovers "that reality is something to which we must be returned at considerable cost."[4]

The marginal is Etty Hillesum in Westerbork, an invisible Jew to the Germans as she worked in the concentration camp, writing letters back to friends in Amsterdam who were only slightly less marginal than Etty herself. She watches as a German guard, just a few feet away on the other side of the fence, with an "enraptured expression" picks purple lupine, his gun on his back, while the matron of the orphanage carries a small child in her arms and places him, alone, on a train bound for Auschwitz.

She writes – miraculously – of this place, Westerbork, as home. Not without a sense of irony, certainly; "this place," she knows, "now a focus of Jewish suffering, lay deserted and empty just four years ago. And the spirit of the Department of Justice hovered over the heath." The first German inmates tell her that "there wasn't a butterfly to be seen here, not a flower, not even a worm." Now, in contrast, she finds an orphanage, a synagogue, a small mortuary, and a shoe-repair factory under construction. With two thousand beds it is an entire city of marginalized workers, a city for those who, like Joyce's Bloom, are permanently keyless citizens.

To describe her own life, Etty Hillesum uses the image of a spider casting the main threads out ahead of itself and then following along from behind. So violently uprooted in her life, it has been this way for her, with all of her expectations for her "real work" shattered:

> The main path of my life stretches like a long journey before me and already reaches into another world. It is just as if everything that happens here and that is still to happen were somewhat discounted inside me. As if I had been through it already, and was now helping to build a new and different society.[5]

It *has* already occurred. Of course: this rain, that new house rising across the street, this music I hear as I type these words; these hands. All of it, all has vanished, like Etty. And you, the reader: the thread's been tossed ahead, reaching into another world. And I'm there too, you're with me as I sit inside this broken city, reading the words of this dead woman who wrote on scraps of borrowed paper with borrowed pens on what she knew was borrowed time. Etty Hillesum knows where she is, which may be one definition of a prophet. From there she reminds us. More courageous than I could ever hope to be, she stretches her hand back from that new world she has been building in eternity.

Briefly, briefly, through the mist of the afternoon rain, I can see them all gathered. Etty Hillesum and William Blake, Hadewijch and Meister Eckhart, Lao-tzu and Chuang Tzu, Changing Woman and Jesus. Just now it's Etty who reaches out from that invisible place within. *You too* she whispers; *you too are one of us.* Her words frighten me, have always frightened me, exhilarated as I am with the possibilities that beckon. I can see her, radiant, standing beside St. Benedict and — who knows? — Jalalludin Rumi and Henry Thoreau. They reach out through her, seeking to claim me, to pull me from this warm home, from this most livable of all American cities, from this richest of all the earth's countries, even from the great globe itself. I know she wants to set me wandering. Homeless, marginalized, mad with a clarity that seeks to burn through the dark cities of this world, mad to reveal the glory within, she reaches out to mark me. She covers my forehead with a cross of ash.

End of a day. End of a year, a century, a millennium. Soon I must leave to pick up my daughter at her friend's house. I remember suddenly an afternoon like this one, some years ago when Katie was five; her first hamster had died, and instead of doing what I call my work I spent the rest of the day mourning with her, and then burying. The earth I dug was soft, moist, and cool in my hands. I held some of the dirt out to my daughter and let her feel how rich this soil is, how good. I cannot explain that, nor can I explain how I felt my daughter's loss, and my own. There is nothing abstract about this. It is the way things are. Bodies turn into other bodies. I sit here composing while Pearl the hamster is in the yard decomposing, which is no different, really, from composing, which means to place together, from *pausis,* a pause, from *pauein,* to stop. And so we do. We must labor to compose ourselves, to pull ourselves together. And sometimes we do that best by stopping.

Dwelling with earth / thinking with depth / helping with kindness / speaking with truth / governing with peace / working with skill.

Such is the nature of earthly, spiritual labor. It's all transformation, like Ariel's vision of Alonso: Those are pearls that were his eyes.[6] Composition, decomposition, like the heads and tails of coins, like the body and its shadow, like the text and its margins, the blank spaces that make meaning possible. I too am composed of pieces of the dead, and I too compose from them, borrowing, much of the time, their words.

For me it's like the monk with Pangur Ban. *Hunting mice is his delight, / Hunting words I sit all night.* I throw my thread ahead, never sure where it will land. And then I follow behind.

Emily Warn

VAGRANT

Locust leaves fall
in the empty city park,
thickly, as if a crow pounds
the podium of the top branches.
Soon rains. Soon wake to darkness.
But today the light resembles California.
I'm stripped to my t-shirt,
enjoying the leaves sift down
with the same pleasure
the boy across the street must feel
pulling his jeans from the line,
burying his face in their smell,
asking, *What are we going to do today, Mother?*

A job application sits on my desk.
A whole day to fill it. I can't.
Instead I invent questions.
Why do pigeons have red feet?
What percentage of a day's sunlight
do locust leaves absorb?
How can I believe in ambition
when the man on the city stairs
whose wife kicked him out needs to talk?
And the wild ripe grapes need to be eaten?
And my shadow wants to walk, admiring
 how it flattens against buildings and stripes trees.

Besides, turning the compost this morning,
I broke a spider web that I promised to fix.
A decade – at least – to weave a web
whose vacancies let wind and rain pour through,
yet snag the occasional fly.

Christian

---

from
THE GOSPEL ACCORDING
TO MATTHEW

No one can serve two masters; for either he will hate the one and love the other, or he will be devoted to the one and despise the other. You cannot serve God and mammon.

Therefore I tell you, do not be anxious about your life, what you shall eat or what you shall drink, nor about your body, what you shall put on. Is not life more than clothing? Look at the birds of the air: they neither sow nor reap nor gather into barns, and yet your heavenly Father feeds them. Are you not of more value than they? And which of you by being anxious can add one cubit to his span of life? And why are you anxious about clothing? Consider the lilies of the field, how they grow; they neither toil nor spin; yet I tell you, even Solomon in all his glory was not arrayed like one of these. But if God so clothes the grass of the field, which today is alive and tomorrow is thrown into the oven, will he not much more clothe you, O men of little faith? Therefore do not be anxious, saying, "What shall we eat?" or "What shall we drink?" or "What shall we wear?" For the Gentiles seek all these things; and your heavenly Father knows that you need them all. But seek first his kingdom and his righteousness, and all these things shall be yours as well.

Therefore, do not be anxious about tomorrow, for tomorrow will be anxious for itself. Let the day's own trouble be sufficient for the day.

Lao-tzu

TAOTECHING #8

The best are like water
bringing help to all
without competing
choosing what others avoid
hence approaching the Tao
dwelling with earth
thinking with depth
helping with kindness
speaking with truth
governing with peace
working with skill
moving with time
 and because they don't compete
they aren't maligned

translated by Red Pine

William Langland

from
PIERS PLOWMAN

Then up came Old Age and whopped me over the head –
Made me bald in front and bare on the crown –
So hard he hit me it would be visible forever.
"Sir evil-bred Oldster!" said I, "discourtesy goes with you!
Since when was this the way – to whop men's heads?
Had you been courteous you would have asked leave!"
"Me – ask permission? – you rascal!" – and he laid on me again
With age, hit me under the ear – scarce can I hear.
He buffeted me about the mouth and beat out my teeth,
bound me with gout – now I can't even walk.
Of the woe I was in my wife had grief
And wished most surely that I was in heaven.
And for that member she loved the most, and loved to feel –
On nights, namely, when naked we went to bed –
For the life of me I had no might to make it rise
– The Old One and she had so enfeebled it.
  And as I sat in this sorrow, I saw how Kynde [Nature] passed,
and I cried to her "Bring me out of care!
Look how that hoary Old One visited me!
Avenge me if you will, for I would be long from him."
"If you would be avenged, wend your way to Unity
And hold yourself with Her – until I send for you."
"Council me, Kynde, what craft be best to learn?"
"Learn to love," quoth Kynde, "and leave all others."

modernized by Douglas Thorpe

EPILOGUE

There was an artist in the city of Kouroo who was disposed to strive after perfection. One day it came into his mind to make a staff. Having considered that in an imperfect work time is an ingredient, but into a perfect work time does not enter, he said to himself, It shall be perfect in all respects, though I should do nothing else in my life. He proceeded instantly to the forest for wood, being resolved that it should not be made of unsuitable material; and as he searched for and rejected stick after stick, his friends gradually deserted him, for they grew old in their work and died, but he grew not older by a moment. His singleness of purpose and resolution, and his elevated piety, endowed him, without his knowledge, with perennial youth. As he made no compromise with time, Time kept out of his way, and only sighed at a distance because he could not overcome him. Before he had found a stick in all respects suitable the city of Kouroo was a hoary ruin, and he sat on one of its mounds to peel the stick. Before he had given it the proper shape the dynasty of the Candahars was at an end, and with the point of the stick he wrote the name of the last of that race in the sand, and then resumed his work. By the time he had smoothed and polished the staff Kalpa was no longer the pole-star; and ere he had put on the ferule and the head adorned with precious stones, Brahma had awoke, and slumbered many times. But why do I stay to mention these things? When the finishing stroke was put to his work, it suddenly expanded before the eyes of the astonished artist into the fairest of all the creations of Brahma. He had made a new system in making a staff, a world with full and fair proportions; in which, though the old cities and dynasties had passed away, fairer and more glorious ones had taken their places. And now he saw by the heap of shavings still fresh at his feet, that, for him and his work, the former lapse of time had been an illusion, and that no more time had elapsed than is required for a single scintillation from the brain of Brahma to fall on and inflame the tinder of a mortal brain. The material was pure and his art was pure; how could the result be other than wonderful?

—Henry David Thoreau, from Walden

Sam Green

————⋙●⋘————

LETTER TO THE EDITOR

BROODING HERON PRESS & BINDERY

Sam & Sally Green, Publishers

Sunday Morning

Dear Doug,

Just after 5:00 here. Woke up alert a little while ago and thinking hard about you, so I figured I'd get up a bit early, grind coffee, and get a letter off. I'm not doing so well with this essay, even in fragments. Admittedly, your assertion that you were thinking about using a poem from *Vertebrae* gave me some relief. Maybe one reason I've been having difficulty working through this thing is that I *have* tackled some of it already in poems from that book (I'm thinking of "Covenant...," "On Hearing Our Plans...," and "Hands Learning to Work" especially, read as a trio; but you're right that other poems deal with it, as well). And perhaps this would be a good solution to my immediate problem, which seems to be an inability to jerk what I know I want to say out of myself in a way that meets your space and deadline requirements.... I've been imposing outside pressures and expectations – the very things that kill good writing for me (which is why I would have made a lousy journalist).

Work on the house progresses still, and still more slowly than we could want. Fall is in our minds, as it always is during the building season, and there is the conflict between needing and wanting to finish, and the demands of *the work* wanting to be done well. Funny we should think of the work asking to be done well, isn't it? When I began putting up the first log for this new addition the familiarity of the work as I maneuvered it took me back instantly twelve years, to when I put the first log onto the house. My neighbors were skeptical about the whole process. The post office here sits at the top of a hill overlooking the county dock. It has a big covered porch where we can stand and watch the rain, or the sun setting behind neighboring Stuart Island. One afternoon, leaning against the wooden railing outside while the postmaster was sorting the bags that had just come in by the mail boat, I turned my back on the view and looked at the way the log walls of the post office worked together, and said to a neighbor, "I've been thinking about building a log house." Fred is our resident mechanical genius and jack-of-all-trades. Back in the good old days he worked for the *Whole Earth Catalogue* and wrote reviews of technical books. Fred is one of the most thoughtful people I've ever met. He can also be blunt: "A log house! Geez, that's a *lot* of work." About that time another neighbor opened the post office door and joined us. "Hey," said Fred. "Sam's thinking about building a log house."

"Man," my other neighbor replied, "that's a lot of work. Can't you think of something a little easier?"

Well, I could. When we made the move from Seattle into the army tent we were to live in for three years on the island, we read up on homemade houses in a number of self-sufficiency books written for back-to-the-landers, and considered a rammed-earth house, a straw bale house, and other equally exotic forms of architecture before settling on a method called "post and beam," largely because we had visited someone who had built one, and who professed as few carpentry skills as I had. But that took lumber, and lumber took money, and we didn't have any. Besides, I had grown up in a log house, and there was something comforting in the idea. There was also something else: a notice on the post office bulletin board that said, "Free Vertical Firewood." The advisory committee for our tiny island school had decided to clear a large patch of woods in order to let more light into the schoolhouse and to expand the size of playground area for the two dozen students. They figured one way to get the trees cut down without a budget was to offer them for firewood. Trouble was, this was fall, and no one wanted green wood, they wanted dry wood, and everyone's energies were focused on downed trees and old snags, so no one had taken the committee up on the idea.

The beauty of a log house is that your interior walls are finished as soon as you put up your exterior walls. There are no troublesome studs, no dry wall, no insulation necessary. Just caulk and chink and there you go. So, despite the fact that it was "a lot of work," I made a deal with another neighbor and I helped him fall the trees. We skidded them out with his tractor. The handy Fred Richardson had constructed a homemade log trailer, and we made a deal with him to haul the logs to our place. Fred and Sally and I loaded the logs onto the trailer up rams using nothing but peevees. We needed mostly thirty-six-foot and twenty-eight-foot logs for the project, but the ridge pole was well over forty feet, and most of the trees were eight to twelve inches through at the butt, so it was difficult. I still remember making the notches for the first log that went onto the sill logs. A neighbor had stopped by to see how things were going. I had rough-cut the notches and was cleaning them out with a gouge made by a blacksmith in Conway. It was a beautiful tool, sharp, and a pleasure to use. My neighbor looked at my work and said, "God, are you going to do *all* of them that way?" I said I was. "Listen," he said, "just keep in mind you want to finish this house in time to *live* in it." He went away shaking his head.

He couldn't understand how I could take so much time with the inside of the notch, which no one was ever going to see. How could I tell him?

Two years later, when I was desperately trying to get the house done enough to move into before winter, another neighbor spent a week helping me put up the rafters after I'd finished all the walls. We were working very fast, and were skipping details, using shims instead of taking the time to correct mistakes. We excused all this with easy banter about what we called "The Rules of Peasant Architecture." When one of us would be too slow, the other would yell, "Hey, remember the axiom: 'Close enough is usually true.'" Or, "It's just a question of mind over matter: Don't mind, and it won't matter." Or, "If it isn't going to show, and it isn't structurally important, don't worry about it."

When I was still in the Coast Guard, I remember being approached by a retired marine sergeant who visited the base from time to time to try and sell insurance policies. We shared a table on the mess deck, drinking the remains of coffee from the huge urn. It was late, and we were the only two there. I was putting a careful spit shine on my dress shoes. The ex-marine talked to me while I worked, making an initial pitch for insurance, but gradually falling into easy conversation when it became clear that I wasn't a mark, that I couldn't possibly afford premiums with my tiny salary and the commitments I already had. He gave me a few pointers on my work. We argued the merits of lukewarm versus cold water, of cotton balls versus strips torn from old cotton skivvies. Finally I finished the shoes and put them down, pleased: I could have shaved in their mirror finish. He frowned at me. "What about the heels?" he asked. "I don't do the heels," I said (nobody could see the heels because the pants hung so low in the back). He leaned close to me across the small round table, putting his considerable weight on both crossed forearms. He had a tattoo on one of them, an exquisite nude with hands cupped demurely to hide her breasts. "Listen to me, kid," he said. "A man who doesn't shine the heels of his shoes is a man who doesn't wipe his ass."

My father always said that work was when you were doing one thing when you'd rather be doing something else. Wendell Berry said it too in the *Mad Farmer's Almanac:* "The world's curse is a man / who'd rather be someplace else." I think it was Berry more than anyone else who made me begin to understand that one's work is not confined to what one does for wages. It takes in *everything* you do. You know these lines from Frost?

> Men work together …
> Whether they work together or apart.

and:

> But yield who will to their separation,
> My object in living is to unite
> My avocation and my vocation
> As my two eyes make one in sight.
> Only where love and need are one,

> And the work is play for mortal stakes,
> Is the deed ever really done
> For Heaven and the future's sakes.

Separation is an illusion. To do less than the best you know how to do isn't just a failure of the self to the self, but a denial of what's possible to others. Poor work is work that doesn't reflect the doer's ability; good work stops only when the limitations of the worker are reached. I've learned this mostly as a poet, coming always to the inevitable point in work on a poem where I know (or believe) the poem could be made better, but I honestly don't know how to do it. As Auden said, "No poem is ever finished; only abandoned." As a father I'm learning this again. But is this just self-satisfaction? Soetsu Yanagi (*The Unknown Craftsman*) said, "Let us do our work so well that all men may be able to discover themselves in it." All right. And yet, in my first years here I went through a time when I thought I could separate myself from others, and when their response to my work didn't matter, directly or indirectly, to me. Still, I tried to work as well as I could, and it wasn't until I began to go through my conversion experience that I began to find an explanation that made sense to me. Hamill quotes that wonderful Latin dictum: *laborare est orare* (and Pound: "There is worship in plowing / and equity in the weeding hoe." *Canto* XCIX). What calls us to pay attention to the *quality* of the work isn't the increase of the value of the offering, though (and the product of work cannot be separated from the process of the labor). It's more than that. And here's where I begin to sound to myself like a hippie-dipshit-pseudo-mystic: our labor is limited to allowing God to work through us as well as He is able; our job is to remove barriers. There's a Rumi poem that makes sense of this for me in which he says:

> The flute player puts breath into a flute,
> and who makes the music? Not the flute.
> The flute player!

Our job is to let the music flow through us. The continuing task. Not to listen and believe we are playing the music ourselves, but to get out of the way.

So, I am back at labor on the house. Yesterday I spent all day trying to get the risers plumb on the back stairs (the northwest corner), the panic of all the other things needing to be done flapping around me like a flock of crows. I kept making tiny adjustments, at one point removing a piece of wood that split, even though it was still structurally sound. Why? Who would see it? No one, probably. Who would know? I would. And the unspoken God. I'm a man who wipes his ass. Most of the time. . . .

And now there's more work to do, other than the work of writing this letter, and thinking, and moving through the day with God-mindfulness. I wish I were a better man. Have you ever read Okakura Kakuzo's little volume *The Book of Tea?* In it he says, "In art the Present is the eternal. The tea-master held that real appreciation of art is only possible to those who make of it a living influence.... Thus the tea-master strove to be something more than the artist art itself." I can't seem to bear the responsibility for that moment to moment, though I'd like to. I fumble through the day. If I am the flute, indeed, then God must shake His head at the off-notes, the wheezings and odd choking sounds. Anyway, I think using a poem if you still want would be fine. Clearly nothing else is going to get finished, and I can't leave you hanging any longer. This letter is pocked with the uncertainties with which I've been wrestling, and you can no doubt see the stumbling. I'll need to let it go for now, and come back to it when it wants finishing. When I can hear the tune plainly.

Love from Here,

Sam

Navajo

from
DINÉ BAHANE
The Navajo Creation Story

Of a time long, long ago these things too are said.

It is said that the people had been continuing their flight from the monsters who pursued them.

By now they were calling themselves *Ha'aznání diné'é*. In the language of *Bilagáana* the White Man that name means Emergence People. Those are the people destined to become known as the ancestors of the Navajo people who now live on the surface of this world.

In trying to escape the *Binaayéé'* they went from place to place and from place to place, thinking themselves safe at each. They would settle and farm the land, planting corn and squash, beans and pumpkins in the spring. And they hoped that in the fall they could harvest what they had planted.

But then those dreaded creatures the *Binaayéé'* would locate them and would again prey upon them. They destroyed and devoured them unrelentingly as hungry wolves gobble sheep who stray.

Thus it was that the last survivors of that unending flight traveled to *Tsé łigaii íí'áhí*. In the language of *Bilagáana* that name means White Standing Rock.

By now there remained only *Áłtsé hastiin* the First Man and *Áłtsé asdzáá* the First Woman along with four other persons. Only an old man had also survived. And only his wife had survived with him. With them only two of their children had survived. One was a young man and the other was a young woman.

Those four were weary and meager. They were frightened and fully without hope. They now wondered what would be the good of clearing yet another patch of land. Surely *Binaayéé'* the Alien Giants would destroy them as they had destroyed everyone else.

"They are sad," said *Áłtsé hastiin* the First Man to *Áłtsé asdzáá* the First Woman. "They have no heart for continuing such an existence."

That is what he said. And this is what she replied:

"Truly they are disheartened," she replied.

"And just as truly are they afraid. Indeed, I am afraid for them, just as I fear for myself and for you."

To which *Áłtsé hastiin* the First Man then had this to say:

"In any case, we must rest here," he said.

"We must try once more to settle. Perhaps the gods will help us somehow."

And *Áłtsé asdzą́ą́* the First Woman had this to say in reply:

"Do not count on them," she replied.

"We do not yet altogether know what pleases them and what annoys them. We do not yet know when they will help us and when they will act against us."

<hr>

So they all settled themselves for the night, scarcely daring to try again to make a home for themselves, and wondering how soon the final misfortune would befall all of them.

Indeed, these were not good times.

In the morning, however, *Áłtsé hastiin* the First Man observed that a dark cloud had covered the top of *Ch'ool'į́'į́* the Giant Spruce mountain which stood yonder by some distance. Saying nothing to others about what he was, however, he merely joined them in their work.

On the second morning he looked and noticed that the dark cloud had descended to the middle of *Ch'ool'į́'į́* and that it was raining on the upper half. But he said nothing to anyone else and joined those who were working.

When daylight brought the third morning, he looked and saw that the dark cloud had now settled further down the sides of *Ch'ool'į́'į́* so that only the base of the mountain lay uncovered. But he still mentioned what he observed to no one, choosing instead to work along with the others.

On the fourth day, however, when he noticed that the dark cloud had now enveloped *Ch'ool'į́'į́* clear down to its base and that rain was falling upon it in torrents, he spoke of what he saw to *Áłtsé asdzą́ą́* the First Woman, saying this to her:

"I wonder what is happening," he said to her.

"For four days *Ch'ool'į́'į́* has been covered with a dark cloud. Only the summit was covered at first. But each day the cloud has forced itself lower and lower, so that now even its flanks are entirely hidden.

"Perhaps I had better go there to investigate."

To which she had this reply to offer:

"It is better that you should stay here," she offered.

"There is great danger out there.

"*Naayéé'* the devouring ones will surely set upon you. Surely you will be devoured like so many others have been."

That is what she replied. And this is what he then had to say:

"Do not be afraid," said he.

"Nothing will go wrong. For I will surround myself with song.

"I will sing as I make my way to the mountain.

"I will sing while I am on the mountain.

"And I will sing as I return.

"I will surround myself with song.

"You may be sure that the words of my songs will protect me."

That is what *Áłtsé hastiin* the First Man said to his wife *Áłtsé asdzą́ą́* the First Woman.

⟫•⟪

So it was that *Áłtsé hastiin* the First Man set out for the cloud-covered mountain of giant spruces. On the very next morning he set out, singing as he went.

"I am *Áłtsé hastiin* the First Man," he sang.

"*Áłtsé hastiin* the First Man am I, maker of much of the earth.

"*Áłtsé hastiin* the First Man am I, and I head for *Ch'ool'į́'į́* the Giant Spruce Mountain, following the dark, rainy cloud.

"I follow the lightning and head for the place where it strikes.

"I follow the rainbow and head for the place where it touches the earth.

"I follow the cloud's trail and head for the place where it is thickest.

"I follow the scent of the falling rain and head for the place where the lines of rain are darkest."

For four days he traveled thus, singing as he went.

"I am *Áłtsé hastiin*," he said, "and I head for Giant Spruce Mountain in pursuit of good fortune.

"In pursuit of good fortune I follow the lightning and draw closer to the place where it strikes.

"In pursuit of good fortune I follow the rainbow and draw closer to the place where it touches the earth.

"In pursuit of good fortune I follow the trail of the cloud and draw closer to the place where it is thickest.

"In pursuit of good fortune I follow the scent of the falling rain and draw closer to the place where the lines of rain are darkest."

On and on he traveled, continuing to sing as he made his way to *Ch'ool'į́'į́* the Giant Spruce Mountain.

"I am First Man and I head for *Ch'ool'į́'į́* in pursuit of old age and happiness," he sang.

"In pursuit of old age and happiness I follow the lightning and approach the place where it strikes.

"In pursuit of old age and happiness I follow the rainbow and approach the place where it touches the earth.

"In pursuit of old age and happiness I follow the dark cloud's trail and approach the place where it is thickest.

"In pursuit of old age and happiness I follow the scent of the rainfall and approach the place where the lines of rain are darkest."

Thus it was that he continued traveling on and on until he reached the foot of the mountain. And thus it was that he continued on and on, making his way up toward the summit. As he made his way he continued singing boldly.

"*Áłtsé hastiin* is who I am," sang he. "And here I am climbing *Ch'óol'į́'į́* in pursuit of long life and happiness for myself and my people.

"Here I am arriving at the place where the lightning strikes, in pursuit of long life and happiness for myself and my people.

"Here I am arriving at the place where the rainbow touches the earth, in pursuit of long life and happiness for myself and my people.

"Here I am where the trail of the dark cloud is thickest, in pursuit of long life and happiness for myself and my people.

"Here I am where the rich, warm rain drenches me, in pursuit of long life and happiness for myself and my people."

So it was that he made his way higher and higher on the mountain called *Ch'óol'į́'į́* because giant spruces grew thick and abundant upon it. And as he climbed he continued to sing with confidence. Even when he reached the very summit he continued to sing.

"Long life and good fortune I attain for my people and for myself," he sang.

"There is long life and good fortune in front of me."

"There is long life and good fortune in back of me."

"There is long life and good fortune above me and below me."

"All around me there is long life and good fortune."

Thus singing as he reached the very point where the peak of *Ch'óol'į́'į́* meets the sky, he heard the cry of an infant.

And at precisely the moment when he first heard that cry lightning was flashing everywhere; so brightly was it flashing that he could not see. Precisely when he first heard the cry the tip of the rainbow showered the peak with intense colors; so intensely did those colors shower him that he could not see. Just when he first heard the infant crying the dark cloud shut out the last bit of remaining daylight; so thick was the cloud's darkness that he could not see. Just at the moment when he heard the crying infant for the first time the rain blinded him; so heavily did it fall that he could not see.

But although he could see nothing he made his way to the spot where it seemed to him that the crying originated.

And as he reached that spot the lightning ceased. The rainbow's intense shroud became a band of pastel softness. The dark cloud evaporated into a sky of blue. The rain stopped and the rays of the morning sun shone upon him.

He looked down at his feet where he had heard the baby crying. But he beheld only a turquoise figure. In it, however, he recognized the likeness of a female. It was no larger than a newborn child, but its body was fully proportioned like a woman's body. Not knowing what else to do, he picked it up and carried it back with him. Back he carried it to *Áłtsé asdzą́ą́* the First Woman and the others.

"Take it," he bid them.

"Keep it and care for it as if it were real.

"Nurse it and nurture it as if it were our very own."

Cormac McCarthy

⋯⟫●⟪⋯

from
THE STONEMASON

It balances out, he says. Yes. The arc of the moral universe is indeed long but it does bend toward justice. At the root of all this of course is the trade. As he always calls it. His craft is the oldest there is. Among man's gifts it is older than fire and in the end he is the final steward, the final custodian. When the last gimcrack has swallowed up its last pale creator he will be out there, preferring the sun, trying the temper of his trowel. Placing stone on stone in accordance with the laws of God. The trade was all they had, the old masons. They understood it both in its utility and in its secret nature. We couldn't read nor write, he says. But it was not in any book. We kept it close to our hearts. We kept it close to our hearts and it was like a power and we knew it would not fail us. We knew that it was a thing that if we had it they could not take it from us and it would stand by us and not fail us. Not ever fail us.

Thich Nhat Hanh

THREE WONDROUS ANSWERS

To end, let me retell a short story of Tolstoy's, the story of the Emperor's three questions. Tolstoy did not know the emperor's name . . .

One day it occurred to a certain emperor that if he only knew the answers to three questions, he would never stray in any matter.

What is the best time to do each thing?

Who are the most important people to work with?

What is the most important thing to do at all times?

The emperor issued a decree throughout his kingdom announcing that whoever could answer the questions would receive a great reward. Many who read the decree made their way to the palace at once, each person with a different answer.

In reply to the first question, one person advised that the emperor make up a thorough time schedule, consecrating every hour, day, month, and year for certain tasks and then follow the schedule to the letter. Only then could he hope to do every task at the right time.

Another person replied that it was impossible to plan in advance and that the emperor should put all vain amusements aside and remain attentive to everything in order to know what to do at what time.

Someone else insisted that, by himself, the emperor could never hope to have all the foresight and competence necessary to decide when to do each and every task and what he really needed was to set up a Council of the Wise and then to act according to their advice.

Someone else said that certain matters required immediate decision and could not wait for consultation, but if he wanted to know in advance what was going to happen he should consult magicians and soothsayers.

The responses to the second question also lacked accord.

One person said that the emperor needed to place all his trust in administrators, another urged reliance on priests and monks, while others recommended physicians. Still others put their faith in warriors.

The third question drew a similar variety of answers.

Some said science was the most important pursuit. Others insisted on religion. Yet others claimed the most important thing was military skill.

The emperor was not pleased with any of the answers, and no reward was given.

After several nights of reflection, the emperor resolved to visit a hermit who lived up on the mountain and was said to be an enlightened man. The emperor wished to find the hermit to ask him the three questions, though he knew the hermit never left the mountains and was known to receive only the poor, refusing to have anything to do with persons of wealth or power. So the emperor disguised himself as a simple peasant and ordered his attendants to wait for him at the foot of the mountain while he climbed the slope alone to seek the hermit.

Reaching the holy man's dwelling place, the emperor found the hermit digging a garden in front of his hut. When the hermit saw the stranger, he nodded his head in greeting and continued to dig. The labor was obviously hard on him. He was an old man, and each time he thrust his spade into the ground to turn the earth, he heaved heavily.

The emperor approached him and said, "I have come here to ask your help with three questions: When is the best time to do each thing? Who are the most important people to work with? What is the most important thing to do at all times?"

The hermit listened attentively but only patted the emperor on the shoulder and continued digging. The emperor said, "You must be tired. Here, let me give you a hand with that." The hermit thanked him, handed the emperor the spade, and then sat down on the ground to rest.

After he had dug two rows, the emperor stopped and turned to the hermit and repeated his three questions. The hermit still did not answer, but instead stood up and pointed to the spade and said, "Why don't you rest now? I can take over again." But the emperor continued to dig. One hour passed, then two. Finally the sun began to set behind the mountain. The emperor put down the spade and said to the hermit, "I came here to ask if you could answer my three questions. But if you can't give me any answer, please let me know so that I can get on my way home."

The hermit lifted his head and asked the emperor, "Do you hear someone running over there?" The emperor turned his head. They both saw a man with a long white beard emerge from the woods. He ran wildly, pressing his hands against a bloody wound in his stomach. The man ran toward the emperor before falling unconscious to the ground, where he lay groaning. Opening the man's clothing, the emperor and hermit saw that the man had received a deep gash. The emperor cleaned the wound thoroughly and then used his own shirt to bandage it, but the blood completely soaked it within minutes. He rinsed the shirt out and bandaged the wound a second time and continued to do so until the flow of blood had stopped.

At last the wounded man regained consciousness and asked for a drink of water. The emperor ran down to the stream and brought back a jug of fresh water. Meanwhile, the sun had disappeared and the night air had begun to turn cold. The hermit gave the emperor a hand in carrying the man into the hut where they laid him down on the hermit's bed. The man closed his eyes and lay quietly. The emperor was worn out from a long day of climbing the mountain and digging the garden. Leaning against the doorway, he fell asleep. When he rose, the sun had already risen over the mountain. For a moment he forgot where he was and what he had come here for. He looked over to the bed and saw the wounded man also looking around him in confusion. When he saw the emperor, he stared at him intently and then said in a faint whisper, "Please forgive me."

"But what have you done that I should forgive you?" the emperor asked.

"You do not know me, your majesty, but I know you. I was your sworn enemy, and I had vowed to take vengeance on you, for during the last war you killed my brother and seized my property. When I learned that you were coming alone to the mountain to meet the hermit, I resolved to surprise you on your way back and kill you. But after waiting a long time there was still no sign of you, and so I left my ambush in order to seek you out. But instead of finding you, I came across your attendants, who recognized me, giving me this wound. Luckily, I escaped and ran here. If I hadn't met you I would surely be dead by now. I had intended to kill you, but instead you saved my life! I am ashamed and grateful beyond words. If I live, I vow to be your servant for the rest of my life, and I will bid my children and grandchildren to do the same. Please grant me your forgiveness."

The emperor was overjoyed to see that he was so easily reconciled with a former enemy. He not only forgave the man but promised to return all the man's property and to send his own physician and servants to wait on the man until he was completely healed. After ordering his attendants to take the man home, the emperor returned to see the hermit. Before returning to the palace the emperor wanted to repeat his three questions one last time. He found the hermit sowing seeds in the earth they had dug the day before.

The hermit stood up and looked at the emperor. "But your questions have already been answered."

"How's that?" the emperor asked, puzzled.

"Yesterday, if you had not taken pity on my age and given me a hand with digging these beds, you would have been attacked by that man on your way home. Then you would have deeply regretted not staying with me. Therefore the most important time was the time you were digging in the beds, the most important person was myself, and the most important pursuit was to help me. Later, when the wounded man ran up here, the most important time was the time you spent dressing his wound, for if you had not cared for him he would have died and you would have lost the chance to be reconciled with him. Likewise, he was the most important person, and the most important pursuit was taking care of his wound. Remember that there is only one important time and that is now. The present moment is the only time over which we have dominion. The most important person is always the person you are with, who is right before you, for who knows if you will have dealings with any other person in the future? The most important pursuit is making the person standing at your side happy, for that alone is the pursuit of life."

Tolstoy's story is like a story out of scripture: it doesn't fall short of any sacred text. We talk about social service, service to the people, service to humanity, service for others who are far away, helping to bring peace to the world – but often we forget that it is the very people around us that we must live for first of all. If you cannot serve your wife or husband or child or parent – how are you going to serve society? If you cannot make your own child happy, how do you expect to be able to make anyone else happy? If all our friends in the peace movement or of service communities of any kind do not love and help one another, whom can we love and help? Are we working for other humans, or are we just working for the name of an organization?

Service

The service of peace. The service of any person in need. The word service is so immense. Let's return first to a more modest scale: our families, our classmates, our friends, our own community. We must live for them – for if we cannot live for them, whom else do we think we are living for?

Tolstoy is a saint – what we Buddhists would call a *Bodhisattva*. But was the emperor himself able to see the meaning and direction of life? How can we live in the present moment, live right now with the people around us, helping to lessen their suffering and making their lives happier? How? The answer is this: We must practice mindfulness. The principle that Tolstoy gives appears easy. But if we want to put it into practice we must use the methods of mindfulness in order to seek and find the way.

I've written these pages for our friends to use. There are many people who have written about these things without having lived them, but I've only written down those things which I have lived and experienced myself. I hope you and your friends will find these things at least a little helpful along the path of our seeking: the path of our return.

Denise Levertov

THE TASK

As if God were an old man
always upstairs, sitting about
in sleeveless undershirt, asleep,
arms folded, stomach rumbling,
his breath from open mouth
strident, presaging death ...

No, God's in the wilderness next door
— that huge tundra room, no walls and a sky roof —
busy at the loom. Among the berry bushes,
rain or shine, that loud clacking and whirring,
irregular but continuous;
God is absorbed in work, and hears
the spacious hum of bees, not the din,
and hears far-off
our screams. Perhaps
listens for prayers in that wild solitude.
And hurries on with the weaving:
till it's done, the great garment woven,
our voices, clear under the familiar
          blocked-out clamor of the task,
can't stop their
                    terrible beseeching. God
imagines it sifting through, at last, to music
in the astounded quietness, the loom idle,
the weaver at rest.

SOURCES

—>◦◦◦<—

EPIGRAPH

The lines from Rumi are Quatrain #82, found in *Open Secret: Versions of Rumi* by John Moyne and Coleman Barks (Putney, VT: Threshold Books, 1984); from Blake, *The Marriage of Heaven and Hell.*

FOREWORD

Thomas Moore is the author of a trilogy of books dealing with matters of the soul: *Care of the Soul, Soulmates,* and *The Reenchantment of Everyday Life.* Earlier books include *Dark Eros* and *The Planets Within.*

PROLOGUE

William Blake's tender personification of the "Minute Particulars" as "the little ones" re-inforces his sense that what we labor upon is indeed living. In *Jerusalem* – here, from plate 55, in *The Complete Poetry and Prose of William Blake,* edited by David V. Erdman (Berkeley: University of California Press, 1982), 205 – the "little ones" that Los (the creative imagination) works upon are his sons and daughters; all creation is intimately related to him.

This selection from Martin Buber's *Tales of Angels, Spirits and Demons* (New York: Hawk's Well Press, 1958), is also reprinted in Parker Palmer's *The Active Life: A Spirituality of Work, Creativity and Caring* (San Francisco: Harper & Row, 1990), 79–81. Palmer comments: "Though some people see the angel as being compassionate from the outset of the tale, I do not. Compassion means, literally, the capacity to be with the suffering of another. Though the angel was 'deeply moved' by human suffering at the beginning of the story, the text says that he was moved only by 'the sufferings he saw below.' His relation to that suffering was both visual and vertical: he saw it rather than touched it, and he kept himself above it rather than entering into it" (83).

The reader might compare this piece with Denise Levertov's "The Task" (page 271).

ORIGINS & FIRST THOUGHTS

This brief excerpt (and those following later) from *Diné bahane': The Navajo Creation Story* is here translated by Paul G. Zolbrod (Albuquerque: University of New Mexico Press, 1984), 47–51. As Professor Zolbrod comments in his own introduction,

> The story tells of the emergence of the insect–like *nítch'i dine'e'* or "air-spirit people" from a primal domain deep within the earth. It describes how they gradually make their way to the surface of the world, where they evolve into *nihookáá'dine'e'* or "earth surface people" and then into an aggregate of human clans.... The story resembles the Old Testament in that its origins reach deep into the inscrutable loam of a primeval past.

> ... The central theme is the attainment of *hózhó*, a fairly untraslatable
> term which can only be approximated in English by combining words
> like *beauty, balance,* and *harmony* (5).

For more on the Holy People, the image of the buckskin, and this account of the origins
of First Man and First Woman, see Zolbrod's notes to this selection. On *hózhó* and, more
generally, on Navajo world views and aesthetics, see Gary Witherspoon's *Language and Art in
the Navajo Universe* (Ann Arbor: University of Michigan Press, 1977).

All translations from Old and New Testaments are from the Revised Standard Version.
With St. Paul's comment ("If any one will not work, let him not eat") compare the Zen
precept: "a day without work, a day without food." See too Sam Hamill's comments in
"Shadow Work" – and this, from Stonehouse:

> the ancients entered mountains intent on the Way
> their constant effort depending on themselves
> weighting their belts with stones to hull rice
> shouldering hoes in the rain to plant pines
> hauling mud and rocks of course
> or water and wood they worked
> the slouches who beg for a living
> don't hang around an old zen monk

Reprinted from *The Zen Works of Stonehouse* (San Francisco: Mercury House, 1998), #41.

From Hesiod, *Works and Days,* translated by Richard Lattimore (Ann Arbor: University of
Michigan, 1959), 53–57. Hesiod's dates are a matter of conjecture; scholars place him between 850 and 775 BC. He tells us that he tended sheep in the foothills of Mount Helikon,
and that his brother Perses tried to cheat him of his portion of inheritance – which might
explain the tone here. In some ways Hesiod's point and style are best summed up in later
lines (502–3):

> While it is still midsummer, give your people their orders.
> It will not always be summer. The barns had better be building.

This excerpt from chapter 18 of the *Gita* is translated by Franklin Edgerton (1944; reprint,
Cambridge: Harvard University Press, 1972), 83–91. The name is derived from the fact that
this poem is the song (*Gita*) of the Blessed One (*Bhagavad*). "Krishna is acting as Arjuna's
charioteer. Arjuna sees in the ranks of the opposing army a large number of his own kins-
men and intimate friends. He is horror-stricken at the thought of fighting against them,
and forthwith lays down his weapons, saying he would rather be killed than kill them.
Krishna replies, justifying the fight on various grounds, the chief of which is that man's real
self or soul is immortal and independent of the body; it 'neither kills nor is killed; it has
no part in either the actions or the sufferings of the body.'" See Edgerton, *The Bhagavad Gita*,
p. 105.

Isha Upanishad. The commentary on this is given by Andrew Schelling himself above, but he
adds in his note to the original translation (in *The India Book: Essays & Translations from Indian
Asia* (Oakland, CA: O Books, 1993) that "the verses of *Isha* ('The Great One') lie among
the oldest strata of the *Upanishads.* They certainly date back 2500 years. A few may be rooted

incalculably deeper, snatches of song from some very distant yogin. Where the astute snatches of rhyme and troubling phrases all come from is anybody's guess — the carefully torqued dialectic, the cryptic glimpses into the limits of work and learning, the nearly strangled cry for vision that finds itself echoed a hundred dynasties later in *Bhagavad Gita.*"

Such a work may — as it moves out of the sunlight and into the deep caves — seem to move outside the scope of direct questions regarding work, but my own feeling is that by moving deeper and deeper beyond the first few stanzas the poem takes us back to that place out of which all questions of work — indeed, of activity, of life itself — originate and resolve. So too, as Schelling suggests, with the *Taoteching* and some of the more cryptic comments of Jesus of Nazareth.

Red Pine (aka Bill Porter), the translator of this version of the *Taoteching* (this is poem #2 in the edition from Mercury House [San Francisco, 1996], 4), notes cryptically that the book "is a vision of what our lives would be like if we were the dark new moon." Such a statement is not arbitrary; as Pine comments in his introduction, the word *Tao* — commonly associated with "road" or "way" — "shares a common linguistic heritage with words that mean 'moon' in other cultures. . . . The symbol Taoists have used since ancient times to represent the Tao shows the two conjoined phases of the moon." The Tao then is moonlike as the invisible influence upon human life, indeed upon all earthly life. An apt symbol for the hidden source of all activity. A work from the sixth century BC, it casts work into the fullest of contexts — philosophical and spiritual.

As Wang Wu-chiu says of this passage, "The sage is not interested in deeds or words. He simply follows the natural pattern of things. Things rise, develop, and reach their end. This is their order" (5).

The selection from *The Rule of St. Benedict* is edited by Timothy Fry, O.S.B. (Collegeville, MN: Liturgical Press, 1981), 159. Included here is a passage from Chapter 48, "The Daily Manual Labor." Jean Leclercq notes that "manual work was one of the most important features of Cistercian ascetic practice" (see *La Spiritualité du Moyen Age* [Paris: Aubier, 1961], 270–71). Their theological arguments in favor of manual labor are succinctly outlined by Christopher Holdsworth in "The Blessings of Work: The Cistercian View," in *Society and Secularity: The Church and the World*, ed. Derek Baker (New York: Barnes & Noble, 1973). He suggests that "manual work appeared to them as an intrinsic part of the life of poverty which they had freely embraced, since having given up all their own possessions they had to work if they were not to be a charge on others" (61–62). The Cistercians also argued that working was not contradictory to a life of prayer, using the story of Martha and Mary (traditionally understood to represent the active and contemplative life) as illustration: "Action indeed was the thing which came first, before contemplation, in the growth of the soul, and St. Bernard found symbolic justification for this idea in the fact that it was Martha, not Mary, who received Jesus in the house" (65). Ailred takes this further by recognizing both sisters in each individual soul:

> Realise, brethren, that never in this life should these two women be separated. When the time comes that Jesus is no longer poor, or hungry, or thirsty, and can no longer be tempted, then Mary alone, that is spiritual activity, will take over the whole house of the soul. This St. Benedict, or rather the Holy Spirit in St. Benedict, saw. This is why he did not confine himself to saying and laying it down that we should be occupied

with reading like Mary, while passing over work such as Martha does; but recommended both to us, and set aside definite times for the work of Martha, and definite times for that of Mary (65–66).

For more on *The Rule*, see too Kathleen Norris's recent *The Cloister Walk* (New York: Riverhead, 1996). Above all, it should be pointed out that the Rule desires to keep things as simple and clear as possible. "Rules" in the rule are few. As one monk said to Norris, "the minute you write something down, you set it in stone. And that's dangerous, because then someone will want to enforce it" (17).

Piers Plowman, my translation from the Middle English prologue. Little is known of William Langland; evidence suggests that his poem (which exists in three versions) dates from the second half of the fourteenth century. Its importance in this turbulent period is clear from the reference to it in a letter written by the leader of the Peasants' Revolt, John Ball, in 1381. A.V.C. Schmidt (in the introduction to his edition of the B Text of the poem) suggests that

> The Prologue's vision sets individual andfield of folk against the stark al-
> ternatives of heaven and damnation (tower and dungeon). Christians at
> all times risk being immersed in the world; Langland sees obsession with
> wealth as the special problem of his day, when the Christian church itself
> was becoming engrossed in temporal possessions (*The Vision of Piers
> Plowman* [New York: Dutton, 1978], xxv).

For further comments on Langland and the "consecration" of manual labor, see Christopher J. Holdsworth in "The Blessings of Work: The Cistercian View," in *Society and Secularity: The Church and the World,* ed. Derek Baker (New York: Barnes & Noble, 1973), especially 71–72. He notes that art historian Emile Male "drew attention to the labours of the months which are found over the portals of churches like Chartres, Paris, and Rheims, in the thirteenth century, where the typical tasks of the rural community are, as it were, hallowed."

This translation of Meister Eckhart (ca. 1260–ca. 1329) is from *Meister Eckhart: Teacher and Preacher,* ed. Bernard McGinn (New York: Paulist, 1986), 296–300.

On "authentic" work, work without a "why," compare Eckhart to (among many others) the *Bhagavad Gita* and the *Taoteching*. Both of these traditions, I believe, remind us that the words *justice* and *just* also suggest accurate, precise – as in a "just measure." Justice, like Tao, and like the Navajo sense of *hózhǫ́,* springs from this inner harmony and alignment with the One.

For more on Eckhart, see the excerpt from Lewis Hyde's *The Gift* on page 240 in this anthology. On Eckhart and justice (and on the Tao) see too Matthew Fox's *Breakthrough: Meister Eckhart's Creation Spirituality in New Translation* (New York: Doubleday, 1980), especially 464–77. He quotes Eckhart: "The just person lives and works without reason of gain. As much as life has the reason for living in itself, in that same way the just person knows no other reason for being just" (472). See too Fox's *The Reinvention of Work* (New York: HarperCollins, 1994), which, like much of his writing, is deeply indebted to Eckhart.

This excerpt from Ananda K. Coomaraswamy's essay on Eckhart is drawn from *The Transformation of Nature in Art* (1934; reprint, New York: Dover, 1956), 87–92. Eckhart's sermons in Coomaraswamy's view could be considered "an *Upanishad* of Europe"; this and his own deep knowledge of Indian theology explain his frequent cross references in the text. His citations from Eckhart come from *Meister Eckhart*, translated in two volumes by C. De B. Evans (London, 1924 and 1931), drawn in turn from the German edition by Franz Pfeiffer (1857). The page references are to the first volume unless otherwise stated.

Coomaraswamy notes elsewhere that *demiourgos* and *technites* "are the ordinary Greek words for 'artist' (*artifex*), and under these headings Plato includes not only poets, painters, and musicians, but also archers, weavers, embroiderers, potters, carpenters, sculptors, farmers, hunters, and above all those whose art is government, only making a distinction between creation (*demiurgia*) and mere labor (*cheirurgia*), art (*techne*) and artless industry (*atechnos tribai*)." He adds that the primary meaning of the word *sophia*, "wisdom," is that of "skill," just as Sanskrit *kausalam* is "skill" of any kind, whether in making, doing, or knowing.

In a footnote to a different essay Coomaraswamy elaborates on the notion of "artless industry":

> The word *tribai* literally means "a rubbing," and is an exact equivalent of our modern expression "a grind." (Cf. Hippocrates, *Fractures* 772, "shameful and artless," and Ruskin's "industry without art is brutality.") "For all well-governed peoples there is a work enjoined upon each man which he must perform" (*Republic* 406c). "Leisure" is the opportunity to do this work without interference (*Republic* 370c). A "work for leisure" is one requiring undivided attention (Euripides, *Andromache* 552). Plato's view of work in no way differs from that of Hesiod, who says that work is not reproach but the best gift of the gods to men (*Works and Days*, 295–96). Whenever Plato disparages the mechanical arts, it is with reference to the kinds of work that provide for the well-being of the body only, and do not at the same time provide spiritual food; he does not connect culture with idleness.

See *Traditional Art and Symbolism*, ed. Roger Lipsey (Princeton: Bollingen Series LXXXIX, Princeton University Press, 1977), 16. For more on this sense of leisure, see also Ivan Illich's illuminating book *In The Vineyard of the Text* (Chicago: University of Chicago Press, 1993) and my introductory comments to The Hunt (page 73 of this book).

This brief version from Jalalludin Rumi is from the *Mathnawi*, Book VI, lines 210–28, and is based on the translation by Reynold Nicholson in *The Mathnawi of Jalaluddin Rumi* (1934; reprint, Lahore, Pakistan: Islamic Book Service, 1989), VI, 269–70. With thanks to Jonathon Omer-man who first introduced me to Rumi some years ago in Cambridge.

Rumi (1207–1273), sharing the same century as Hadewijch and Eckhart, was born in what is now Afghanistan, which his family fled at the threat of a Mongol invasion, settling at last in Konya, Turkey. His poetry has won a large readership in this country through the translation work and commentaries of Robert Bly, Andrew Harvey, and especially Coleman Barks. See too the studies by Annemarie Schimmel, in particular *The Triumphal Sun*.

This excerpt is drawn from *Hadewijch: The Complete Works*, translated with an introduction by Mother Columba Hart, O.S.B. (New York: Paulist, 1980), 80–81. As Mother Hart notes, this thirteenth-century Belgian woman was "not a nun but a Beguine – that is, she was one of the devout women of her day who chose to lead a life of apostolic poverty and contemplation without taking vows as nuns. This movement came into being towards the end of the twelfth century, originating largely among women of noble and patrician families. Apparently they rejected not only the narrow life of the lady in the castle, but the strict obligations of the nun in the cloister. The Beguines sought not vows or enclosure, but a new way of life to be arranged by themselves, in which to the recitation of the Hours they could add manual work, study, or teaching, according to their desires" (3).

At the heart of Hadewijch's understanding of work is her profoundly mystical understanding of love, which in turn deeply influenced the mystic John of Ruusbroec (1293–1381) and his disciples. She writes (in Letter 17): "you must still labor at the works of Love, as I long did, and as his friends did and still do. For my part I am devoted to these works at any hour and still perform them at all times: to seek after nothing but Love, work nothing but Love, protect nothing but Love, and advance nothing but Love. How you are to do or omit each of these things, may God, our Beloved, teach you" (84).

I have eliminated a few footnotes from the Paulist edition.

From E.F. Schumacher, *Small Is Beautiful: Economics as if People Mattered* (New York: Harper & Row, 1973), 53–62. On "Buddhist Economics," see also Gary Snyder's book *Real Work* on his humorous attempts to "improve" the work at the monastery by making it more efficient.

From Dorothee Soelle (with Shirley A. Cloyes), *To Work and to Love: A Theology of Creation* (Philadelphia: Fortress Press, 1984), 83–91. For more on Thomas Aquinas, see Matthew Fox, *The Reinvention of Work* (New York: HarperCollins, 1994). He quotes Aquinas in his epigraph: "Everything gives pleasure to the extent that it is loved. It is natural for people to love their own work . . . : and the reason is that we love *to be* and *to live*, and these are made manifest in our *action*." In short, Aquinas says, "To live well is to work well" (*Sum. Theol.* I–II, q. 57, a.5). On Thomas Carlyle see his *Past and Present*, the chapter on "Labour":

> For there is a perennial nobleness, and even sacredness, in Work. Were he never so benighted, forgetful of his high calling, there is always hope in a man that actually and earnestly works: in Idleness alone is there perpetual despair. Work . . . is in communication with Nature; the real desire to get Work done will itself lead one more and more to truth.

I myself find Carlyle a bit too energetically Victorian here, reminding me of Alfred Lord Tennyson's version of the endlessly striving Odysseus. On Dorothy Day and *The Catholic Worker*, see her autobiography, *The Long Loneliness* (1952; reprint, New York: Harper & Row, 1980), especially "Paper, People and Work," 182–204. Asked by a devout young woman whether she had "ecstasies and visions," she replied, "Visions of unpaid bills" (188).

Wendell Berry, "Health and Work," excerpted from the longer essay, "The Body and the Earth," which in turn makes up an important section of Berry's book *The Unsettling of America* (1977; reprint, New York: Avon Books), 137–40. "The Body and the Earth" is also available in Berry's *Recollected Essays 1965–1980* (San Francisco: North Point, 1981). "Connection is health," Berry writes; it should be clear from my introduction how indebted to him I am.

Walt Whitman. This is out of chronological order, but feels right for the aesthetic order. See also his "A Song for Occupations": "In the labor of engines and trades and the labor of fields I find the developments, / And find the eternal meanings."

Olav Hauge, "Everyday," from *Selected Poems*, translated by Robin Fulton (Fredonia, NY: White Pine Press, 1990), 43. Born in 1908, Hauge has spent his life in western Norway, making a living off the apple crop from his orchard, an acre in size. If one hears influences, it's likely to be to ancient Japanese and Chinese poets, as the references here would suggest. "Old Laertes" is the father of Odysseus, who left his palace and returned to his garden when his son left Ithaca for the war in Troy.

THE HUNT

The images of animals – in particular of bulls and stags – on the walls of caves in Lascaux (in the Dorgogne reigon of France) have a peculiar potency, even in reproduction. Dating from approximately 15,000 BC, it is thought that the images had a religious or magical function, helping the hunters through a ritual of slaying (painting as a form of capturing the spirit) – or, perhaps, the paintings may have been a means of assuring a continual supply of animals at a time when the animals were becoming scarce.

"Magic Words For Hunting Caribou" is a translation by Edward Field from a number of Eskimo sources. See Jerome Rothenberg, ed., *Shaking the Pumpkin: Traditional Poetry of the Indian North Americans* (1986; reprint, Albuquerque, NM: University of New Mexico Press, 1991), 43, and Rothenberg's notes, 350–51. Field's original source is Knud Rasmussen, *The Netsilik Eskimos*, Report of the Fifth Thule Expedition, Copenhagen, 1931, *passim*.

It's important to note here that these words are understood to put the hunter into relationship with the hunted animal; this is, in Martin Buber's terms, an I-Thou relationship established in part *through* the power of the words. See Rothenberg's note to Rasmussen's note:

> "Translating magic words is a most difficult matter [writes Rasmussen] because they often consist of untranslatable compounds of words, or fragments that are supposed to have their strength in their mysteriousness" – *coefficient of wierdness* is Malinowski's good term for it – "or in the manner in which the words are coupled together." Obviously comprehension by others isn't the issue here "as long as the spirits know what it is that one wants" (351).

See too the comments of Leslie Marmon Silko on animal pictographs:

> Pictographs and petroglyphs of constellations or elk or antelope draw their magic in part from the process wherein the focus of all prayer and concentration is upon the thing itself, which, in its turn, guides the hunter's hand. Connection with the spirit dimensions requires a figure or form that is all-inclusive. Only the elk *is* itself. A *realistic* rendering of an elk would be only one particular elk anyway. The purpose of the hunt rituals and magic is to make contact with *all* the spirits of the elk.

See "Interior and Exterior Landscapes" in *Yellow Woman and a Beauty of the Spirit: Essays on Native American Life Today* (New York: Simon & Schuster, 1996), 28–29.

An excerpt from Barry Lopez, "Saint Lawrence Island, Bering Sea," the epilogue to *Arctic Dreams: Imagination and Desire in a Northern Landscape* (New York: Scribners, 1986), 407–11. See also Sherman Paul's *For Love of the World* (Iowa City: University of Iowa Press, 1992), 67–107, for a detailed analysis of Lopez's writing.

Richard Nelson, "The Gifts of Deer." This essay is excerpted from Nelson's book *The Island Within* (San Francisco: North Point, 1989), 256–77. It can also be found in *On Nature*, ed. Daniel Halpern (San Francisco: North Point, 1986), 117–31, where I believe it first appeared.

As a young anthropologist Nelson went to study the Eskimos of Wainwright, Alaska, and came away forever altered. He records his experiences with these and other northern hunters in earlier books: *Hunters of the Northern Ice* (1967), *Hunters of the Northern Forest* (1973), *Shadow of the Hunter: Stories of Eskimo Life* (1980), and *Make Prayers for the Raven* (1983), which became a PBS television documentary. One can see in this sequence of books that Nelson grows increasingly dissatisfied with the objective, distanced stance of the anthropologist; his books turn more and more to story as the author grows closer to his subject, until at last there is no "subject" left: Ethan, his son, is "boy made of deer." For a lengthy and insightful commentary on Nelson, which includes a long response by Nelson, see Sherman Paul's chapter "The Education of a Hunter: Reading Richard Nelson," in *For Love of the World: Essays on Nature Writers* (cited above, under Lopez), 135–76.

"Wild Trout" is from the *Parabola* issue on *The Hunter*, XVI (Summer, 1991). P.V. Beck is the author of *The Sacred: Ways of Knowledge, Sources of Life* (Tsalie, AZ: Navaho College Press, 1977).

Pam Houston's introduction to the collection she edited, *Women on Hunting* (New Jersey: Ecco Press, 1995), beautifully illustrates the complicated relationship women and men have with hunting, the wilderness – and with each other.

Susan Griffin's "His Power: He Tames What Is Wild" can be found in Houston's book, but also in Griffin's earlier *Woman and Nature* (New York: Harper & Row, 1978), 103–5. It suggests the link between the literal hunt and the metaphorical erotic hunting that men (and women) do.

Galway Kinnell's "The Bear" appears as the final poem in his early volume *Body Rags* (Boston: Houghton Mifflin, 1967), 60–63, and is reprinted in his *Selected Poems*. Here the hunt is evocatively re-imagined by the poet, who sees the hunter "take on" the bear in a quite literal fashion, until in dream he becomes the bear. The final lines of the poem make it clear that this process is also to be seen as a metaphor for the work of the poet himself – and, by extension, perhaps, for the work each of us must do. In our work we become that "other" that we hunt down. This is sacrificial labor (from *sacere + facere*: "to make sacred"). For a similar understanding of this relationship between bear and human see N. Scott Momaday's *The Ancient Child* and (more theoretically) Calvin Luther Martin's *In the Spirit of the Earth: Rethinking History and Time.*

Linda Hogan's poem is also found in *Parabola's The Hunter*, 58–59, and in her volume *The Book of Medicines* (Minneapolis: Coffee House Press, 1993), 25–26.

The interview with John Haines is reprinted in his book *Fables and Distances: New and Selected Essays* (St. Paul: Graywolf, 1996), 218. This single paragraph links many of the topics in this book, and reveals their underlying foundation: through work we may reach this "half-conscious intuition that ... life extended far beyond that moment and that immediate activity." One of the great American poets, Haines spent decades homesteading, hunting, and trapping in Alaska. The collection of essays is splendid, as is his collected poems, also published by Graywolf (*The Owl in the Mask of the Dreamer*, 1993).

"To Make a Living ..." is from *The Dance of the Dust on the Rafters: Selections from Ryojin-hisho*, translated by Yasuhiko Moriguchi and David Jenkins (Seattle: Broken Moon Press, 1990).

18. *Ryojin-hisho*, the editors tell us, is "one of Japan's great masterpieces of literary folk art. ... [It is] a collection of songs of faith and love that first appeared as an anthology in the late twelfth century" (xv). This particular piece reflects the ambivalence in the act of hunting – killing in order to feed oneself – and beyond that, then, the ambivalence regarding the cycles of life itself – that this Buddhist feels.

CULTIVATION

Claude Monet's *Grainstacks*. See my comments on the introduction to this section (page iii).

"Corn Mother" is a creation myth (see *American Indian Myths and Legends*, selected and edited by Richard Erdoes and Alfonso Ortiz [New York: Pantheon, 1984], 11–13). The editors note:

> Derived from a wild grass called *teosintl*, corn was planted in Mexico's Tehuacan Valley as early as 8000 years ago. The oldest corn found north of the border was discovered in New Mexico's Bat Cave. It is about 5500 years old. The Hopis say: "*Moing'iima* makes corn. Everything grows on his body. He is short, about the height of a boy. He has a female partner. Every summer he becomes heavy, his body is full of vegetables: watermelon, corn, squash. They grow in his body. When the Hopi plant they invariably ask him to make the crop flourish; then their things come up, whether vegetables or fruit. When he shaves his body, the seeds come out, and afterward his body is thin. He used to live on this earth and go with the Hopi. When things grow ripe, he becomes thin and is unhappy. He stays in the west."

See too this interesting note in *The Native Americans: An Illustrated History*:

> Geneticists tell us that plants grow best in disturbed soil such as the pits, mounds, and middens surrounding Indian campsites; these became home to the weedy species, which turned into America's earliest cultivated and domesticated foods....
>
> [I]t was the hand of woman that first domesticated the plants of the Eastern Woodlands. Throughout native America, it was always the woman who retained the botanical information. She knew exactly what plants to feed her family. She knew what plants made the best clothing and dyes, and when to harvest materials for making cordage and weaving textiles. She knew which leaves, bark, roots stems, and berries could cure disease (82).

This familiar passage from Genesis 4 should be compared to the excerpt from the Navaho Creation Story, printed in Arts, Crafts & Hand-Work (page 180). We see in both a story about the origins of human culture.

The Odyssey, translated by Robert Fitzgerald (New York: Vintage Books, 1963), Book IX, 148–49. We hear quite distinctly in these lines the voice of the landowner and agriculturist who scorns the laziness of the "savages" and cannibals who fail to take advantage of fertile land. "Sea-going folk would have annexed it and built their homesteads on it." The comparison to the attitude of Anglo-Saxon Americans upon encountering the Plains Indians in the nineteenth century should be evident. For a curious comparison, go back to Laura Ingalls Wilder's *Little House* books and Pa's great love of that Midwestern virgin soil.

See too the succinct comment from Indian agent N.A. Cornoyer working in the land of the Umatillas, along the Columbia River: "Many of the Indians, seeing that nothing is done by the government, constantly evince a desire to roam about and cannot be induced to settle down to their farms and adopt the habits of civilization" (Click Relander, in *Drummers and Dreamers* (Seattle: Caxton Printers, 1986), 133.

"A Kalapuya Prophecy" is a reworking of material in Melvile Jacobs's *Santiam Kalapuya Ethnologic Texts* in Jerome Rothenberg's *Shaking the Pumpkin*, 337. Again, many passages in *Drummers and Dreamers* are relevant here. See, for example, the Dreamer Smohala's comments to Major MacMurray, recorded in a paper the major gave in 1886 on "The Dreamers of the Columbia River Valley in Washington Territory."

> You ask me to plough the ground? Shall I take a knife and tear my mother's bosom? Then when I die, she will not take me to her bosom to rest.
> You ask me to dig for stone. Shall I dig under her skin for her bones? Then when I die I cannot enter her body to be born again.
> You ask me to cut grass and make hay and sell it and be rich like white man, but how dare I cut off my Mother's hair? (139)

In a subsequent conversation another military man, Captain Huggins, attempted to convince Smohala that he should leave his land and accept the ways of the cultivated whites. "The country," the captain argues, "is filling up with white people and their herds. The game is nearly all gone. Would it not be better for your young Indians to learn the white man's work?"

> "My men shall never work," Smohalla said. "Men who work cannot dream and wisdom comes to us in dreams."
> "You say that wisdom comes in dreams and that they who work cannot dream; yet the white man, who works, knows many things of which the Indian is ignorant."
> "His wisdom is that of his own mind and thoughts. Such wisdom is poor and weak," replied Smohalla (143).

To give Captain Huggings his due, I should report his final comment: "*Vale*, Smohalla. Not in the least do I blame thee for hating my race.... And, if I were an Indian, I should be strongly tempted to become thy disciple" (145). It should also be noted that "even before Smohala's death, some of the Wanapums slipped from the Prophet's strict teachings and plowed and planted small fields.... Game had become scarce and the root-digging grounds had been destroyed. The Wanapums had to till the soil or die of starvation" (241).

Owen Thomas notes (in the Norton Critical Edition of *Walden*, [New York: 1966]) that *Rans des Vaches* is a song for calling cattle, sung or played by Swiss cowherds; Pythogaras reputedly forbad his followers to eat beans; the Latin (*patrem familias* ...) is from Cato, *De Agri Cultura*: "A householder should be one who sells, not one who buys."

One gets the clear sense from this chapter, as in so much of the book, that any single activity, such as working on the bean field, never stands isolated for Thoreau. The work also involves viewing the night-hawk circling overhead, and the extended reflections that the sight of the hawk gives rise to.

"The Making of a Marginal Farm" is the final essay in Wendell Berry's *Recollected Essays* (San Francisco: North Point, 1981), 329–40, and was the only new essay in that volume. What Berry says here reinforces what Monet meant in his use of the verb *eprouver* to describe his relationship with the grainstacks. In his commentary to the exhibition catalogue *Monet in the 90's: The Series Paintings* (Boston: Museum of Fine Arts, 1989), Paul Hayes Tucker stresses Monet's comment that in these paintings he was trying to render *"ce que j'eprouve,"* noting that this verb suggests "not only participation in or perception of an event ... but ... with things revealing themselves slowly so that they become known in their fullest dimensions." Berry writes about the difference "between knowing a place and living in it."

This brief excerpt from *Work and Worship: The Economic Order of the Shakers* by Edward Deming Andrews and Faith Andrews (Greenwich, CT: New York Graphic Society, 1974), 48–49, reminds us that the Shakers first gained fame for the excellence of their seeds. The authors note that the Shakers "advocated 'frequent shifts in duties' ... a practice 'facilitated by the fact that nearly every adult male was quite conversant with almost all the tasks of the farm.'" They quote here from Russell H. Anderson's "Agriculture Among the Shakers, Chiefly at Mount Lebanon," in *Agricultural History*, vol. 24 (July 1950), 120, and then from William Hepworth Dixon's *New America*, third edition (Philadelphia, 1867), 301–2:

> You see that the men who till these fields, who tend these gardens ... have been drawn into putting their love into the daily task; and you hear with no surprise that these toilers, ploughing and planting in their quaint garb, consider their labor on the soil as a part of their ritual, looking upon the earth as a strained and degraded sphere, which they have been called to redeem from corruption and restore to God.

Not all would agree with this language, but here certainly is the notion of work as spiritual transformation. And how far from Rainer Maria Rilke's cry is this? "It is our task to imprint this temporary, perishable earth into ourselves so deeply, so painfully and passionately, that its essence can rise again, 'invisibly,' within us."

The Mennonites make for an interesting comparison to the Shakers. See Calvin Redekop's essay "Mennonites, Creation and Work" in *Christian Scholar's Review* (22.4, June 1993), 348–66. Redekop (and others) show how the Mennonite "'adoption' of the land and the agrarian way of life ... resulted from a history of persecution" (353). See too, from another perspective, *The Findhorn Garden: Pioneering a New Vision of Man and Nature in Cooperation* (New York: Harper & Row, 1975).

Pieter Bruegel's *The Harvesters* (1565) is in the Metropolitan Museum in New York City.

William Carlos Williams's poem "The Corn Harvest" is part of his late *Pictures from Bruegel* (see *The Collected Poems Volume II* [New York: New Directions, 1988], 389–90). I deeply love Williams's drawing our attention to the young man lying under the tree, "the / resting / center of / their workaday world." Pushed farther, one suddenly sees the tree itself (tree of life?) as the still center of this activity, and the man then linked to the tree in a kind of ultimate rest, while all around him time and activity continue to spin. The painting (and the poem) partake of that quality T.S. Eliot struggles to depict in *The Four Quartets* – that "still point of the turning world." Even as it depicts action, the painting – like the poem, and like the young man – rests in this stillness of completion, and thus points us to: "The inner freedom from the practical desire, / The release from action and suffering, release from the inner / And the outer compulsion, yet surrounded / By a grace of sense" (Eliot). It points us, in fact, to Sabbath, the goal and end point of creation.

HOME-WORK

Jan Vermeer's *Woman Pouring Milk*, found in Amsterdam's Rijksmuseum, is described by Edward Snow (also a translator of Rilke) as "a melody of contrasting physical textures and sensations" (see *A Study of Vermeer* [Berkeley: University of California Press, 1979]). Its "play of natural and manufactured forms and textures (the bread and milk against the various containers and their supports; the wicker basket against the metal one ...) implies a concern with the ontological categories and values imbedded in the sensuous immediacy of the object-world, and with the spiritual life that world acquires through its commerce with the human" (10–11). I'm not sure that the "object-world" here depicted "acquires" spiritual life through human contact, but I do feel that this painting calmly and luminously radiates that deeper life. Before such simple presence it feels foolish even to speak of symbol, to mention bread and milk as archetypes of nourishment, of the maternal. Here we approach the enlightened mind of the Zen master, where we realize in complete simplicity that bread is bread, milk is milk. See the next piece in this section, Layman P'ang's famous "My miraculous power and spiritual activity: / drawing water and carrying wood."

Layman P'ang is P'ang Yun, an eighth-century Chinese Zen Master. This translation comes from Stephen Mitchell's anthology of sacred poetry, *The Enlightened Heart* (New York: Harper, 1989), 35. Mitchell tells us this about Layman P'ang:

> Upon his retirement in middle age, he gave away his house for use as a Buddhist temple, put all his money and possessions onto a boat in a nearby lake, and sank it. "Since his wealth was great," one ancient account says, "he worried about it. Once he had decided to give it away, he thought to himself, 'If I give it to other people, they may become as attached to it as I was. It is better to give it to the country of nothingness.'" After this, he and his wife, son, and daughter earned their living by making and selling bamboo utensils.

St. Teresa of Avila (1515–1582), from *The Letters* (in four volumes, translated by the Benedictines of Stanbrook, London: Thomas Baker, 1924), II, 175. E. Allison Peers comments, in her general introduction to *The Autobiography of St. Teresa of Avila*, "no mystical writer before her day ... nor any who has written since, has described such high matters in a way so apt, so natural" (New York: Image Books, 1960), 40. "For the love of God," she once protested when asked to write, "let me work at my spinning wheel.... I am almost stealing the time for writing, and that with great difficulty, for it hinders me from spinning and I am living in a poor house and have numerous things to do" (41, 122–23). The book she reluctantly penned was *The Interior Castle*, one of western Christianity's greatest mystical texts.

Brother Lawrence was born Nicholas Herman in French Lorraine, was unschooled, served as footman and soldier ("He was a great awkward fellow who broke everything"), and became a lay brother among the Carmelites in Paris in 1666. His work was in the kitchen, where people came to find him, looking for whatever it was that he had found. His "Gathered Thoughts," is here published in a small volume with *The Practice of the Presence of God* (Old Tappan, New Jersey: Fleming H. Revell, 1958, 1967).

Denise Levertov, "The Conversion of Brother Lawrence," can be found in *Sands of the Well* (New York: New Directions, 1996), 111–13. "Not work transformed you; work, even drudgery, / was transformed." It appears to be another, and different, idea of work than we find in other writers here, where the work itself is seen as transformative. This is a kind of absorption where the worker becomes the worked-upon: "A stone before the carver."

It's also true, however, that this idea of briefly stepping back from the work into sheer Presence or mindfulness (to use a Buddhist term) is also recommended by Thich Nhat Hanh and others. The ringing of a bell or chimes often functions this way – cutting into time with a reminder of the timeless.

Chuang Tzu is translated by Burton Watson in *Basic Writings* (New York: Columbia University Press, 1964), 46–47. Little is known of Master Chuang; he was, apparently, a contemporary of Mencius (fourth century BC). If the central question of life is freedom (both inner and outer), then, Watson suggests, the primary tendency of the Confucian schools is to "seek for concrete social, political, and ethical reforms. . . . Chuang Tzu's answer to the question is: free yourself from the world" (3). And the way to do this is summed up in the idea of *wu wei*, "or inaction, meaning by this term not a forced quietude, but a course of action that is not founded upon any purposeful motives of gain or striving. In such a state, all human actions become as spontaneous and mindless as those of the natural world. Man becomes one with Nature, or Heaven, as Chuang Tzu calls it, and merges himself with the Tao, or the Way, the underlying unity that embraces man, Nature, and all that is in the universe" (6).

As Watson further notes, Chuang Tzu often describes this state through "the analogy of the artist or craftsman":

> The skilled woodcarver, the skilled butcher, the skilled swimmer does not ponder or ratiocinate on the course of action he should take; his skill has become so much a part of him that he merely acts instinctively and spontaneously, and without knowing why, achieves success (6).

Thomas Merton, in *The Way of Chuang Tzu* (New York: New Directions, 1965), interestingly compares Chuang Tzu's emphasis on *wu wei* and the "relation of virtue to the indwelling Tao" with "St. Paul's teaching on faith and grace, contrasted with the 'works of the Old Law'" (24–25). This, perhaps, is true atonement, at-one-ment.

The Zen Works of Stonehouse, translated by Red Pine (San Francisco: Mercury House, 1998). The translator comments: "Stonehouse, whose Buddhist name was Ch'ing-hung, was a thirteenth-century Chinese monk who spent forty years living in a hut in the coastal province of Chekiang. Near the end of his life, he compiled nearly 300 of his poems into a collection he called Mountain Poems. These selections are from that collection, due out from Mercury House in 1998, together with a second collection of his poems as well as his Zen sermons, delivered while he was abbot of Fuyuan Temple in Chiahsing."

"The Sacredness of Chores" comes from Brenda Peterson's collection of essays, *Nature and Other Mothers: Reflections on the Feminine in Everyday Life* (New York: HarperCollins, 1992). See too Kathleen Norris's comments on laundry in *The Cloister Walk* (New York: Riverhead

Books, 1996), 283–86. "I know what I want on my tombstone," a clergy friend said to her. "At last my laundry's done."

Thoreau, again from *Walden*, cited above, p. 76 (from "Sounds").

Linda Hogan's "Waking Up The Rake" comes originally from *Parabola* (XIII, 2, 92–95), and has been included in her collection of essays, *Dwellings* (New York: Norton, 1995), 147–54.

Marc and Helen Hudson were living in Omak, Washington, in the Okanogan region, when their boy Ian was born in 1983, drowning, inhaling meconium. They now live and teach in Indiana. Helen is a scholar of the Icelandic Sagas; Marc a poet and naturalist (his books include *Afterlight, Journal for an Injured Son*, and a translation of *Beowulf*).

Louise Erdrich's *The Blue Jay's Dance: A Birth Year* (New York: HarperCollins, 1995), 11–12.

"Sumangala's Mother" is an anonymous Pali poem, translated by Willis Barnstone; see *A Book of Women Poets From Antiquity to Now* (New York: Schocken Books, 1980), 71.

In the Near East in the Neolithic "women spent so many hours of their lives at hard labor over heavy stone grinders that the work permanently deformed their bones. Archeologists have found the toe, knee, and shoulder bones of the women in the early farming villages of northern Mesopotamia to be squashed and deformed in ways caused by pressure from kneeling and pushing heavy objects with the arm and shoulder – clearly the metatelike stone grinders we find on the sites" (Barber, *Women's Work*, 96).

ARTS, CRAFTS & HAND-WORK
CRAFTS

This Mimbres pot, reproduced courtesy of the Logan Museum at Beloit College, has a hole in the bottom to "symbolically release the spirits of the painted figures." These potters "used the ribbon or coil method in making their bowls ... rolling a long, thin strip of clay, coiling and braiding it layer on layer to the desired shape, then smoothing and burnishing it. When the pot was dried, coated, and reburnished, it was ready for painting." The earliest Mimbres pottery dates from AD 750 to 1000. See *The Native Americans: An Illustrated History* (Atlanta: The Turner Publishing Company, 1993), 64. For a more detailed account, see also *Mimbres Pottery: Ancient Art of the Southwest* (New York: Hudson Hills Press, 1983).

Leslie Marmon Silko says about Pueblo pottery in relation to the land:

> The squash blossom itself is *one thing*: itself. So the ancient Pueblo potter abstracts what she saw to be the key elements of the squash blossom – the four symmetrical petals, with four symmetrical stamens in the center. These elements, while suggesting the squash flower, also link it with the four cardinal directions. Represented only in its intrinsic form, the squash flower is released from a limited meaning or restricted identity. Even in the most sophisticated abstract form, a squash flower or a cloud or a lightning bolt became intricately connected with a complex system of relationships that the ancient Pueblo people maintained with each other and with the populous natural world they lived within.

See "Interior and Exterior Landscapes," in *Yellow Woman and a Beauty of the Spirit: Essays on Native American Life Today* (New York: Simon & Schuster, 1996), 28.

Paul G. Zolbrod, *Diné bahane': The Navaho Creation Story* (Albuquerque: University of New

Mexico Press, 1984), 53–54. Regarding the term "hermaphrodite" (*nádleeh*), Zolbrod notes that one earlier writer defined hermaphrodites in this context as men "performing a woman's labor." "They are not without status in the Navajo creation cycle and seem to have no particular stigma to overcome. Later in Berard Haile's account of the quarrel between the sexes they exercise a great deal of authority. Before First Man and First Woman work out a reconciliation, they must get the hermaphrodites to agree" (354).

Another piece (#11) from Red Pine's translation of the *Taoteching* (Mercury House, 1996), 22. Red Pine comments in his introduction upon the link between Tao and moon; here the association of the thirty spokes suggests not just the wheel but the lunar cycle of days. He also includes two comments well worth adding here, the first from Te-Ch'ing (1546–1632):

> Heaven and Earth have form, and everyone knows that Heaven and Earth are useful. But they don't know that their usefulness depends on the emptiness of the Great Way. Likewise, we all have form and think ourselves useful but remain unaware that our usefulness depends on our empty, shapeless mind. Thus existence may have its uses, but real usefulness depends on nonexistence. Nonexistence, though, doesn't work by itself. It needs the help of existence.

And this, beautifully, from Huang Yan-chi (1820–1874): "What is beyond form is the Tao, while what has form are tools. Without tools we have no means to apprehend the Tao. And without the Tao there is no place for tools."

Compare such comments to Eckhart (a reminder not to misunderstand this idea of "empty mind" or "nonexistence"), and of course to M.C. Richards. See too my comments in the introduction to this section (page 175), and John Haines's comments on art coming out of silence – "to take thought means that we must, for a while, stop doing" (page 224).

M.C. Richards's *Centering in Pottery, Poetry and the Person* (Middletown, CT: Wesleyan University Press, 1964) is one of those indescribable books that once encountered become permanently lodged in one's body and mind. I found my copy years ago in a used book store for $3.00. I often find it in used book stores, which leads me to wonder: Have those who sold this book transcended to another plane? Why else would they part with it?

On pottery as an alchemical process, see too the story David Whyte retells in *The Heart Aroused: Poetry and the Preservation of the Soul in Corporate America* (New York: Doubleday, 1994):

> There is an ancient Chinese story of an old master potter who attempted to develop a new glaze for his porcelain vases. It became the central focus of his life. Every day he tended the flames of his kilns to a white heat, controlling the temperature to an exact degree. Every day he experimented with the chemistry of the glazes he applied, but still he could not achieve the beauty he desired and imagined was possible in the glaze. Finally, having tried everything, he decided his meaningful life was over and walked into the molten heat of a fully fired kiln. When his assistants opened up the kiln and took out the vases, they found the glaze on the vases the most exquisite they had ever encountered. The master himself had disappeared into his creations.

Soetsu Yanagi, *The Unknown Craftsman: A Japanese Insight into Beauty*, adapted by Bernard Leach (Tokyo: Kodansha International, 1972), 145–46. A wise book, with essays on theoretical subjects ("Pattern," "Seeing and Knowing," "The Buddhist Idea of Beauty") as well as on "The Crafts of Okinawa" and "The Way of Tea."

"The Master Carver" is again drawn from Burton Watson's *Basic Writings of Chuang Tzu* (New York: Columbia University Press, 1964), 126–27. Thomas Merton writes: "In 'The Woodcarver,' we see that the accomplished craftsman does not simply proceed according to certain fixed rules and external standards.... [T]he superior work of art proceeds from a hidden and spiritual principle which, in fasting, detachment, forgetfulness of results, and abandonment of all hope of profit, discovers the tree that is waiting to have this particular work carved from it. In such a case, the artist works as though passively, and it is Tao that works in and through him" (31). See also my comments in the introduction to this book (page 9), and Parker Palmer's essay on "The Woodcarver" in *The Active Life: A Spirituality of Work, Creativity and Caring* (San Francisco: Harper & Row 1990), 73–77.

"Wood Grain and Carving," by Robert Garrison, is borrowed from *Going for Coffee: Poetry on the Job,* an anthology by Tom Wayman (Madeira Park, B.C.: Harbour Press, 1981), 190–91. Thanks to Rose Reynoldson for the loan.

This short piece from Richard D. Derby comes from *The White Pine Series of Architectural Monographs,* II.3 (June 1916), 5–10, courtesy of Jay Coupard. This series was intended in part to promote the use of white pine in building on the East Coast – a reminder of what used to be.

I have referred to the Shakers in earlier sections (both on cultivation and home-work, at both of which they excelled). To refer to them here with pictures of their artistry in wood is only fitting, and again reminds us that such categories may fragment the reality. The work is one, and is toward one end, whether we call it justice, just-ness, righteousness, or beauty.

A painter friend of William Carlos Williams, Charles Sheeler, had a collection of Shaker furniture and artifacts in his house, and often painted them. See Williams's interesting comments about this partly reproduced in *William Carlos Williams and the American Scene, 1920–1940* by Dickran Tashjian (New York: Whitney Museum of American Art, 1978). Williams comments that this collection of Sheeler's was not merely for show but intended "to transfer values into a new context, to make a poem again" (109).

Ananda K. Coomaraswamy's "Shaker Furniture" is a review of *Shaker Furniture: The Craftsmanship of an American Communal Sect,* by Edward Deming Andrews and Faith Andrews. See *Traditional Art and Symbolism,* edited by Roger Lipsey (Princeton: Bollingen Series LXXXIX, Princeton University Press, 1977), 255–59. Footnotes have been eliminated.

Thomas Merton's comment on the Shakers is succinct: "when you expect the world to end at any moment, you know there is no need to hurry – you take your time, you do your work well."

Studs Terkel, from *Working: People Talk About What They Do All Day and How They Feel About What They Do* (New York: Pantheon, 1974), xl–xlix. Compare Carl Murray Bates's comments about learning from his elders to *Wen Fu,* to Gary Snyder's "Axe Handles," and the comments of Lewis Hyde in *The Gift:* "Artists are brought to their vocation when their own nascent gifts are awakened by the work of a master.... Most artists are converted to art by art itself." (Arts, 240) "Model / And tool, craft of culture, / How we go on," Snyder says. Of course part of the moral of the stonemason is that there aren't many to follow him.

Compare too Cormac McCarthy's play, *The Stonemason* (Epilogue, 261). This is the voice of the mason, Ben, who has learned his trade from his grandfather Papaw:

> For true masonry is not held together by cement but by gravity. That is to say, by the warp of the world. By the stuff of creation itself. The keystone that locks the arch is pressed in place by the thumb of God.... He talks to me about stone in a different way from my father. Always as a thing of consequence. As if the mason were a custodian of sorts. He speaks of sap in the stone. And fire. Of course he's right. You can smell it in the broken rock.... According to the gospel of the true mason God has laid the stones in the earth for men to use and he has laid them in their bedding planes to show the mason how his own work must go. A wall is made the same way the world is made. A house, a temple.... For we invent nothing but what God has put to hand ([Hopewell, NJ: The Ecco Press, 1994], 8–10).

The just man makes for just work and right work makes the right man.

Donald Hall, from *Life Work* (Boston: Beacon Press, 1993), 32.

This information on Athena and weaving is from Elizabeth Wayland Barber, *Women's Work: The First 20,000 Years* (New York: Norton, 1994), 239–44. See also her comments in the chapter "Courtyard Sisterhood" on the process of preparing dried flax or hemp for spinning. Textiles, she concludes, "flourished in the early horticultural economies of southeastern Europe between 6000 and 2000 BC, when the women could handle the subsistence farming and the crafts while the men could go out of the community to hunt, fish, tend flocks, and barter for luxuries such as shell beads and obsidian blades."

See too Barbara Newman's *Sisters of Wisdom: St. Hildegard's Theology of the Feminine* (Berkeley: University of California Press, 1987), 95: "Women's function as weaver is literal as well as metaphorical," Newman writes; "man receives not only the garment of flesh from the mother's womb but also garments of linen and wool from her hands. Discussing the division of labor between the sexes, Hildegard intimated that man is of the earth, earthy, so his portion is to till the earth from which he was taken. But woman, created as flesh from flesh, was made the mother of all flesh. In addition she is distinguished by her skilled handiwork (*artificiosium opus manuum*), probably referring to the feminine arts of spinning, weaving, sewing, and embroidery. This fusion of symbolic and social functions," she concludes, "is typical of Hildegard's perspective. Woman's work is socially indispensable, but it is also a revelation of God's work. Just as the cosmos is Wisdom's vesture, or God's visible glory, so the body born of woman is the glory of the soul – or would be, had there been no fall." Barber notes:

> "The owl eyed goddess Athena girdled her." Note that the first and apparently most important garment for this young woman is the girdle, as everywhere else in the early Greek texts; I suspect this is some traditional form of the ancient string skirt, with all its significance for mating. Unfortunately we are seldom told more, because everyone at *that* time, of course, knew all about it and didn't need to have it explained.

Arachne and spinning: the English word for spider means "spinner"; our culture has fastened on to a different aspect of the spider's repertoire. Biologists, on the other hand, call all spiders by the name arachnids. Poseidon: Modern scholarship has made it clear that Poseidon is a local Aegean deity of earthquakes and tidal waves, who got grafted onto the pantheon of the incoming Greeks in the spot where the Indo-European god of fresh water belongs (Roman Neptune, etc.). "Raging waters" are the point of crossover. Big rivers were major forces to Indo-Europeans living around the Volga, Don, Danube, etc., but there are no such enormous rivers in Greece. The most fearsome body of water there is the sea, especially when seismic activity whips it up into a killer tidal wave.

Owl-eyed Athena: This much-disputed epithet, *glauk-opis,* is often translated "bright-eyed" or "gray-eyed," which is etymologically a possibility, but the term has good company in Hera's epithet *bo-opis,* which can only mean "cow-eyed." (The word for *owl* is *glauks.*) Such animal forms for deities are common in the layers of European culture that preceded the classically Indo-European populace, persisting here and there in dark corners even up to the present.

Another brief excerpt from *The Rule of St. Benedict* (Chapter 57).

Hayden Carruth, "Regarding Chainsaws," from *Collected Shorter Poems* (Port Townsend, WA: Copper Canyon Press, 1992), 211–213.

ARTS

Denise Levertov, "The Artist," from *With Eyes at the Back of Our Heads* (New York: New Directions, 1959), 4. The Toltec were one of a number of Nahuatl tribes (the Aztec being another) who flourished in southern Mexico a thousand years ago.

The Preface to Lu Chi's *Wen Fu* (*The Art of Writing*) is here translated by Sam Hamill (Minneapolis: Milkweed, 1987), 9. Born AD 251, Lu Chi's word *wen* (according to Hamill) "is one of the oldest words in Chinese, going back at least three thousand years to the time of the oracle bones where it meant, even then, art — literary as well as plastic art. In its most general sense, *wen* is simply 'form or pattern' wherein meaning & form are united in an inseparable unity" (36).

"Axe Handles" is the title poem of Gary Snyder's North Point volume (San Francisco: 1983), 5–6. This too, like Parker Palmer's comments on Chuang Tzu, moves easily from craft to teaching.

Mirabai (1498–1550), an Indian princess who wrote fiercely beautiful and erotic love lyrics to the god Krishna. Her songs are still celebrated — and sung — throughout India. This translation by Andrew Schelling comes from his *For Love of the Dark One* (Boston: Shambhala, 1993), 37.

The paragraph by John Haines is from the essay "Roots" in *Living Off the Country: Essays on Poetry and Place* (Ann Arbor: University of Michigan Press, 1981), 86. "Good poems come from roots," he writes here, meaning "that the work, and the life, must have their origin in a place of conviction."

The passage from Rainer Maria Rilke's letters comes from the volume *Letters on Cézanne,* translated by Joel Agee (New York: Fromm International, 1985), 50–51. In this context I want to suggest that Rilke's comments to paint not "I love this" but "here it is" suggest not naturalism but something closer to what Yanagi refers to as the Buddhist idea of beauty: the "I" must vanish ...

Perhaps too we might recall here the comment of Paul Cezanne's father – an immensely successful banker – to his son: "Think of the future; one dies with genius, but one eats with money." As John Walker comments, "After his father's death, Paul, perhaps with subconscious irony, altered this aphorism into his only eulogy for his parent: 'My father was a man of genius; he left me an income of twenty-five thousand francs'" (*The National Gallery of Art* [New York: Abrams, 1975], 504).

Donald Hall, again from *Life Work*, 51–54.

Kathleen Norris, from *The Cloister Walk* (New York: Riverhead Books, 1996), 141–47. On the bodily nature of monastic reading, see also Ivan Illich, *In The Vineyard of the Text* (Chicago: University of Chicago Press, 1993).

Sam Hamill's "Shadow Work," from *A Poet's Work: The Other Side of Poetry* (Seattle: Broken Moon Press, 1990), 35–43, suggests the close link between the marginal work that has been ascribed to women for generations and the marginal work of the artist. Once again categories collapse.

The reader is encouraged to look up Ivan Illich's *Shadow Work* as well (Boston: Marion Boyers, 1981), from which Hamill quotes.

I might add here that the book-making process itself is an example of a revived craft, as the extraordinary handcrafted Brooding Heron Press books of poetry published by Sam and Sally Green up on Waldron Island, Washington, testify. The *feel* of the book in one's hands is part of the reading process. I'm grateful for the inexpensive Penguins that make Sophocles and Shakespeare accessible, but I am also grateful for the resurgence of the small presses that remind us that the book is the word embodied.

Lewis Hyde's *The Gift: Imagination and the Erotic Life of Property* (New York: Vintage, 1983), 46–47, 54–55, referred to in the preceding essay by Sam Hamill, is another unclassifiable work. It touches on many of the points raised by others in this anthology – Hamill, of course, but also Eckhart (referred to by Hyde) and Everson (see the next entry). Hyde's references to Eckhart are drawn in part from Reiner Schurmann's study, *Meister Eckhart, Mystic and Philosopher* (Bloomington: Indiana University Press, 1978), and in part from an older translation of Eckhart.

This reflection on vocation by William Everson is drawn from "Meditation Two: Identity," in his book *Birth of a Poet* (Santa Barbara: Black Sparrow Press, 1982), 30. As a point of departure, see also on the idea of vocation or calling Chapter 3 of Max Weber's *The Protestant Ethic and the Spirit of Capitalism* (New York: Scribners, 1930), especially 79–81, on "Luther's Conception of the Calling."

"Karl Barth's Dream" is from Thomas Merton's *Conjectures of a Guilty Bystander* (Garden City, New York: Image Books, 1968), 11–12. Merton's epigraph (from Kabir, the fifteenth-century Indian poet and mystic) to this section of his journals also deserves a place in this volume, especially as we prepare to leave behind the quest for vocation:

> The servant Kabir sings: "O Sadhu!
> finish your buying and selling, have done
> with your good and your bad – for there
> are no markets and shops in the land
> to which you go!"

FROM THE CITY TO SABBATH

It is possible to read this collection as moving ever upward on a kind of cultural spiral, arriving at last here, with William Blake's biblical and visionary sense of the city as the ultimate expression of what it means to be human. For Blake the true city was an imaginative state of ongoing (and even furious) labor: Sabbath seems not to exist in this eternal and infinite state of creativity, which he also conceived as "mental war."

It is also, of course, possible to read this volume as bearing witness to a steady decline from the Edenic glory days of hunting and gathering, arriving at last at the nadir of human existence in the city. Many have suggested that with the coming of the Neolithic and agriculture, humanity took a wrong turn; see, for example, Calvin Luther Martin's *In The Spirit of the Earth*, 82–83: "The tools of our civilization are artifacts of the Neolithic imagination which succumbed to the illusion of self-nonself.... they had lost, not Eden, as they claimed, but the discipline and ability to image, to envision all as self."

Blake knew both cities, the "real" and the imagined: He lived in poverty in late eighteenth- and early nineteenth-century London, and much of his work is a powerful outcry against that outward manifestation of the fallen and degraded humanity. For the political and social dimension of Blake's work, see above all David Erdman's *Prophet Against Empire*, but also Michael Ferber's *The Social Vision of William Blake*, and David Punter's essay, "Blake: Creative and Uncreative Labor" in *Studies in Romanticism* 16 (1977), 535–61. Punter concludes: "The fragmentation of society cannot, for Blake, be fought by writing in terms of political economy, or of religion, or of moral codes, but only by establishing a language ... wherein these realms can be placed in imaginative synthesis" (560). This defines the task of *Jerusalem:*

> Trembling I sit day and night, my friends are astonish'd at me.
> Yet they forgive my wanderings, I rest not from my great task!
> To open the Eternal Worlds, to open the immortal Eyes
> Of Man inwards into the Worlds of Thought: into Eternity
> Ever expanding in the Bosom of God. The Human Imagination

This short passage from Eric Gill's autobiography, collected in *A Holy Tradition of Working* (Hudson, NY: Lindisfarne Press, 1983), 138–39, is a footnote to Blake. The anthropomorphism expressed here is questionable, depending on how one reads Gill's phrase "material things."

This poem from Emily Warn is previously unpublished – my thanks to Emily for her permission to use it here. Her second volume from Copper Canyon Press, *The Novice Insomniac*, was published in 1996. In reference to the poem's title, it's worth noting the comment that Kathleen Norris makes (Arts, 231) about "degenerate art" and the "extravagant, loving gesture" of Jesus' friend who bathes his feet in expensive oil. "Vagrant" and "extravagant" share the same root, after all – *vagari* is "to wander," and *extra vagari* is "to wander beyond": to exceed the boundaries. The vagrant has much to teach us.

Matthew 6:24–34. This excerpt from Matthew's gospel moves us toward our end and approaches the spirit of the *Taoteching*.

This piece from the *Taoteching* is #8 in Red Pine's translation (San Francisco: Mercury House, 1996), 16. Han Fei (died 233 BC) sums up the paradox of water as The Way: "If a drowning man drinks it, he dies. If a thirsty man drinks it, he lives." How does one say whether in itself it is good or bad?

William Langland's passage from *Piers Plowman* (from Passus XX) brings us full circle. *Kynde* here can be taken as reference to "Nature" but understood more broadly as a representative of Truth, Law, and God. When Will (the protagonist) speaks of his desire to "go hence" – to get away from old age – he has finally learned through *Kynde* "the knowledge derived from experience," in A.V.C. Schmidt's words, "to desire what the ascetics knew from the outset ... detachment from the transience of worldly things" (356). (See Source Notes, 276.)

Unite – Schmidt notes that the key place "Unity" receives in this poem may well be a desire on the part of Langland to "arouse attention to the doctrine of the Church as Christ's body" (see Ephesians 4.1ff). "The word," Schmidt concludes, "had a poignant significance in 1378, the year in which Christendom was rent by the Great Schism – the period in Church history when the Papacy was challenged by antipopes residing in Avignon" (355).

It is also clear, in the simplicity of Will's final question (and in *Kynde's* blunt answer) that only now, after an entire lifetime, has Will learned the meaning of this *craft*. (See Schmidt, 357.)

EPILOGUE

"There was an artist ..." From *Walden*, the conclusion. As Owen Thomas notes (in the Norton Critical Edition), this legend was probably composed by Thoreau himself, borrowing names and places from the *Bhagavad Gita*. I first borrowed the Heritage Club edition of *Walden* from the family bookshelf when I was in high school twenty-five years ago. I look forward, at some appropriate point, to loaning it permanently to my daughter. And so the culture goes on.

This letter from Sam Green is published – with my gratitude – through his permission. As the letter suggests, Sam and his wife, Sally, have homesteaded on a piece of land up on Waldron Island in Washington State.

This excerpt from *Diné bahane': The Navajo Creation Story* is translated by Paul G. Zolbrod (cited above, page 267), 171–75, and is found as well in Brian Swann's excellent collection *Coming To Light: Contemporary Translations of the Native Literatures of North America* (New York: Vintage, 1994), 619–23. I have eliminated footnotes.

The "child" found at the end of this section by First Man is identified with Changing Woman, who is (perhaps) here seen as the child of those two on (or of) the mountain that First Man seeks out (in this translation called "old age" [or long life] and "happiness" – in Navajo, *są́'ah naagháii* and *bik'eh hózhǫ́*). You might call them "Long Life Boy" and "Happiness Girl" since (in Gary Witherspoon's wonderful study, *Language and Art in the Navajo Universe* [Ann Arbor: University of Michigan Press, 1977], 202) the former is associated with the static male and the latter with the active female. "Hence," concludes Zolbrod, "Changing Woman can be seen as the 'child' of two basic Navajo ideals" (see 384–85). She is identified with life itself and thus with the powers of creation.

Note too that "singing up the mountain" here suggests First Man (in Zolbrod's words) "as the prototype of the Navajo chanter or medicine man." He continues:

> It is worth observing that the shamanic act is in many instances seen as a vicarious quest wherein the chanter-healer departs from his own body and ventures to a world apart where only spirits dwell. At the very least, the act of singing, praying, chanting and reciting is one involving a certain kind of psychic transportation" (383).

Cormac McCarthy, *The Stonemason* (Hopewell, NJ: Ecco Press, 1994), 32–33. See also above, in the notes on Studs Terkel's stonemason (Sources, 288). This speech by Ben Telfair about his grandfather climaxes Act 1 of McCarthy's play. It returns us – as so much of the best thinking and writing about work does – to the underlying relationship between true work and the ideas – the *actions* – of harmony, justice, "rightness." Such words have both an aesthetic and an ethical dimension to them. Good work is *just* in all senses.

Thich Nhat Hanh's retelling of Tolstoy's story – itself a fair representation of spiritual cross-pollination – comes from his book *Miracle of Mindfulness* (Boston: Beacon Press, 1975, 1976), 69–76.

Denise Levertov's "The Task" is from her volume *Oblique Prayers* (New York: New Directions, 1984), 78. See her comments on this poem in her essay "Work That Enfaiths" (in her *New & Selected Essays* [New York: New Directions, 1992], 252):

> In a somewhat earlier, related poem called "The Task" I had pictured God as a weaver sitting at his loom in a vast wilderness, solitary as a bear in the Alaskan tundra, listening to the cries of anguish far off, audible above the clack of the loom because all else is so quiet – and hastening his task; for the cloth must be woven before the "terrible beseeching" can cease. A friend's description of the heavenly but awesome quiet of the wilderness near Mount Denali was one source for this poem. Another source was what Julian of Norwich tells us she learned in one of her "showings": that there is a divine plan, both temporal and transcendent, which will account for the unchecked miseries of the world, a plan which our finite minds are incapable of grasping. God informs her, you remember, to trust this and tells her that "All shall be well and all manner of thing shall be well." The time is not yet ripe for us to comprehend this mystery, she is told. But meanwhile all manner of thing is not well, and "The Task" images the toil of a lonely God.

This poem brings me back to Martin Buber's tale of the sorrowing angel – and to Sabbath rest.

PERMISSIONS

NOTES

INTRODUCTION

1 The janitor speaks to Raymond Good in Peter L. Berger, ed., *The Human Shape of Work* (New York: Macmillan, 1964), 43. It doesn't take the second coming of Marx to see how thoroughly alienating much of modern industrial (or technological) labor can be. But to take this as the norm is to reduce all of life to servility. Wendell Berry: "Men who drudge all their lives in order to retire happily are the victims of a cheap spiritual fashion invented for their enslavement. It is no more possible to live in the future than it is to live in the past. It is impossible to imagine 'how it will be,' and to linger over that task is to prepare a disappointment. The tomorrow I hope for may very well be worse than today." See his *Recollected Essays 1965–1980* (San Francisco: North Point, 1981), 71.

2 Ananda K. Coomaraswamy, in *The Transformation of Nature in Art* (1934; reprint, New York: Dover, 1956), 91.

3 Rainer Maria Rilke, *Duino Elegies*, from the ninth elegy. Translated by Stephen Mitchell, in *The Selected Poetry of Rainer Maria Rilke* (New York: Vintage, 1984), 203.

4 Wendell Berry, in *Home Economics* (San Francisco: North Point, 1987), 143–44.

5 Gary Snyder, *The Real Work* (New York: New Directions, 1980), 82.

6 Kathleen Raine, quoted in Berry, *Home Economics*, 145.

7 The axe handle: see Gary Snyder's poem of that name in *Axe Handles* (San Francisco: North Point, 1983), 5–6, and reprinted later in this collection. See too, on the "wayless Way," Snyder's comments in his essay "On the Path, Off the Trail," where he reminds us that the meaning of *dao* (tao) is not just road or path but also the practice of an art or craft — as in *kado*, "the way of flowers," or *sado*, "tea ceremony." To go off the trail is a reminder that "there is a point beyond which training and practice cannot take you.... This is the surprise of discovering oneself needing no self, one with the work, moving in disciplined ease and grace. One knows what it is to be a spinning ball of clay, a curl of pure white wood off the edge of the chisel — or one of the many hands of Kannon the Bodhisattva of Compassion. At this point one can be free, with the work and from the work." *The Practice of the Wild* (San Francisco: North Point, 1990), 145, 148.

8 Chuang Tzu, in Thomas Merton, *The Way of Chuang Tzu* (New York: New Directions, 1965), 110–111.

ORIGINS & FIRST THOUGHTS

1 Leslie Marmon Silko, "Interior and Exterior Landscapes: The Pueblo Migration Stories," in *Yellow Woman and a Beauty of the Spirit* (New York: Simon & Schuster, 1996), 36–37.

2 Wendell Berry, from *The Long Legged House*, excerpted in *Recollected Essays 1965–1980* (San Francisco: North Point, 1981), 57.

3 John Milton, *Paradise Lost* XII, 646–649.

4 "The Flight," in Denise Levertov's *Collected Earlier Poems 1940–1960* (New York: New Directions, 1979), 34.

5 Hayden Carruth, *Selected Essays and Reviews* (Port Townsend: Copper Canyon, 1996), 24.

6 Quoted by Laura Coltelli in her interview with Jay Harjo. See Harjo's *The Spiral of Memory* (Ann Arbor: University of Michigan Press, 1996), 61.

7 E.F. Schumacher, *Good Work* (New York: Harper & Row, 1979), 3.

8 Ibid.

9 Ibid., 119.

10 Ibid., 27.

11 Ibid., 42.

12 Marc H. Ellis, *Peter Maurin: Prophet in the Twentieth Century* (New York and Toronto: Paulist Press, 1981), 106.

13 Schumacher, *Good Work*, 50.

14 William D. Miller, *Dorothy Day: A Biography* (New York: Harper & Row, 1982), 228.

15 Peter Maurin, *Easy Essays*, essays selected and reprinted from the Catholic Worker by the people at the Catholic Worker Farm, West Hamlin, Virginia, 1974.

16 Ellis, *Maurin*, 114.

17 Ibid.

18 Pope John Paul II, *Laborem exercens*, as printed in *The Priority of Labor: A Commentary on "Laborem Exercens," Encyclical Letter of Pope John Paul II*, by Gregory Baum (New York and Toronto: Paulist Press, 1982), 93–152. It should be noted that the moral viability of the papal analysis of work is undermined by its blatant sexism. The encyclical refers to human beings exclusively as men and to work almost entirely in terms of the male labor force. The pope's understanding of the social role of women is clear: Their province is the family. Sexist, even misogynist, statements from the Vatican are historical commonplaces. The importance of Laborem exercens lies in its progressive vision of human work, a vision that will ultimately prove to be subversive of the global domination of women. The pope's emphasis on the creative, self-realizing aspect of human labor stands in direct contradiction to his rigid conservatism where sex roles are concerned.

19 Gregory Baum, *The Priority of Labor: A Commentary on "Laborem Exercens," Encyclical Letter of Pope John Paul II* (New York and Toronto: Paulist Press, 1982), 17.

20 *Laborem exercens,* 95.

21 Ibid., 103–4.

22 Ibid., 105.

23 Ibid.

24 Ibid., 105–6.

25 Baum, *Priority of Labor,* 30.

THE HUNT

1 Richard Nelson, *The Island Within* (San Francisco: North Point, 1989), 277.

2 Ivan Illich, *Shadow Work* (Boston: Marion Boyars, 1981), 102.

3 Paul Shepard, *Man in the Landscape* (New York: Knopf, 1967), 36. Shepard in turn is relying here on Josef Pieper's book *Leisure, the Basis of Culture.* See too, more recently, the striking comments on leisure in Illich's *In the Vineyard of the Text.* Here he associates leisure (in the medieval monastic world) not with vacation in the modern sense, but with freedom (*vacare*), which "can be found only by those who give themselves to wisdom." He quotes St. Augustine, who, shortly after his conversion founded a small community, the purpose of which was "to be deified by leisure" (*deificari . . . in otio*). "My leisure," Augustine writes, "is not spent in nurturing idleness, but in exploring wisdom . . . I draw back from distracting activities, and my spirit devotes itself to heavenly desires" (Chicago: University of Chicago Press, 1993), 62.

4 For Leslie Marmon Silko's essay, see "Interior and Exterior Landscapes: the Pueblo Migration Stories" in *Yellow Woman and a Beauty of the Spirit* (New York: Simon & Schuster, 1996), 45–47. "Storyteller" has been often anthologized, but is available in Silko's collection *Storyteller.* On the relationship between the sexual hunt and the hunting of animals, see also Susan Griffin's chapter, "His Power: He Tames What Is Wild" in *Woman and Nature: The Roaring Inside Her* (New York: Harper & Row, 1978), especially 103–5, excerpted in this anthology.

5 All quotations from Tuan Mac Cairill are from "The Story of Tuan Mac Cairill," in *Irish Fairy Tales* by James Stephens (New York: Macmillan and Company, 1968).

6 Jamie de Angula, *The Pit River Indians* (San Francisco: Turtle Island Foundation, 1973).

7 "The Battle of the Trees," from the *Book of Taliesin,* quoted in *The Quest for Merlin,* Nikolai Tolstoy (New York: Little and Brown, 1985).

8 *The All of It* by Jeannette Haien (New York: Harper & Row, 1986).

CULTIVATION

1 *Monet in the Nineties: The Series Paintings* (Boston: Museum of Fine Arts, 1989), 34.

2 Wendell Berry, "Conserving Communities," in *Another Turn of the Crank* (Washington D.C.: Counterpoint, 1995), 8.

3 John Berger, *Into Their Labours* (New York: Pantheon, 1991), xvi.

4 Paul Shepard, *Nature and Madness* (San Francisco: Sierra Club Books, 1982), 43.

5 See John Haines, *Living Off the Country: Essays on Poetry and Place* (Ann Arbor: University of Michigan Press, 1981), 51. The Ortega y Gasset quotation can be found in *Man and Crisis* (New York: W. W. Norton, 1958).

6 *Collected Poems 1957–1982* (San Francisco: North Point, 1985), 248.

7 See "The Necessity of Wildness" in *The Unsettling of America* (cited above) 130–31, as well as the essay "Writer and Region" in *What Are People For?* (on, among other things, Huckleberry Finn and "lighting out for the territory"), and the beautiful short story "The Wild Birds" in the collection of that title. Here it is evident that his character Burley Coulter represents this force of the wild running through everything, and the lawyer Wheeler Catlett is the civilizing force who must learn to take Burley as and who he is.

8 Vicki Hearne, *Adam's Task: Calling Animals by Name* (New York: Knopf, 1987), 135.

9 See Gary Witherspoon, *Language and Art in the Navajo Universe* (Ann Arbor: University of Michigan Press, 1977), 23–28.

10 On Athena, see the comments of Elizabeth Wayland Barber from *Women's Work*, excerpted below in the section on Arts, Crafts & Hand-Work.

HOME-WORK

1 As Elizabeth Wayland Barber comments in *Women's Work: The First 20,000 Years* (New York: Norton, 1994), 185, Herodotus more or less "invented the notion of history as an independent form of study, using the word *historia* – literally 'research, a seeking-out' – at the start of his book on the Greco-Persian Wars of 490–480 BC." The translation is hers.

This passage about men and women at work is worth comparing to the passage in the Hebrew Book of Proverbs (31.10–25), also quoted by Barber (184): "Who can find a virtuous woman? ... She seeketh wool, and flax, and worketh willingly with her hands. ... She considereth a field, and buyeth it: with the fruit of her hands she planteth a vineyard." Here we get a clear (if idealized) image of "an independent-minded middle class of free women" who "continued for centuries to create handsome, salable textiles for the busy commercial caravans run by their equally business-oriented menfolk."

2 This paragraph from Leslie Marmon Silko's recent essay "Yellow Woman and a Beauty of the Spirit" (in *Yellow Woman and a Beauty of the Spirit: Essays on Native American Life Today*, p. 66) stands of course as counterpoint to Herodotus – and, insofar as Herodotus (and the Bible) stand as representatives of Western ideas of work and gender, as counterpart to a tradition of which we are the descendents.

3 Louise Erdrich, *The Blue Jay's Dance: A Birth Year* (New York: HarperCollins, 1995), 4–5.

4 W.B. Yeats, "Adams' Curse," in *The Collected Poems* (New York: MacMillan, 1956), 78.

5 Yeats, "The Circus Animals' Desertion," in *The Collected Poems* (New York: Macmillan, 1956), 336.

6 Thich Nhat Hanh, *The Miracle of Mindfulness: A Manual on Meditation* (revised edition, Boston: Beacon Press, 1987), 4–5.

7 [Arthur] Waley (*Three Ways of Thought in Ancient China*, 73) takes this whole paragraph to refer to the working methods of a mediocre carver, and hence translates it very differently.

There is a great deal to be said for his interpretation, but after much consideration I have decided to follow the traditional interpretation because it seems to me that the extreme care and caution which the cook uses when he comes to a difficult place is also a part of Chuang Tzu's "secret of caring for life." (Translator's note.)

ARTS, CRAFTS & HAND-WORK

1 D.M. Dooling, ed., *A Way of Working* (1979; reprint, New York: Parabola Books, 1986), x.

2 Adrienne Rich, *The Dream of a Common Language* (New York: Norton, 1978), 72–77. See also Kathleen Norris's comments about the vocations of monks and poets in the excerpt from *The Cloister Walk* (Arts, 228).

3 Carla Needleman, *The Work of Craft* (1979; reprint, New York: Arkana, 1986), 48–49.

4 Needleman, 51–52.

5 Needleman, 60.

6 Bobette Perrone, H. Henrietta Stockel, and Victoria Krueger, *Medicine Women, Curenderas, and Women Doctors* (Norman, OK: University of Oklahoma, 1989), 37.

7 Soetsu Yanagi, *The Unknown Craftsman: A Japanese Insight into Beauty* (Tokyo: Kodansha International, 1972), 131.

8 David V. Erdman, ed., *The Complete Poetry and Prose of William Blake* (Berkeley and Los Angeles: University of California, 1982), 724–25.

9 That is, matching up his own innate nature with that of the tree. (Translator's note.)

10 Edward Deming Andrews and Faith Andrews, *Shaker Furniture; The Craftsmanship of an American Communal Sect* (New Haven, 1937) [reprinted New York, 1950]. Cf. Edward Deming Andrews, *The Gift to Be Simple: Songs, Dances and Rituals of the American Shakers* (New York 1940) [reprinted New York, 1962].

FROM THE CITY TO SABBATH

1 *The Collected Poems of William Carlos Williams Volume I: 1909–1939* (New York: New Directions, 1986), 100–4.

2 Eugen Herrigel, *Zen in the Art of Archery* (New York: McGraw Hill, 1964), 104–5.

3 Jane Elizabeth Sammon in *Religion & Intellectual Life*, VII. 2, 21.

4 Flannery O'Connor, *Mystery and Manners*, 112.

5 Etty Hillesum, *Letters From Westerbork* (New York: Pantheon, 1986), 24, 55, 78.

6 Shakespeare, *The Tempest*, I, 2.

ACKNOWLEDGMENTS

This is a project that goes back to the summer of 1989 and a Coolidge Fellowship in Cambridge, Massachusetts, sponsored by ARIL – the Association of Religion and Literature. While there I began to re-read Walden and to think, read, and write about what work has meant over the millennia – and what it has meant to me.

It was a subject of more than academic interest to me; I had recently left a tenure-track teaching job at St. Mary's College (Notre Dame) to accompany my wife and four-year-old daughter back to Seattle, where my wife had been offered a job. Upon arriving in Seattle, I found myself with primary child care, part time teaching, and a second, afternoon job cleaning up at the Honey Bear Bakery – an arrangement that was, for a time, quite delightful, combining as it did a fair amount of intense head-work in the morning followed by hours of intense kid and body work.

It was in this context that I found myself asking a lot of questions about work: why – beyond necessity – we do it, what it means, and why so often it *doesn't*.

My thanks to the folks at ARIL (especially Nancy Malone), to Denise Levertov for first calling my attention to the Fellowship, and for many subsequent conversations and suggestions with and from her; to Jane Hirshfield for helpful ideas early on in the process; and to those authors whose works appear here, especially those who helped with new material, with still more suggestions, and with absurdly low fees: Andrew Schelling, Bill Porter, Sam Hamill (and Copper Canyon Press), Sam Green, Marc and Helen Hudson, Kathleen Norris, Brenda Peterson, Linda Hogan, Donald Hall, Emily Warn – and to Tom Moore for graciously supplying a foreword.

To the staff and students at Seattle Pacific University, especially Beryl Carpenter, Sheila Chapman, Angeline Niwa, Lisa Harlow, Daphyne Shimeall, Sage Rogers, and to the DOR. To friends in the English Department – both at SPU and at St. Mary's – who embody collegiality.

To my friends in the Community – those like Molly who helped out with typing, and to all of those – Laurie and Julian, Jerry and Kay, Cathy and the rest – who know the beauty of the single Body.

And to my family, especially Judy and Katie, who endure and love and teach the great art of ongoing transformation.

Designed and typeset in Adobe Centaur by
Thomas Christensen and Kirsten Janene-Nelson
at Mercury House, San Francisco, and printed on
55# Glatfelter Natural paper by Bang
Printing, Brainerd, Minnesota